This book is about the practice of grade retention in elementary school, a particularly vexing problem in urban school systems, where upward of half the students may repeat a grade. *On the Success of Failure* addresses whether repeating a grade is helpful or harmful when children are not keeping up. It describes the school context of retention and evaluates its consequences by tracking the experiences of a large, representative sample of Baltimore schoolchildren from the first grade through middle school.

In addition to evaluating the consequences of retention, the book describes the cohort's dispersion along many different educational pathways over this eight-year period, the articulation of retention with other forms of educational tracking (like reading group placements in the early primary grades and course-level assignments in middle school), and repeaters' academic and school adjustment problems before they were held back. Focusing on the experience of first, second, and third grade repeaters, the volume finds that the effects of retention are mainly positive. Test scores and marks, which are low to begin with and get worse over time, improve when retainees get back into the regular promotion sequence, and in most instances repeaters remain above where they had been before being held back. The comparisons are especially favorable for single repeaters held back after first grade. In the socioemotional realm, no great stigma is attached to retention. Instead, when children are held back their attitudes about self and school improve, probably because their marks and test scores have improved.

On the success of failure

On the success of failure

A reassessment of the effects of retention in the primary grades

KARL L. ALEXANDER
The Johns Hopkins University

DORIS R. ENTWISLE
The Johns Hopkins University

SUSAN L. DAUBER
Northwestern University

CAMBRIDGE
UNIVERSITY PRESS

Published by the Press Syndicate of the University of Cambridge
The Pitt Building, Trumpington Street, Cambridge CB2 1RP
40 West 20th Street, New York, NY 10011-4211, USA
10 Stamford Road, Oakleigh, Melbourne 3166, Australia

First published 1994

Printed in the United States of America

Library of Congress Cataloging-in-Publication Data
Alexander, Karl L.
On the success of failure : a reassessment of the effects of
retention in the primary grades / Karl L. Alexander, Doris R.
Entwisle, Susan L. Dauber.
p.   cm.
Includes bibliographical references (p.   ).
ISBN 0-521-41504-7
1. Grade repetition – United States.   2. Education, Primary – United
States.   I. Entwisle, Doris R.   II. Dauber, Susan L.   III. Title.
LB3063.A54   1995
371.2'8 – dc 20   94-10730
                                                        CIP

A catalog record for this book is available from the British Library.

ISBN 0-521-41504-7 Hardback

Contents

Preface

This volume examines the effect of grade retention on children in the Baltimore City Public School System (BCPS). Early retention is supposed to help children who are having a hard time catch up before they have fallen too far behind. Whether it does so is the topic of this book.

In Baltimore, as in other large, urban school systems, retention is a serious problem, mainly because the public schools fall heir to the city's problems (Szanton 1986: 11). Despite being underfunded relative to more affluent suburban and exurban communities, these school systems shoulder far greater burdens. For example, a recent series of *Baltimore Sun* articles spotlighted one BCPS middle school (Diggs–Johnson) with more low-income students (450 of its 601 pupils) than the total in three nearby Baltimore County schools with enrollments more than four times as large. Another *Sun* article reviewed the burdens of special education borne by the city system, which services 20% of the special education children in the state while enrolling just 15% of its students.

The *Sun* articles portrayed a system besieged and in need of help: "In teacher pay, city trails by thousands"; and "Crumbling buildings greet children at city schools" (*Baltimore Sun*, "Bright Faces, Faded Dreams," June 7, 1992, through June 13, 1992). The city's average per pupil expenditure on books in 1990–91 was $92, about three-fourths of the state average ($121). The state's wealthiest county, Montgomery, spent $211, well over twice as much.

There are similar disparities in per pupil expenditures, with $4,947 in Baltimore City versus $5,515 statewide. Baltimore County, a largely white jurisdiction that wraps around the city on three sides, averaged $6,695; Montgomery County averaged $7,591.

More than three-fourths of the enrollment in the city system is

African-American. The 1990 poverty rate in Baltimore for children under 18 was 32.5% overall, but 39.1% among African-Americans (Children's Defense Fund 1992). In the 1989–90 school year, 60% of the city's elementary school children qualified for the federal government's free lunch program. In almost half the city's 106 elementary schools, the proportion qualifying was above 70%; in 26 schools it was more than 80% (Citizens Planning and Housing Association 1990).

Under such circumstances, many children begin school poorly prepared. In the 1989–90 school year, 14% of elementary school students received special education services and 9% were retained in grade. In some schools both figures were much higher.

How should such a system respond when children are not keeping up? Is repeating a grade helpful or harmful? In 1977, following a national trend, Baltimore's Board of School Commissioners announced its opposition to social promotion (Bowler 1991). Since then rates of retention have remained high, but not without controversy. In 1989, for example, an *Evening Sun* headline read: "15,000 students failed despite debate over promotions" (Kelly, July 25, 1989: C1). These 15,000 repeaters included 16% of that year's first graders, a ratio that is not unusual (e.g., Epstein 1987; Shepard and Smith 1989: 8). In school systems like Baltimore's, many children enter first grade already "behind" – their academic skills are weak, and for them the life-style of the school is quite foreign. But is holding these youngsters back a year a reasonable response?

Serious charges have been raised against retention: that it is sometimes implemented unfairly; that the stigma associated with it weighs heavily on young children; and, perhaps most critically, that it does not work, in the sense of helping children do better in the long run. Indeed, for many critics of retention the matter is already settled, and some school systems have begun moving away from the practice.

Are the critics right? Should schools stop holding children back? For guidance in answering questions about retention, this book reports the experience of about 800 Baltimore children who were randomly selected to take part in the "Beginning School Study." We began this research project in 1982, when the youngsters were starting first grade. Their academic progress and socioemotional development have been carefully followed from then until now. By the time they entered high school, about 40% had been held back at least once, so there is a large sample of retainees upon which to base a study of retention. The other 60%, those who did not repeat at any point, constitute a natural comparison group. The BSS research design provides a strong scientific foundation for posing questions about retention's effects, but to tease out these consequences is not easy.

Chapters 1 and 2 review the design of the research and assess its strengths and weaknesses as an archive for assessing the antecedents and consequences of retention. Here we mention just a couple of its features. This is a *prospective* study. We began following these 800 children *before* any of them were held back. It turns out that the repeaters were not doing as well as their classmates even before being retained. Knowing where children stood before retention allows us to say whether problems are more severe after retention, whether they merely represent continuation of difficulties that predated retention, or whether problems seem less severe after retention. The study also spans many years – the first eight years of these children's schooling – so it can shed light on the long-term consequences of retention, and there do appear to be some. Finally, it is important that our study focuses on children in a typical urban school system where rates of retention are high. The sample is more than half African-American and most of the youngsters come from low-income families. These are the kinds of children most often held back. Their problems would not be expected to be the same as those of middle class children in schools with low rates of retention, although middle class children are the ones who have most often been examined in prior retention research.

As the reader will see, our results run counter to much current thinking about retention. We find that while not a cure-all, retention appears to be a reasonably effective practice. Spending two years in a grade does not bring repeaters up to acceptable levels of performance, so problems – serious problems – remain. Nevertheless, most youngsters who are held back do much better the second time through a grade, and for several years afterward they continue to show improvement over their standing before retention. We have detected no emotional scars from the retention experience. In fact, because of their improved performance, repeaters' self-confidence went up, not down.

We respect the good intentions of those who take a negative view of retention, but we believe they are mistaken, at least for children like those in Baltimore. We are especially eager to disabuse educators of the idea that retention leads to problems that drag disadvantaged youngsters down. These children are burdened by circumstances beyond their control before retention. It falls to the schools to try to help. Obfuscation on the retention question is a disservice to all concerned: to the policymakers and practitioners who want desperately to help, but even more to the children, whose well-being hangs in the balance, and to their parents.

High rates of retention in the early grades are a symptom of a school system's or a city's problems. Retention does not cause those problems, nor, so far as we can tell, does it aggravate them. Repeating a grade does not help as much as we might want, but its usefulness, however limited, should be appreciated. Notwithstanding the prevailing climate of opinion, at times it makes sense to hold children back a year. The extra time helps them catch up and puts them in a better position to keep up later.

Acknowledgments

We are indebted, first, to the people in the Baltimore City Public Schools for their support and cooperation. A project of uncommonly long duration, the Beginning School Study (BSS) has continued through the administrations of several superintendents, in years when budgets were severely curtailed, and through political controversy. Despite all, support from the superintendent's office has held firm, and principals, teachers, guidance officers, and support staff throughout the system have been extraordinarily generous, patient, and understanding. It is they who allowed the idea of the Beginning School Study to become a reality. The BSS youngsters and their parents also have been remarkably supportive. Since the fall of 1982, when the BSS youngsters began first grade, they have given generously of their time and have worked with us in partnership. We are pleased to dedicate this volume to them.

Financial support has come from several sources over the years. *On the Success of Failure* covers the first eight years of the BSS youngsters' schooling, and the overall project is now finishing its twelfth year (1993–94). The BSS embodies our conviction that issues of schooling need to be studied over the long haul. The effort has been sustained through a series of overlapping, multiple-year awards, including several grants from the National Institute of Child Health and Development (HD29343, 23728, 21044, 16302), two from the W. T. Grant Foundation (83079682 and 82079600), and one from the National Science Foundation (SES8510535). We trust this volume, and other BSS publications, justify the confidence placed in us by those who have shared our sense of the importance of the project.

Special thanks go to Anna Stoll, who has contributed to the effort in a multitude of ways over the years, including her extraordinary patience and skill in preparing this manuscript. Our thanks also go to the other BSS "core staff" members: Joanne Fennessey, Linda Olson, Mary Ann Zeller, and Binnie Bailey. Their contributions in various capacities have been invaluable in keeping the enterprise going, as were those of Patricia Gucer, Doris Cadigan, Jane Marie McCormack, Barbara Izzo, Gloria Zepp, and Gail Fennessey in earlier years. We are grateful to Aaron Pallas for his thoughtful critique of the manuscript at various stages.

Finally, one very special 1982 beginning first grader deserves particular mention. From the first field testing of our questionnaires in her preschool class, Karen Alexander has cheerfully and graciously served as the project's human guinea pig – a one-person focus group who has helped guide us as we tried to understand children's and teenagers' reactions to school. All three authors appreciate her help, and one loves her very much.

1

Retention: many questions, few answers

Each spring, tens of thousands of children across the country receive the
same dark message: they are failures. They will be held back, retained,
repeat a grade – all of which are synonyms for failing.

Retention implies that children have somehow fallen short and are
unprepared for the next level of schooling. Unlike many other educational decisions, this one is highly public. The pupil's friends go on, but
the retained child must start over with new classmates, most of whom are
younger, smaller, and smarter. The new teacher knows the child is repeating, as do the new classmates. Furthermore, the judgment of failure is
almost never reversed. The child who repeats a grade will likely be "off
time" for the rest of his or her schooling.

Schools use retention to help children who have fallen behind catch
up, but does it really help? There are many skeptics, who do not see the
child catching up, but rather suffering humiliation and harm. Are these
apprehensions warranted? Despite strong opinion on both sides and
much study, the issue is not decided. Later in this chapter we will review
what is known (and believed) about the consequences of retention. Before
getting into those materials, however, we need to sketch out the dimensions of the problem. Though there is disagreement about the pros and
cons of retention, no one disputes its seriousness. We first consider
retention rates, then some of its "costs."

Falling behind: the magnitude of the problem

Over the past 25 years the average percentage of children off time at least
one year by the end of elementary school has risen (see Table 1.1).
Estimates vary, but by the late eighties probably about one youngster in

Table 1.1. *Percentage of children one or more years below modal grade*

Age (years)	Grade	1964–66		1979				1990					
				White		African-American		White		African-American		Hispanic	
		Male	Female	Male	Female	Male	Female	Male	Female	Male	Female	Male	Female
6	1	3.4	3.2	8.5	6.5	4.4	5.9	18.6	14.8	18.8	16.0	15.3	18.3
7	2	12.7	8.7	16.9	10.6	15.5	11.7	30.0	20.0	24.3	21.1	23.0	18.6
8	3	20.8	13.5	20.6	13.6	24.0	13.3	27.2	22.3	26.8	25.6	28.4	26.1
9	4	22.8	14.1	19.4	16.8	29.8	21.0	32.0	20.1	30.1	25.9	36.2	27.8
10	5	23.7	15.4	22.9	14.7	43.0	23.0	29.3	22.8	38.3	27.6	28.2	35.1
11	6	23.5	16.0	20.5	16.2	41.1	21.2	32.4	24.0	42.8	32.7	46.9	37.5

Source: Data derived from CPS School Enrollment Surveys in October. Table D, U.S. Bureau of the Census, Current Population Reports, Series P-20, No. 167, *School Enrollment – Social and Economic Characteristics of Students: October 1966* (Washington, DC: U.S. Government Printing Office, 1967). Table 16, U.S. Bureau of the Census, Current Population Reports, Series P-20, No. 360, *School Enrollment – Social and Economic Characteristics of Students: October 1979* (Washington, DC: U.S. Government Printing Office, 1981). Table 3, U.S. Bureau of the Census, Current Population Report, Series P-20, No. 460, *School Enrollment – Social and Economic Characteristics of Students: October 1990* (Washington, DC: U.S. Government Printing Office, 1992).

five failed a grade before entering middle school or junior high. Next to dropping out, failing a grade is probably the most ubiquitous and vexing issue facing school professionals today. These days, children can "fail" kindergarten (see Epstein 1987), and in many school systems failing first grade is quite common.

Astonishing though it is, the prevalence of retention is uncharted on a national basis, a victim of what Weiss and Gruber (1987) call the "managed irrelevance of federal statistics." The Common Core of Data, the primary set of federal statistics on elementary and secondary education, does not include data on sensitive matters like retention. Weiss and Gruber report that "in a delicately balanced political environment . . . they [the NCES] have enough trouble getting local districts to categorize grade levels and instructional staff in comparable ways without getting into emotionally laden issues" like grade retention. Every school district keeps its own statistics, but retention data rarely see the light of day. Why? Because retention signals the failure of the school and teacher, as well as of the student.

Although there are no comprehensive national statistics on retention per se, the Bureau of the Census regularly monitors children's grade in school in relation to their age. These data have been collected regularly since 1966 in the Current Population Survey (CPS) school enrollment supplements. They are representative of the civilian noninstitutional U.S. population in the 50 states plus the District of Columbia. These enrollment data can be used to identify children who are in a grade below the modal grade of children their age, and so permit educated guesses at overall retention rates. Collected from households, with no allowance for differences across states or districts in age of school entry, cutoff dates, late starts, and the like, these figures are approximate at best when used to estimate rates of retention.

The first of the CPS reports on modal age (Table 1.1, first panel) shows patterns for grades 1 through 6 separately for the two sexes, in 1964, 1965, and 1966, for "all races combined." At that time a little more than 3% of 6-year-olds were below modal grade, and about 2% were reported not to be enrolled.[1] These data indicate that many children had fallen behind by grade 3, a pattern in all later enrollment data as well. The proportion of males off time exceeds the proportion of females in this period, a finding that also persists. In the mid-sixties about 24% of males and 16% of females were at least 1 year behind by age 11 (sixth grade).

Data from the late seventies, available for African-Americans and whites separately, allow us to consider age and gender trends for these two major racial/ethnic groups (middle panel Table 1.1). Again at every age the rate for males exceeds that for females. For ages 6, 7, and 8, the off-time rates for African-Americans and whites are not startlingly different, and the male-to-female ratio looks about the same. At age 9 and above, however, the off-time rates for African-Americans continue to increase (to about 40% for males by age 10), while the rates for whites appear to level off at about 20% for males and 16% for females.

By 1990, enrollment data by age and sex categories are available for whites, African-Americans, and Hispanics separately. The Hispanic data are somewhat disorderly (e.g., the low figure for 10-year-old males) and inconsistent with the other trends in some respects (e.g., the higher percentages for females over males among 6- and 10-year-olds). Aside from concluding that the rate for Hispanics is greater than that for whites – indeed higher even than African-Americans among 11-year-olds – their profile is difficult to interpret.[2]

In 1990, similar proportions of African-American and white 6-year-olds are over age for grade, with the figures for all groups considerably higher than in 1979. That somewhat more white and African-American males than females are in kindergarten (and even nursery school) at age 6 may represent a recent tendency to let later-maturing youngsters, most often boys, wait a year before starting first grade. Middle class parents, especially those whose children are born in the late months of the calendar year, often delay school entry (Entwisle and Hayduk 1981).

For whites, in 1990 just as in 1979, most of the falling behind takes place over the first 3 years of schooling, with an off-time rate by the end of elementary school hovering around 30% for males and 22% to 24% for females, both of which figures are up some from 1979 levels. The 1990 rate for 6- and 7-year-old African-American males is much higher than it was in 1979. About 30% of African-American boys were off time by age 9 in 1990, which was not much different from the figure for whites. However, among African-American boys, the percentages continue to rise, while among whites they level off. As a result, among 11-year-olds, African-Americans register a much higher over-age percentage than whites: 42.8 versus 32.4. The 1990 rates for African-American girls rise steadily year by year, but even at age 11 the rate for females (32.7%) lags well behind that for males. Still, the 1990 rate for African-American girls is half again their 1979 rate.

Though these figures on off-time enrollments are high, they do not signify retention only, and so for our purposes they must be used with caution. It is likely, for example, that many of the 6-year-olds who are off time in October of the school year are "late starters." Age requirements vary from one district to another and also from one year to another. The most conservative view would be that all off-time 6-year-olds in 1990 are late starters. Even with this conservative assumption, by age 11 about 10% to 14% of whites and about 17% to 24% of African-Americans are off time, depending on sex.

In analyzing CPS enrollment data, Bianchi (1984) found that in an "average household" (a husband–wife family with income above the poverty level, in which the wife has a high school education and either does not work outside the family or works part-time) about 18% to 19% of males age 7 to 15 are enrolled below their modal grade. A recent national survey of eighth graders (the NELS-88 project) asked retrospectively about grade retention, and 17.7% of the respondents acknowledged having repeated at least one grade (National Center for Education Statistics 1990: 9). Retrospective accounts of this sort probably are not completely reliable, but neither is inferring retention from over-age enrollments, as must be done with the CPS data. That figures from two such different data sources are so close suggests these estimates are reasonably accurate.

In Bianchi's analysis retention rates were about the same for "average household" whites, African-Americans, and Hispanics, but rates escalated rapidly as other risk factors increased. For children of high school dropout parents living in poverty, for example, the rate was about 50% for males of all three racial/ethnic groups, and around 40% for comparably disadvantaged females. Bianchi's findings thus reveal that the likelihood of retention differs greatly according to the level of a child's family resources. The NELS-88 survey confirms this, as 26.1% of African-American youngsters reported having repeated a grade versus 15.6% of whites. Also, 31.3% of children in the lowest family socioeconomic status (SES) quartile had repeated a grade versus 8.2% in the highest quartile (NCES 1990: 9).

Another sense of these patterns can be derived from data at the state level (Rose, Medway, Cantrell, and Marus 1983; Shepard and Smith 1989). Grade-specific retention rates (K through 12) for fifteen states in the 1979–80 and 1985–86 school years generally held steady through the decade of the eighties, increasing less than 1% overall, although in some states rates shot up (e.g., Arizona). These data on retention at the state level show that high retention rates prevailed through the eighties compared to earlier decades, and imply an even higher cumulative risk of retention. For example, grade-specific retention rates of 7% to 8% are common. If these are cumulated over 6 elementary years, then the risk of retention by middle school probably hovers around 50% in many localities. Though retention rates at the national level are hard to nail down precisely, impressions grounded in these various data sources nevertheless are highly congruent: rates are high overall, probably have increased substantially from the fifties and sixties, and are especially high for poverty-level and minority youngsters – the so-called at-risk students, whose academic problems have dominated educational policy discussions in recent years.

Shepard and Smith (1989: 9) credit high rates of retention to the eighties' education reform movement, ushered in by the National Commission on Excellence in Education's 1983 report, *A Nation at Risk*. Although widely credited with prompting the "excellence movement" of the eighties, this report probably instead helped crystallize trends already gathering steam. A "swelling chorus of complaints" about social promotion in the public schools had begun in the seventies (see Larabee 1984, for citations). From a historical perspective, enforcing rigorous promotion standards represents a return to practices that prevailed in the nineteenth century.

The Excellence Commission's report focused attention on a narrow set of policy options like the "New Basics" high school curriculum and higher educational standards (with students more often being held to them). In consequence, "social promotion" has declined. But the educational reform movement probably is not the only factor behind increased rates of retention. There also have been large demographic shifts in the school-age population, and those too have no doubt influenced retention rates. In 1966, 13% of elementary school students were African-American, and the 87% classified as "white" include Hispanics, Orientals, and Native Americans, as well as whites. By 1986 about 70% of elementary school children were white, about 16% African-American, and 10% Hispanic. Demographic projections anticipate continuing shifts in the proportion of minority and majority children between now and 2020. At that point only about 50% of children will be non-Hispanic whites, with 25% Hispanic and 25% African-American. The number of children living in poverty also is expected to increase – by 37% (Pallas, Natriello, and McDill 1989).

Minority group youngsters who are poor are at great risk of school failure, so in the next few decades rates of retention may rise considerably above current levels unless preventive steps are taken. Even now, though, as many as half of some school systems' students are not promoted from one grade to the next (for a survey of practices in several large urban school systems see Hammack 1986). Is it practical or wise to hold back so many youngsters? How can marginal students who have experienced only failure be shielded from further failure? For many of these youngsters enforcing rigid standards will backfire: they are encouraged to drop out, to act out, or both (McDill, Natriello, and Pallas 1986; Pallas, Natriello, and McDill 1987). Poor, inner-city minority youths are those whose promotion prospects are most in jeopardy. For many of them, flunking a grade could well shape life chances and incur costs for years to come. The next section reviews some of these possible costs.

Some costs of retention, in dollars and otherwise

Although retention is commonplace, not much is known about its costs and benefits. Some costs are clear-cut, but others are hard to assess because firm evidence is lacking. One obvious consequence of retaining youngsters is increased national education costs. In the mid-eighties, the price tag for having a student repeat a grade was about $3,500 (Harvard Education Letter 1986; Mueller 1989). As per pupil expenditures increase, this figure will rise as well. Retaining up to half of the children in a district one or more times by the fifth year of elementary school is roughly equivalent to increasing the district's elementary school population by 10%. The associated costs probably exceed 10%, however, because special programs are often provided for retained children.

One cost especially hard to calculate is a deferred one: school discontinuation. Failing a grade in school is an important predictor of dropping out of high school (Consortium for Longitudinal Studies 1983; Pallas 1987; Rumberger 1987; Wagenaar 1987), perhaps because repeating a grade increases children's adjustment problems in school (Kellam, Branch, Agrawal, and Ensminger 1975). One national study showed a dropout rate of about 40% among those who had failed a grade, compared to only 10% among those who were never held back (Bachman,

Green, and Wirtanen 1971). In a study of dropouts in Washington, D.C., more than 78% had been retained at least once, and more than 52% had been retained two or more times; only 22% of the dropouts had never been retained (Tuck 1989; see also Fine 1991). Young people who drop out of high school have lifetime earnings far below those of youngsters who continue. One study estimates the loss of lifetime earnings for dropouts to be around $100,000 even after adjusting for other related disadvantages (McDill, Natriello, and Pallas 1986; on some of the costs to society associated with dropout see Catterall 1987). Young people drop out for many reasons, but being behind in school is one of the strongest predictors even when other risk factors like minority status and poverty background are taken into account (Grissom and Shepard 1989; Pallas 1984). There are even connections between dropping out and early retention specifically (Cairns, Cairns, and Neckerman 1989; Lloyd 1978; Stroup and Robins 1972).

Retention affects success after high school in other ways as well. For example, Royce, Darlington, and Murray (1983: 444–45) report that, compared with similar students who had not repeated a grade, repeaters were more likely later to be unemployed or not seeking work, to be living on public assistance, or to be in prison. Delayed entry into the work force may be another cost of retention. Beginning work at 19 instead of 18 loses a year's salary, a cost that often will be passed along to parents who have to support their children for an additional year. Too, dropouts are less likely to get postsecondary schooling, another route to higher earnings. The direct excess educational costs for teaching students who repeat a year is thus in actuality only a small fraction of the long-term costs to the student and to society.

Beyond costs calculated in dollars, there may be psychological costs involving self-esteem or happiness, too. These costs are borne by both children and their families – parents because dreams for their children are compromised, and children because they come to see themselves as failures or misfits. Teachers and parents worry a great deal about the socioemotional consequences of children being off time in school, and with good reason. Repeating a grade seems to increase children's adjustment problems in school (Kellam et al. 1975), perhaps because it disrupts peer relations. When children move from grade to grade they generally keep the same peers, but retention separates children from their peers. Evidence indicates that school performance deteriorates when peer groups are disrupted (Felner and Adan 1988; Felner, Ginter, and Primavera 1982).

Does retaining pupils in a grade accomplish enough good to warrant the risks and costs it entails? No one knows. Despite extensive study and strong opinions, the jury is still out.

Retention: solution or problem?

When children fail to master the curriculum at an acceptable level of proficiency, there are at least three courses of action. The first is to alter policies so students will not have to be held back; that is, redesign the schooling process so everyone can be promoted. So far this has not proved feasible in the United States. Retention is not common in most other countries, even developed ones whose educational systems are seen as equal to or better than our own (Haddad 1979). Clearly, having children repeat a grade is not the only option, but promoting everyone has thus far not proved practical on a broad scale in the United States.[3]

Another possibility is to have students who fail go to summer school to make up ground. However, for reasons that are not well understood, summer programs at the elementary level are not very successful in making up for academic deficiencies (see Heyns 1987). To give an example, about 10% of Cincinnati children who participated in such a program after first grade achieved satisfactory levels of reading achievement in the summer session and went on to second grade, but for the other 90%, attending summer school did not prevent having to repeat first grade (Mueller 1989).

The third solution when performance is below standard is for youngsters to repeat the school year. As reviewed earlier, this is far more common in the United States than most people realize, indeed applying to up to 50% of poor, minority children in many school systems (see Hammack 1986).

Repeating a grade: the fairness issue

Popular sentiment (and probably most practitioners) would have youngsters repeat a year rather than pass them along ill prepared for the work that lies ahead. A Gallup poll (1986), for instance, reported that 72% of those queried felt that "promotion from grade to grade should be more strict than it is now." Moreover, in their study of kindergarten teachers' attitudes about retention, Smith and Shepard (1988: 330) found that most teachers, too, subscribe to an achievement ideology: "Teachers believe . . . the pupil career should be driven by competence or readiness rather than by social promotion and . . . for the most part, they act according to these beliefs." Is this unreasonable? Promoting children who clearly are not prepared simply sets them up for further failure.[4] Social promotion also creates management problems for teachers, who then must instruct children with widely varying competencies. It could even encourage the attitude among other students that anyone can slip through, although early research suggests this is not a serious risk (Hall and Demarest 1958; Otto and Melby 1935). Even if such concerns are exaggerated, they hardly reflect a mean-spirited desire to penalize those who cannot make the grade; yet from the existing research and commentary on the topic, one could conclude that harm is the actual, if unintended, result.

The "mean spiritedness" idea subsumes two themes. The first is "effectiveness," the surface concern. Sometimes this expands to "cost effectiveness," but whether cast in bookkeeping terms or not, there is a general expectation that educational interventions will do more good than harm, and preferably at least some good and no harm. Most of the research on retention takes this perspective: if retained youngsters are no better off than they would have been if passed along, then the intervention is judged unsuccessful or ineffective.[5] And if this could reasonably have been anticipated by those responsible for the decision, then "mean spirited" would seem an apt characterization.

But with "harm" and "good" on the table, we also need to ask, "To whom?" and "For whom?" This brings us to the second theme, which involves fairness or equity issues. Schools in the modern era shoulder many responsibilities, one being to help children from impoverished backgrounds who enter school poorly prepared. Many of these also will be minority youngsters. For such children, doing well in school can be a Herculean struggle, and schools must be meticulous in serving their needs.

Impressive progress has been made over the years in furthering equal opportunity for the less advantaged, but vigilance still is required. Even if most teachers rated children strictly in terms of classroom performance, there is always the possibility of so-called institutionalized discrimination – that is, of practices that are taken for granted as right and proper, but which nevertheless deny opportunities to poor and minority young-sters. In the minds of some, retention is one of these. Smith and Shepard (1987: 133), for instance, conclude that practices such as retention and homogeneous grouping by ability "[help] advantaged groups, [create] further barriers for the disadvantaged, and [promote] segregation and stratification."

Such concerns are long-standing (see, e.g., Abidin, Golladay, and Howerton 1971), and of course are not peculiar to retention. In fact, the potential for unfairness is present whenever instructional and organiza-tional interventions separate youngsters from one another on the basis of skill or achievement level and treat them differently thereafter. This is because academic and social disadvantage overlap. Minority and disad-vantaged youngsters almost always come out lower than whites and ad-vantaged youth on so-called merit selection criteria, and so the former will lag behind under merit-driven reward systems. To mention only the most obvious examples, there is disproportionate assignment of disad-vantaged youngsters to special education classes, to low-ability instruc-tional groups, and to general or vocational tracks at the secondary level. Minority and/or disadvantaged youngsters are underrepresented in pro-grams for the gifted and talented, and in admission to select colleges and universities. These young people are more likely to drop out and also, of course, to be held back, the focus of our interest here.

Some critics view merit criteria as either unnecessary or inappropriate, because using them has the effect of perpetuating historic inequalities, and of legitimating them under a veneer of equal opportunity. Even though it may be an unintended consequence of well-intended pro-cedures, relying on merit criteria tends to relegate minority and disad-vantaged youngsters to the bottom rung of practically every education ladder.

"Meritocrats," though, view these same selection criteria as necessary and appropriate. While they may regret that minority and disadvantaged youths fall at the low end, such an outcome is viewed as society's failing, not a reason to compromise academic standards. In fact, the argument goes, relying on merit standards serves all children's interests, because such standards channel young people into the education "slots" best suited to their talents and aptitudes. Put differently, this view holds that more youngsters will make better use of their potential under merit-based sorting than they would under any reasonable alternative.

This particular debate will be with us for many years to come, and properly so. Equity concerns almost always hover in the background when educational practices are being scrutinized, and this holds true especially for practices involving a remediation component. Under such circumstances, questions of "effectiveness" take on added significance. If retention is harmful rather than helpful, this needs to be known. This sentiment is echoed by Shepard and Smith (1988: 142): "Special placements require evidence of effectiveness . . . good intentions are not sufficient." The reason is straightforward: an intervention that has good consequences for its recipients is not likely to be deemed unfair. Fairness and effectiveness thus are joined. The analyses presented in this volume speak most directly to the question of effectiveness. In the narrow context of program evaluation, this sort of separation is possible, but whether a particular practice is good or wise is much more complicated. The concluding chapter addresses some of these broader questions that surround retention.

Prior research on repeating a grade: strong opinions, weak evidence

What does the available research say about the effects of retention? Three comprehensive reviews convey the tenor of a wide range of prior research. A paper by Holmes (1989) covers 61 studies, extending the coverage in two of his earlier papers (Holmes 1986; Holmes and Matthews 1984). The Harvard Graduate School of Education's Education Letter (1986) reviews 60 studies conducted since 1911. Jackson (1975) discusses 44 studies classified according to three types of research design: comparisons of retained versus promoted students; studies of how retained youngsters fare over time; and "true" experiments with random assignment of at-risk pupils to either retention or promotion groups.

None of these reviews favors retention as a strategy for helping poor-performing students do better, and over time the tone has gotten harsher and harsher (an exception is Karweit's [1992] recent overview of retention research, which will be mentioned later in this chapter). For example, in 1975 Jackson (p. 627) concluded that "there is no reliable body of evidence to indicate that grade retention is more beneficial than grade promotion for students with serious academic or adjustment difficulties." Almost a decade later, with even more studies at hand, Holmes and Matthews (1984: 232) wrote, "Those who continue to retain pupils at grade level do so despite cumulative research evidence that the potential for negative effects consistently outweighs positive outcomes. . . . the burden of proof legitimately falls on proponents of retention plans to show there is compelling logic indicating success of their plans where so many other plans have failed." Stronger still was Smith and Shepard's (1987: 134) indictment:

> The evidence is quite clear and nearly unequivocal that the achievement and adjustment of retained children are no better – and in most instances are worse – than those of comparable children who are promoted. *Retention is one part of the current reform packages that does not work.* (Emphasis in original)

This is strong language to be sure, but is the evidence really that clear and unequivocal? Summary judgments aside, the research studies on which these conclusions are based reflect a familiar pattern of conflicting and contradictory results. Most of the studies covered in the three reviews actually show insignificant differences between retained and nonretained children; some studies favor retention by a small margin, others do not, and significant differences point in both directions. More studies find in favor of promotion, but there are many exceptions.

In fact, after saying that there is no evidence in favor of retention, Jackson (1975: 627) goes on to say, "This conclusion should not be interpreted to mean that promotion is better than retention but, rather, that the accumulated research evidence is so poor that valid inferences cannot be drawn." It would appear that almost 20 years of further study have not done much to change the situation, as virtually the identical sentiment can be found in Karweit's (1992: 1117) recent review of the literature.

At issue here is the quality of research studies on retention (Harvard Education Letter 1986). Some studies, for example, examine students only after retention occurs, so if retained students have a lower effort level or feelings of competence below those of other students, it could be that retained students displayed these same characteristics before retention. Without knowing their preretention status, it is impossible to conclude how retention may have affected them.

Another serious failing is that many studies do not follow a comparison group of nonretained youngsters. If *only* retained children are followed, their performance could reflect a general decline in performance with age that would be seen for any group, whether or not retained (e.g., Simmons and Blyth 1987). For example, on average, all students' liking for school tends to decrease with age (e.g., Epstein and McPartland 1976; Harvard Education Letter 1992b). How retention affects children can be determined only if a comparable group of children who are not retained is also followed; but appropriate comparisons are difficult to accomplish, and studies inevitably fall short of the optimum. These points are developed more fully in the next section.

Meaningful comparisons: same age, same grade

Evaluating the effects of retention requires tracking the same students over time, and trying to isolate the effects of retention. The way comparison groups are formed is crucial. Comparison groups often are composed of "same grade" students. Same–grade comparisons evaluate retained pupils against their new classmates. For example, first graders who are repeating the grade are compared with first graders who are entering the grade for the first time. This type of comparison has obvious drawbacks, because it compares retainees with youngsters who generally will be a year or so younger. However, it can be useful for deciding whether an extra year in a grade brings children up to grade-level expectations.

A second kind of comparison, the "same age" variety, evaluates retainees against promoted members of their original class at some later point. For instance, how do retained pupils fare after 2 years in first grade in comparison with their promoted classmates, who would be finishing second grade? Same-age comparisons involve children of roughly similar age, but at different grade levels. Obviously this type of comparison also has drawbacks. How can we expect children who have seen only the first grade curriculum to perform on the same level as children who have seen both a first and second grade curriculum?

The distinction between same-grade and same-age comparisons is important, as is the need for both types. There is no single ideal comparison: it is impossible to have retained and nonretained youngsters be of the same age and in same grade. The two types of comparison are illustrated in Figure 1.1, which tracks two successive cohorts of school beginners for 3 years. In this example, all members of the study group (cohort 1) start out together as first graders (point A). At year's end most of the cohort has moved up to second grade (point C), but some were

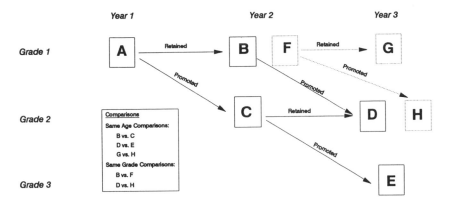

Figure 1.1. Illustration of same-age and same-grade comparisons involving retainees in the early primary grades. Solid lines: members of cohort 1; dotted lines: members of cohort 2.

held back, and hence in the second year are still first graders (point B). Between the second and third years the study group continues to spread out. By the third year most first grade repeaters will have joined some second grade repeaters in second grade (point D), while their "on time" peers have moved into third grade (point E).

Meanwhile, in the second year a new beginning cohort has begun to work its way through the system. In Year 2, these "new" first graders from cohort 2 (point F) are joined by repeaters from cohort 1 (point B). In Year 3, some members of cohort 2 still are in first grade (point G), but those who move on to second grade (point H) are assigned to classes with first and second grade repeaters from the first cohort (point D).

The picture gets more complicated still as time goes on, but the snapshot in Figure 1.1 is sufficient to set up the contrasts of interest. Point B locates first grade retainees from the first cohort at the end of their repeated grade. To see how they are faring relative to their original cohortmates, we would compare their performance with the youngsters at point C; this is a same-age comparison. The corresponding comparison 2 years postretention involves points D and E; these youngsters are the same age, but have just finished grades 2 and 3 respectively.

Same-grade comparisons can be made two ways. An example from Figure 1.1 would be at points B and F, where first grade repeaters from cohort 1 are evaluated at the end of their repeated year against their new grademates from cohort 2, who have just gone through first grade for the first time. Another such comparison would be at the end of second grade, points D and H, which carries the comparison a year beyond retention for first grade repeaters from the first cohort. In both instances, retainees are compared with their new classmates, who generally will be about a year younger but similar in terms of their location within the grade structure.

A second strategy for making same-grade comparisons would be to evaluate retainees' performance at the end of a particular grade against that of their original cohortmates a year earlier, when they successfully finished the same grade. In Figure 1.1, one such comparison would evaluate retained youngsters at point B against the promoted youngsters at point A. This is the type of same-grade comparison used in the present research, which examines data on the experiences of a single cohort over time.

The same-age and same-grade comparisons afford complementary perspectives on retention. Same-age comparisons may tilt results against retention because the agemates are at different grade levels, so the promoted group will have been exposed to more of the elementary school curriculum. Same-grade comparisons may tilt results in favor of retention because the retained youngsters have advantages: being older than their grademates, having gone through the curriculum twice, receiving special remedial efforts, and perhaps being test-wise if the same evaluation instrument is used repeatedly. It is important that many of the more recent studies reviewed in Holmes's 1989 literature update favored retention, and most of these employed a strategy of same-grade comparisons. Karweit (1992) also comments on these more recent studies, noting that positive results most often are obtained when retention is joined with a planned remediation program. Karweit mentions specifically in this regard the evaluation reported by Peterson, DeGracie, and Ayabe (1987), which we discuss later in this chapter.

Holmes discounts these positive results, however, partly because of the same-grade strategy. In such comparisons, retainees generally will be a year or so older than children in the comparison group, which gives them a developmental advantage. But there are organizational advantages, too, and with the possible exception of test-wiseness, these reflect the logic of retention as an intervention. The idea is to give children a chance to catch up, and the time it takes to reach this goal should not be the only factor weighing on the merits of the practice. If repeating a year brings performance up to the requisite standards, and if children thereafter progress like others who were able to meet that standard in just 1 year, then retention may have fulfilled its purpose.[6]

Of course, meeting performance standards is not the only concern. There also is worry about being labeled a "failure." However, in schools where retention is relatively commonplace, the stigma from repeating a grade could be cushioned, and retained children's day-to-day classroom experience even could be ego building if the classwork after retention is more within their capabilities. Such children could show up well against their new, younger classmates. If they are on average getting B's and the rest of the class is getting C's, they will be experiencing "success." If this relative advantage persists beyond the year of retention, we might conclude that repeating a grade was beneficial, even if children were thrown off schedule as a result.

The "matching" strategy and its problems

Beyond the same-grade / same-age issue for framing comparisons, there are further challenges. For example, to make a fair comparison of a group that was retained with one that was not, the groups should be about the same on ability tests and on other relevant qualities *before* retention. This is a tall order because it is not sensible to think that promoted children who test at the same ability level as retained children are in other ways the same: if they were the same in every way, they presumably would also be retained. For example, those who are low in ability but nevertheless promoted may do well by trying hard, or because they are more emotionally mature. Equating the two groups only in terms of the ability to achieve high test scores will not provide a fair comparison, as the later success of promoted students could be due to these other qualities, and not to their having been spared the stigma of retention.

As this example suggests, it is hard to separate the effects of retention from those of other problems that may have led children to be retained in the first place. One approach would be to list all the youngsters whose performance puts them at risk for retention, and then randomly place them into two groups: one group to be retained and another group to be promoted. If the pool of students were large enough, then the two groups should be equivalent (within sampling fluctuations) with respect to the risk factors that prompt a retention decision. Because of the random assignment, later on, when school performance is compared across these randomly constituted groups, the influence of other factors should be equivalent. If the promoted youngsters were doing better than the repeaters in the year after retention, and if the difference was too large to be due to chance, we would conclude that retention had an adverse effect. This conclusion would be justified because other likely sources of uneven performance would have been equated in the two groups by the earlier random assignment. Other risk factors should not contribute to group differences in performance.[7]

Random assignment, though, is not a viable strategy (on the impracticality of this approach for assessing effects of retention, see Harvard Education Letter 1986: 3). It is hard to imagine parents being willing to have a child pass or fail at the toss of a coin, even for a scientific experiment; and even if they were, most scientists would eschew this strategy for ethical reasons. The alternative is to identify the complicating factors that cloud comparisons, then somehow adjust for their influence in the research design or by statistical means. As a practical matter, there is no way to begin except to compare retained and promoted groups that are *not* equivalent.

With strict random assignment ruled out, an intuitively appealing strategy is to "match" youngsters so as to mimic the kinds of groups that would result from a random assignment. That is, after the retained youngsters are identified, the investigator looks at the (larger) pool of promoted children and selects a comparison group of promoted youngsters who are similar to their retained classmates. Using this kind of "matched control" group is common in research on retention, but there is a fundamental difficulty with this approach: a comparison group of "at risk but promoted" children will never be matched perfectly to a group of retained youngsters. For one thing, even with a large group to select from, it is impossible to match children on more than a few characteristics at a time. It would be hard, for example, to match exactly on age, sex, ethnic group, parents' socioeconomic status, and test performance, even with a pool of several hundred youngsters. Moreover, matching on these criteria does not match students on teachers' marks, family size, peer popularity, and many other potentially critical factors. No matter how extensive the matching, there can be no guarantee that something else of importance is not matched and that this "something," rather than retention, is the cause of differences that are found later between the promoted and the nonpromoted students. This is a fundamental dilemma, with no sure way out.

Other weaknesses in prior studies

The available evidence on retention has weaknesses beyond those involving the nature of comparison groups. Much of the literature is dated; the major reviews, for example, typically include studies that now are more than a half century old! In light of the demographic shifts and changes in school organization and curriculum that have occurred in the past few decades, the current applicability of these older studies is suspect. A contemporary urban school with a high minority enrollment and a 40% retention rate is far different from one of a few decades ago enrolling no minority students and having a 5% retention rate.

Another problem is that, of the many current studies, a large majority is unpublished. Of 63 studies reviewed by Holmes (1989), only 20 were published. The others were unpublished dissertations, master's theses, and the like. There is some quality assurance in published research, in that it goes through a refereeing process in which researchers in the same field examine it and decide whether or not it merits publication. That so much of the evidence about retention comes from unpublished sources is cause for concern.

Still another weakness in retention research is sampling, that is, how the youngsters are selected. Rarely has research on retention used nationally representative, or even especially diverse, samples. Years ago Jackson (1975: 628) mentioned the "failure to sample from a population large and diverse enough to allow broad generalization" as a weakness that future studies should try to correct, but the literature still is weak on this score. Bianchi's (1984) study is the only one known to us based on a national probability sample, but her research deals with being off time, not exactly the same topic as retention, and it considers only risk factors, not consequences. The recent NELS-88 study of eighth graders is national in scope, but covers retention in the primary grades through retrospective questions asked of the pupils and their parents (e.g., Meisels and Liaw 1991; Stevenson, Schiller, and Schneider 1992). This methodology has obvious drawbacks. The evidence now available on effects of retention is especially weak with respect to groups at particular risk for retention (e.g., minority youngsters from disadvantaged circumstances; for relevant comment, see also Reynolds 1992).

Another problem is that most evaluations of retention extend only a semester or a single year after children are held back. Since what happens during the child's repeated year may be unlike what happens in subsequent years (the child is going through the curriculum for the second time and adjusting to the new peer group), a short-term followup will not give a full reading of the impact of retention. The long-term consequences of retention could be different from, and more important than, its immediate consequences.

There is already solid evidence that retention in the early grades leads to dropping out in secondary school. What about other long-term outcomes? For example, what about the youngsters retained in first grade who at the time of puberty mature earlier than their grademates? They may have made a satisfactory adjustment to that point, but at the adolescent transition be conspicuous because of their off-time status. On the other hand, there may be long-term positive consequences as well. Retention could lead to less need for special education later on, or to better reading proficiency in high school.

The research literature offers little guidance about long-term consequences. In addition, most studies consider retention from a limited vantage point, focusing either on children's academic performance or on some aspect of their socioemotional adjustment. Rarely are both considered. However, cognitive and affective development go hand in hand, and retention could affect both children's intellectual growth and their socioemotional and personal functioning. On the one hand, there is some indication that children who are held back tend to have fewer friends than those not held back (Harvard Education Letter 1986). Such children could also suffer a loss of self-esteem or of parents' confidence, both of which could undermine school performance. On the other hand, children who are held back could also get better marks in school as they repeat a grade, and perhaps this would begin to draw out their academic potential. Many such questions remain unanswered.

Same-grade comparisons, same-age comparisons, and matching in recent research

Despite these serious problems with the retention literature, recent research appears to be improving in quality. The report by Peterson, DeGracie, and Ayabe (1987) already mentioned illustrates this improvement and also highlights the trade-offs required when "matching" is used to make comparisons. The question these authors address is whether public school children in Mesa, Arizona, who are retained in the first, second, or third grade, do better in reading, language, and math after 4 years of schooling than do other children not retained. In the Mesa school system, retainees get special remedial assistance. This project began in 1981, and includes all youngsters retained that year for whom California Achievement Test (CAT) data are available in at least one subject over a 4-year period. The number of students is not exactly the same for every type of performance, but the analysis includes about 65 first grade retainees, 26 second grade retainees, and 14 third grade retainees.[8]

To afford a base of comparison, matched samples of promoted youngsters were identified at each grade level. Criteria used in the matching included information on the pupils' sex, ethnicity, and age, as well as reading, math, and language scores from the spring 1981 CAT administration. Although it is hard to tell exactly how the matching was implemented, the use of several test domains along with students' personal demographic characteristics is uncommonly inclusive, and there is good correspondence between retained and promoted subsamples on all matching criteria.

Peterson et al.'s analysis is straightforward. They present test means and standard deviations from the spring of each year from 1981 through 1984, separately for retainees and matched controls. The averages are reported in normal curve equivalent units (performance relative to that of the norm group taking the same-level test). This mode of presentation enables use of the two comparisons discussed earlier, that is, same-age and same-grade. The first compares the performance of retained youngsters with that of the promoted members of their cohort at the same time.[9] The second compares retained pupils with promoted youngsters at the end of a particular grade level – first or second, for example. This kind of comparison could be against the previous years' scores of promoted members of their original cohort, or against the current scores of the cohort repeaters moved into when they were held back. Peterson et al.'s analysis uses the first of these approaches, but in either case the retainees will be older than the youngsters they are being compared with.

At the end of the repeated grade, Peterson et al. find significant advantages favoring held-back youngsters in terms of their position relative to their former classmates *at the same point in time* (B vs. C from Figure 1.1, for example). These same-age advantages diminish in subsequent years, however, and by the third year they are no longer significant. Even so, there is no indication in these data that retained students are falling behind their promoted peers.

In same-grade comparisons these researchers again find significant advantages for held-back youngsters at the end of their repeated grade, especially for those held back in first grade. Retainees, for example, did better at the end of the second time through first grade than their original, promoted grademates had when they finished first grade the year previously. This would be the B-versus-A comparison from Figure 1.1.

This comparison is potentially misleading, however, because the matched first grade students who were promoted were matched partly in terms of their poor performance on the CAT in the spring of that year. Hence, if retained pupils advanced at all during the repeated year, as they would be expected to, they would necessarily outdistance their matched classmates, whose scores would be the same low average from spring 1981 that was the basis for their selection. The appearance of a first-year advantage thus reflects mainly the consequences of the matching procedure. This is one of the pitfalls of matching.[10] Significantly, though, Peterson et al.'s results also show small advantages for these repeaters when they finished the second and third grades, compared to their promoted classmates when *they* finished second and third grades, so there are indications that the advantages of repeating a grade persisted for 2 or 3 years. These comparisons, unlike those for the baseline year, probably are meaningful.

This study, then, shows some positive consequences for retention. Same-grade advantages are found for retainees for several years, while same-age comparisons indicate improved relative performance in the repeated year. However, by the third year after retention, retainees were performing at about the same level as their matched-control agemates. As is typical, Peterson et al. accept this last detail as a negative indication in the evaluation. Since the later testing levels of retainee and control groups were not significantly different, it cannot be said that retention accomplished anything useful in these instances.

But is this last conclusion really warranted? This is arguable, because for retainees just to be holding their own may be an accomplishment.

Much hinges on what would have happened if these youngsters had not repeated a year, and not been given the opportunity to consolidate their skills. The logic of using matched controls is intended to afford a window on this counterfactual possibility, but at this point the power of experimental versus nonexperimental studies becomes clear. Had the retained youngsters not been obliged to repeat a year, would we really expect their achievement profiles to look like those of their poor-performing but promoted matched peers? The very fact that retainees were designated for retention and the controls were not suggests that retained youngsters' difficulties were more severe. As already mentioned, it is impossible to match retained and promoted students on all the relevant factors; the promoted students, for example, might be more mature, have fewer family problems, or be less aggressive than the held-back students.

Under a social promotion policy, retained youngsters might have fallen farther and farther behind, as their skill deficiencies, poor work habits, low self-esteem, and other characteristics continued to hinder their progress. If this were the expectation, then to find that children who have been held back were performing more or less on a par with their classmates 3 years afterward would be impressive.

Other information gaps

The Peterson et al. study thus suggests that retention may well accomplish some good, although results from other recent studies are mixed (e.g., Mantzicopoulos and Morrison 1992; Meisels and Liaw 1991; Pierson and Connell 1992; Reynolds 1992). The issue still is very much open, and many, many questions remain. For one thing, as noted earlier, information on achievement levels that predates retention is essential. Knowledge of the child's status before retention affords a frame of reference for inferring what might be anticipated in the absence of retention, as well as an empirical baseline against which to weigh postretention performance.

Also, most prior research concentrates on how retention affects achievement-test scores, ignoring children's emotional and affective responses to retention. Concerns about the stigma of retention must be high on the agenda, because a youngster who is harmed emotionally may bear permanent scars. At issue here are students' feelings about themselves. There is first their public identity as "failures." Do those who are retained suffer loss of self-esteem, or have reduced feelings of efficacy?

There is ample evidence that children who believe they can succeed are more likely to do so. Another issue is that children of a given age are expected to be in a particular grade. "Off time" youngsters are "deviant" according to the schools' regular timetable, and this could cause them problems for many reasons: their level of physical development is not the same as that of their classmates, they may be in the same grade as one of their younger siblings or friends who started school later, and so on.

These kinds of responses – experiencing losses in self-esteem or being harmed socioemotionally in some other way – are hard to measure but are clearly important. In fact, most laypersons think mainly of these consequences of retention rather than of those involving school performance, yet prior research has little to say about socioemotional repercussions.

Retainees in the Beginning School Study

The purpose of this book is to answer some of the questions about retention that have been raised in this chapter, using information from the Beginning School Study (BSS), a large-scale study of students in Baltimore who began first grade in 1982. Evaluating the consequences of retention is our primary objective, but we will also see what kinds of children most often are retained, and will sketch the contours of the retention experience by describing retention patterns in the elementary and middle school years. We will describe how retention intersects other aspects of "administrative sorting" in these years, including assignment to special education classes, ability-group placements for instruction in reading, and curricular placements in middle school. The broader system of educational tracking within which retention is embedded is typically neglected in research on retention, which almost invariably studies retention apart from these other placements. This is a potentially serious oversight, however, as these interventions are joined, not separated, in children's experience. Tracking patterns in the elementary school and middle school years are examined in Chapter 8.

The BSS, which is an ongoing study, was not designed specifically to study retention. Rather, it is a long-term prospective study of young children's academic and socioemotional development, and was undertaken to see what helps or hinders children as they go through school. This broad sweep, it turns out, is extremely useful as we explore the consequences of retention.

When the BSS children started first grade, no one knew who would fall behind, but in the 8 years covered in the present volume, about half of them did. The Baltimore system follows a K–5, 6–8 grade organization, so 8 years of schooling coincide with the end of middle school if nothing goes wrong. But being held back throws repeaters off schedule, so at the end of 8 years they will not be finishing middle school. Unlike their "on time" peers, it will take them 9 or more years to make it into high school, and some very likely will drop out before then. This book looks to see what happens to them along the way, prior to the high school transition.

By virtue of its inclusiveness and duration, the BSS contains information on the academic performance and personal development of retainees and nonretainees alike, both before and after retention. This information, moreover, has been obtained directly from the retained children and from their promoted classmates, from teachers and parents, and from school-system records. There is a rich set of data for studying retention, and because the study is long-term, the impact of retention can be traced over many years.

The sample

A stratified random sample of just under 800 students was selected from the pool of youngsters entering first grade in Baltimore City Public Schools in 1982. The 20 schools in the study were chosen at random from within strata defined by the school's integration status (i.e., "mostly white," "mostly African-American," and "racially integrated") and by community socioeconomic level (i.e., "blue collar" and "white collar") (see Table 1.2). Random samples from the previous year's kindergarten rosters were chosen in each of the twenty schools in the summer before children started first grade; in the fall, supplemental samples of new first grade registrants in each school also were drawn. Every first grade classroom in the 20 schools was included in the sampling. The summer sampling gave us time to obtain parental consent for most of the students before the start of the school year.

The two-stage random sampling plan (first schools were picked randomly, then students were picked randomly within first grade classrooms) strengthens the study because it ensures a nonvolunteer sample; parents did not volunteer their children or otherwise secure their own admission to the study. All but 3% of the parents selected did agree,

Table 1.2. *Socioeconomic and racial classification of schools in the Beginning School Study sample*

	Predominantly African-American		Integrated		Predominantly White		Total
Community type	No. of schools	Av. parent education (years)	No. of schools	Av. parent education (years)	No. of schools	Av. parent education (years)	
Blue collar	5	11.6	4	10.9	5	10.6	14
White collar	1	12.8	4	14.2	1	12.7	6
Total	6		8		6		20

Note: Based on data on entire first grade enrollments, African-American children in the integrated schools ranged from 13% to 85%, with an average for the eight schools of 45%. Figures based on the BSS sample range from 12% to 97%, averaging 51%. Data on parents' educational level are from the parent interviews conducted summer through early fall 1982.

however, when we requested their permission to study the children identified in the random selection process. In other studies of retention, neither schools nor parents are picked randomly.

Without random sampling, schools and parents that are most concerned about retention (or about students) are likely to be the ones studied. This kind of selection bias is a serious concern. If parents of retained children recruit themselves and their children into a study, or if a principal volunteers the school as a study site, there may be biases in terms of the attention that parents and school devote to retained children. They may be unusually aware of retention or the problems it breeds, for example, or know exactly which children have been retained, whereas in other schools where retention is not a focus of attention retained children might be much less visible. Parents who volunteer their children for educational studies also are apt to be more concerned about their children's educational progress, and therefore more motivated to do things that might help their children, than are parents who do not volunteer.

The BSS sample intentionally overrepresents whites and higher SES youngsters with respect to the Baltimore City school population. About 55% of the BSS sample is African–American, as contrasted to about 77% of the entire city system enrollment at the time the project commenced (U.S. Bureau of the Census 1983). A simple random sample of Baltimore children in 1982 would have had too few well-off students and too few white students to permit SES or racial/ethnic comparisons. A stratified design maintains representativeness, but also guarantees adequate coverage of the major racial groups and the full range of SES levels.

Strengths and weaknesses of the BSS for studying retention

The BSS data and design have much to offer in trying to understand the impact of retention. For one thing, the data are longitudinal. We know these children's histories from a point before any were retained. The students' preretention status on many characteristics – achievement level, classroom deportment, self-regard, and others – can be assessed. Also, their parents' and teachers' views of them before they were retained are known. This is of great importance, since youngsters who are retained typically have academic or adjustment problems that predate retention.

Failure to take account of preexisting problems in comparing retained with nonretained pupils could give a false picture of retention's impact, as we have discussed. Because coverage in the BSS starts at the beginning of first grade or even earlier, before anyone has been held back, there is an important safeguard against misconstruing some children's long-standing academic and adjustment problems as consequences of retention.

The BSS data also are timely, spanning the decade of the eighties. The youngsters in this sample began first grade in 1982, and this book covers information about them through the spring of 1990.

The sample itself is another asset. The BSS is a large, diverse, representative, nonvolunteer sample of children attending public schools in a major urban center. The majority are African-American, but a large number are white. Many of them are poor, but a significant fraction are not. Poor, urban, minority children are most at risk for being off time in school, and figure prominently in policy discussions of at-risk pupils, yet they have not often been the targets of retention research. Rather, retention studies often use convenience samples of middle class children who are more readily accessible. The BSS sample ought to provide a solid foundation for drawing conclusions about what retention does to and for the kinds of children most typically held back. The data are from Baltimore exclusively, but we suspect the day-to-day situation in Baltimore is broadly similar to that in other large city school systems with high enrollments of poor and minority children.

Our analysis plan also is different from that used in most prior retention research because we rely mainly on statistical adjustments to make "fair" comparisons between retainees and other children rather than try to match cases on a one-to-one basis to form "comparison groups." This strategy preserves the representativeness of the sampling base, and ideally also avoids the problems discussed earlier in connection with matched comparison groups in weighing retention's consequences. Also, we make several kinds of comparisons, rather than relying on just one. The quality of the baseline information and the size of the BSS sample are sufficient to permit the necessary statistical adjustments, and the overtime data allow us to consider possible effects from several vantage points (see Chapters 4 and 5).

That the BSS is longitudinal and also long-term is another plus. The data in the present volume cover 8 years of schooling, and focus on the experiences of an entire cohort as it moves along. Early retainees (first, second, and third grade repeaters specifically) are followed for several grades beyond the repeated year.

We have said that the repeated year is special in many ways. Only after it is behind them can we judge how students are faring in a "regular" environment. For first grade retainees, we can track subsequent performance and adjustment through the completion of seventh grade – 2 years in first grade, plus 1 year each in grades 2 through 7. Having an especially long time to study first grade repeaters, and the opportunity to compare them with youngsters held back in second grade or later, will allow us to see whether retention in grade 1 stands apart from that in later years. There are reasons to suspect it might. Certainly the fact that retention rates are much higher in first grade than later seems to suggest so (for grade-by-grade comparisons covering 13 states, see Morris 1993; Shepard and Smith 1989).

The year of transition into formal schooling – first grade – carries special pressures and demands. Faring well or poorly at this point has consequences that echo far into the future. In higher grades, students have already made various accommodations to the academic routine; as a result, later retention may have less of an impact. The combination of transition pressures overlaid on a formative stage of schooling sets first grade apart. In addition to examining whether retention has different effects according to the grade in which it occurs, we can also say a little about children who are moved into special education after retention, and how this relates to retention. We can pose questions, then, about the scheduling of retention and about how retention ties in with other interventions, like special education.

Finally, and perhaps most important, the BSS data allow academic and socioemotional consequences of retention to be examined together, with coverage of multiple topics in both areas. In the academic area, we will consider children's gains on standardized tests and report card marks. Teachers' marks are certainly related to test performance, but they also capture other aspects of the child's performance, such as the degree of effort expended and the ability to solve problems independently, work consistently toward a goal, and cooperate with others in group work.

In terms of socioemotional outcomes, the possible stigmatizing effects of retention are of great concern. In this volume we consider retainees' own reactions to the retention experience, their academic "sense of self,"

self-regard more generally, and their future expectations with respect to schooling. If retention is as punishing for children as some fear, this should be detectable in children's ideas about themselves and their future prospects. Many questions about self-regard and hopes for the future were asked in individual interviews with children both before and after they were held back. We therefore can look specifically for changes in outlook that surround the retention experience.

The data come mainly from school records, from one-on-one interviews with the BSS youngsters and their parents, and from self-administered questionnaires in the case of their teachers. We have talked directly with the individuals involved many times over the years. For many questions surrounding retention this is an exceptionally strong data base. With test scores and report card marks for 8 years, for example, we can cover children's academic progress all through the elementary grades and well into middle school. The pupil interviews allow us to monitor changes in repeaters' thinking over this same period.

The BSS project has some weaknesses too, however, and these are important to acknowledge. There are issues that cannot be addressed with the BSS data, at least not as fully as we would want, and the present volume will have little to say about them. Probably the main shortcoming is that we have not done detailed classroom observations. Consequently, we can comment on pupil–teacher interactions and retainees' relations with their classmates only in terms of what they have told us. Survey respondents may not always be candid or forthcoming, especially when they are being queried about potentially sensitive issues. There is also the risk that problems will go undetected, either because they are not covered in the interview or because the questions have not been framed properly. Then too, there are matters that simply do not lend themselves to an interview format because they are too nuanced, too sensitive, or involve concerns about which the respondents might not even be aware.

In our case, the risk of deliberate distortion probably is slight. We did not set out in the BSS to study retention, and none of our queries was cast in those terms. Children were selected for participation in the study because they started first grade in the fall of 1982, not because of their standing as repeaters. Our questioning similarly had little to do with retention. When exploring children's self-attitudes, feelings about school, and the like, questions were asked of everyone, and none dealt with retention per se. The same is true of questions posed of parents and teachers. Some youngsters were repeaters and others were not, but this was was never an issue in any of our fieldwork, so participation in the study should not have heightened sensitivity to the subject.

To the extent that concerns about retention can be addressed this way, the BSS should be a good source. However, the day-to-day details of children's classroom experience are not well covered in this approach. Survey and observational studies are complementary. We will be able to detect problems surrounding retention that show up in children's performance on standardized tests, in the marks they receive, and in the more global reactions of self and others. Other dimensions of the problem are beyond the scope of this volume.

There also are concerns that involve problems encountered in implementing our research design. The BSS extends over many years and draws data from many sources. Our procedures generally have worked well. Indeed, through Year 8 almost 80% of the original sample was still participating in the study. Nevertheless, information from all sources is not available each year. Our testing data, for example, come from the school system's regular testing schedule. When children were absent on the testing days, or were missed because they moved between schools, scores are not available for them. Similarly, not all parents and children were able to be interviewed on each occasion (mainly because of difficulty locating them). Not all teachers consented to participate in the study as respondents, although none refused to allow their pupils to be interviewed.

Gaps in cov< age thus are a concern throughout, especially for the many youngsters who left the city schools during the 8 years covered in this volume. In Chapter 2, where the children's movement up the grade structure and through the school system is plotted in detail, we will see that some 40% are gone by the end of Year 8. School record data are not available for most of these youngsters after leaving the BCPS, and interview coverage for them and their parents is spotty. How these missing data affect our conclusions will be explored in detail throughout the volume.

Another concern is that school record data on grade-level progressions are sketchy or unreliable for some children. Fifteen children, in fact, had to be excluded from the entire investigation because we could not track them well enough using school records to be certain what happened to them. The inability to track these children, and other problems of incomplete data, alerted us to an important issue not acknowledged in previous studies of retention: the sorting of children in the first few years of schooling that places many of those with the most severe problems outside normal recordkeeping procedures. Some with severe family problems move frequently from one school to another. This leads to their records being lost or mislaid. They also miss taking tests on regular schedules. These children would be completely overlooked in conventional studies of retention or, for that matter, in most research on schooling, because students are sampled by grade rather than by cohort. Cohort sampling is based on the total potential population in a grade. Problems of missing data and sample attrition will be taken up in the next chapter, where we trace students' "pathways" through their first 8 years of school.

Another drawback is that our data on parents' economic standing are not as detailed as we would like. Coverage of students' social demographic characteristics is important for describing who is retained, and also for making statistical adjustments when we try to isolate effects of retention from possible confounding factors. From parent interviews we have data on education, but to cover economic well-being we rely mainly on school records pertaining to eligibility for reduced-price school meals, which lets us place parents into high- and low-income categories. Other aspects of these youngsters' family circumstances, such as regularity of income, total amount of income, or whether they are on welfare, are not known.[11]

We also know little about any special services provided youngsters before, during, or after their retention year. We know a bit about their receipt of remedial instruction in math or reading, but little more. Some may have gone to special summer programs, for example. Our analysis will have little to say about such supplementary services.

Plan of the book

Chapter 2 charts children's movement through the school system during the elementary and middle school years, with particular attention given to the separation of retainees from their original cohortmates. In Chapter 3 we look to see exactly who the retainees are, in terms of their social demographic characteristics and school-readiness problems. Then, in Chapters 4, 5, and 6 we consider how retention affects school performance as measured by results of standardized tests and by teachers' marks. In Chapter 7 we examine possible stigmatizing effects of retention, and in Chapter 8 we examine how retention ties in with other forms of administrative sorting such as assignment to special education classes, group placements for instruction in the first grade, the level of children's instruction in reading throughout the primary grades, and curricular assignment across "remedial," "regular," and "advanced" English and math classes in middle school. In the concluding chapter we reflect broadly on the findings and their policy implications.

2

Children's pathways through the elementary and middle school years: retention+

We saw in Chapter 1 that repeating a grade in elementary school is commonplace, and that for minority and disadvantaged youngsters in urban centers it is often the rule rather than the exception. However, the picture is sketchy at best because at the national level we know virtually nothing about retention trends. Instead, the data cover overage and underage enrollments, which leaves considerable room for slippage. A recent national study of eighth graders (NELS-88; see NCES 1990) asked students and their parents about prior retention, and this survey will help answer some questions about prevalence. Nevertheless, retrospective recall is no substitute for frequent, detailed monitoring of what is actually happening in the lives of children as they move through the elementary grades.

This chapter plots the BSS cohort's history of retentions over an 8-year period. For children who remained on schedule and who attended K–5, 6–8 schools (the typical grade organization in the Baltimore system), this time frame covers all of elementary and middle school. However, many children are thrown "off schedule" because of retention and other complications, and so will not move out of middle school on time. One consequence is that the transition between levels of schooling (e.g., from elementary to middle school, and from middle school to high school) is also delayed. Most retainees will not be with their age peers or with their entering cohort when they move from one level of schooling to the next, and their integration with new classmates could add to the adjustment challenges that attend such transitions even under ordinary circumstances (Eccles and Midgley 1989; Simmons and Blyth 1987).

We will also describe how retention ties in with other "sorting" or "tracking" experiences students have over this period, especially assignment into, and sometimes out of, special education classes. The link between retention and special education is of particular interest because many youngsters are assigned to special education *after* being held back. These youngsters very likely have especially severe problems, either academic or emotional, and so the special education connection may be important for understanding how retention works. If these children are the "worst cases," not keeping track of them could be a serious oversight when weighing retention's successes and failures. Provision of special education "pull out" programs for retained children in regular classrooms will also be considered. In Baltimore, these programs provide instruction in math and / or reading.

Grade acceleration after retention – midyear promotion and skipping of grades between years – also will be examined. These "irregularities" would be easy to miss in a cross-sectional or retrospective study, yet they, too, could be important for understanding how retention works.

The main purpose of this chapter is to trace children's schooling history in light of administrative sorting. This sorting includes school transfers, between Baltimore schools and also out of the system. School moves are important in their own right, because moves impose heavy burdens on young children, with serious academic consequences (see Alexander, Entwisle, and Dauber 1994; Wood et al. 1993).

Sample attrition is another, procedural reason for examining moves. Not all children in the cohort are covered for the entire 8 years, and the consequences of this have to be weighed carefully. Most attrition from the BSS panel is due to transfer out of the city's school system. Examining school moves allows us to see how many children have left, who they are (the matter of selective sample loss), and whether the representativeness of our sample has been seriously compromised as a result.

Children's promotion histories: e unum pluribus?

Children in the BSS all began first grade in the fall of 1982. From that point forward, their school careers diverged along many varied pathways. Some of this complexity is conveyed in Figure 2.1, which maps students' moves over the years (column headings) and across grade levels (row headings) for 8 years. The intersection between columns and rows highlights on-time and off-time patterns. The chart also shows movement out of the school system, which is the major source of sample attrition.

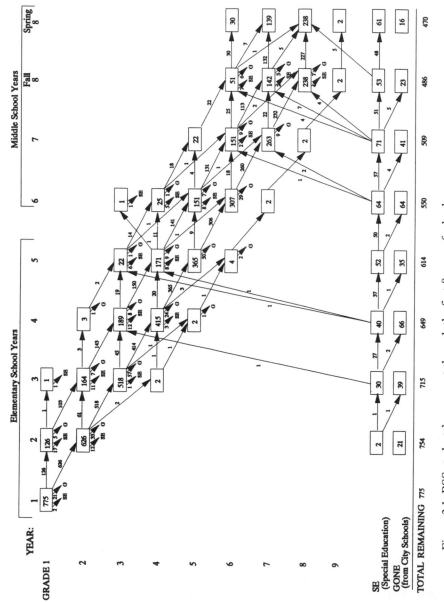

Figure 2.1. BSS students' movement through the first 8 years of school.

Although initially we sampled 790 youngsters who began first grade in the fall of 1982, only 775 are covered in the chart. Fifteen youngsters have been excluded because of gaps in the record of annual grade assignments that could not be filled from other sources, or because of inconsistencies that could not be reconciled.[1] To keep the display manageable, Figure 2.1 tracks fall-to-fall placements. Midyear gaps will be filled in later.[2]

Educational sorting in the elementary grades

Figure 2.1 is the main record of the BSS cohort's history of administrative sorting. It spans the elementary grades – in most schools grades 1 through 5 – and middle school, grades 6, 7, and 8. The "775" entry in the first cell indicates the number of children who started as first graders in the fall of 1982. The arrows plot subsequent movement, with the "SE" trail indicating assignment to separate special education classes. These assignments are made during the school year, and refer to classes in the spring of that year. Some SE children eventually return to regular classes, but not until at least a year after being assigned to special education.[3] The "G" trail identifies transfer out of the BCPS ("G" means "gone" from the BCPS). The timing of out-transfer is determined from school records.

The main path from Year 1 to Year 2 is from first to second grade, with 626 children remaining "on schedule" at this point. The 126 students who are still in first grade in the fall of the second year are first grade repeaters, as is one of the two children assigned to special education classes in the first year. The total retention rate for the first year, just over 16% (127 of the 775 students in the sample),[4] is the highest annual rate of first retention in the entire figure; correspondingly, it yields the largest single group of retainees.

In Year 3, 61 children are identified as second grade repeaters (not shown are 7 more youngsters put in special education classes at the end of the second year who were also retained). They are joined in second grade by 103 of the first grade repeaters, who have been promoted after 2 years in first grade. One other first grade repeater was held back again in the third year, and so is identified in the third column as a double retainee (still in first grade). Other first grade repeaters (13.4% of the original 127) have been moved into special education classes. In comparison, only

12 of 626 Year 2 second graders, or just under 2%, were in special education in Year 3. The connection between retention and special education is established early.

In the third year we also see our first "skips": two children who had been second graders in Year 2 are identified in Year 3 as fourth graders. The cohort thus is spreading out. In 3 years its members are dispersed across four grade levels, and many are in special education. At the same time, and despite this dispersion, most youngsters are in second (164) or third (518) grade in Year 3. The 518 who have remained on schedule through 3 years constitute 72% of the 715 children still in city schools at this point. Because 60 children left the city schools by the fall of Year 3 (21 in Year 1; 39 in Year 2), these 518 make up 67% of the original sample of 775.[5]

Between the third and fourth years the fan spreads yet further. Only 415 youngsters are fourth graders in the fourth year; this is 54% of the original total, or about 64% of the 649 sample members still in BCPS through Year 4 (66 more left city schools between the beginning of Years 3 and 4). Of the various off-time possibilities, 45 involve children repeating third grade in the fourth year (two other students are also third grade repeaters, but both were assigned to special education before the third year, one in the first year, and one in the second). In the figure, the 45 third grade repeaters not in special education are joined by 143 first and second grade retainees, who in the fourth year have made it into third grade. One other child has moved into third grade out of special education. In addition, three youngsters still in second grade at this point are double repeaters, whereas 13 more children have moved into special education (11 second grade retainees, 1 on-time third grader, and 1 child who after three tries is still in first grade).

By the fifth year the sample of students still in BCPS has shrunk to 614, about 79% of the original 775. Only 365 of these are in fifth grade (60% of the total). Another 171 of them are in fourth grade. This total includes 20 fourth grade repeaters. There also are 22 double retainees at this point, youngsters still in third grade in the fifth year. Also, the number of special education students has increased to 52, up 12 from the previous year despite the return of two pupils to regular classrooms and the departure of one from the school system. Twelve of the 15 new special education students were retained before being assigned to special education classes (they were already a year behind in the fourth year).

All told, we thus find an off-time rate of some 40% through 5 years, the typical elementary school span in the Baltimore school system.[6] Though these children all entered the system together, after 5 years those still in city schools are spread across four grades, and many are in special education classes. Another 161 (21%) have left the system.

This dispersion of students is striking, and revealed only by monitoring prospectively the grade-level progressions of a well-defined cohort. Such detailed tracking is extremely rare in educational research. A cross-sectional survey of children in a particular grade level, or even a longitudinal study of a selective panel, would miss the complicated history of retainees and probably many special education students. A simple tally of repeaters by grade almost certainly will underestimate both the number and the consequences of the administrative sortings that occur in the first few years of school.

Educational sorting in the middle school years

During Years 6, 7, and 8, which ordinarily are middle school years in the Baltimore system, many children are still finishing elementary school.[7] Figure 2.1 uses fall grade placements to identify children's standing in the first 7 years. In Year 8, fall and spring grade placements are covered.

Each year more children fall behind: there are 9 fifth grade repeaters in Year 6; 18 sixth grade repeaters in Year 7; and 22 seventh grade repeaters in Year 8.[8] Though these figures generally are lower than those seen in the elementary grades, the case base also has dwindled. There were only 263 seventh graders in Year 7, for example, and so the 22 retainees that year constitute 8% of the pool, still a significant fraction.

We also see a large jump in the number of double retainees in this period, especially among sixth graders in Year 7. In Year 7, there are 151 sixth graders who have already repeated one grade. In the fall of Year 8, 25 of them still are in sixth grade. This represents a 17% retention rate in a group that already has been retained once. Although only two students are assigned to special education classes for the first time in the seventh year, 13 new special education assignments are made in the eighth year, 7 of whom are double retainees.

The jump in retentions toward the end of middle school probably reflects teachers' reluctance to pass children along to the next level of schooling if they are deemed unready. Although the high rates of middle school retention seen here may be intended to shield struggling students from the pressures of high school, one consequence is that many youngsters will still be in middle school, or barely into high school, when they reach the legal dropout age. The average age of never-retained students when they enter ninth grade will be 14 years, 5 months, students retained once would average 15 years, 5 months, and students retained twice would be 16 before entering high school. The legal school-leaving age in Maryland is 16, and it takes at least 9 months to get a court decision on chronic truants. Effectively, all the retainees would have little trouble dropping out, if they chose to, before entering high school.

In these years we also see the first significant outflow from special education: 3 at the end of Year 6, 15 in the spring of Year 7, and 5 in the spring of Year 8. Although all five of the students who leave special education in Year 8 are placed in eighth grade, the 15 youngsters who are moved back into regular classes at the end of Year 7 are dispersed across three grade levels. Only four are put into eighth grade, which gets them back on time. Another four are put into sixth grade, which is the equivalent of double retention because they are 2 years behind schedule. Seven youngsters are put back 1 year, and so are in seventh grade in Year 8.

These assignments probably reflect a desire to get children back into regular classes before high school, but many of them still are behind: 12 of the 23 children moved out of special education classes during the middle school years remain off time, so special education has not helped these youngsters get back on schedule. Too, most children who were in special education in Year 7 are still there in Year 8 (51 of 71, with 5 others leaving the system), so the placement of children back into regular classes is highly selective.

A similar organizational imperative probably is behind the modest number of "skips" seen among former retainees during the middle school years. There are seven of these altogether, five of which have children returning to their regular grade levels (the other two involve double retainees, who remain one grade behind). In contrast, all six of the skips registered in elementary school involved on-time youngsters, and hence represent genuine acceleration.

In middle school, then, the volume of sorting activity increases: more children are held back; some previously held back are moved up; and for the first time, appreciable numbers of children return to regular classrooms from special education. Since high school generally begins in ninth grade, all this activity very likely anticipates that upcoming transition. The intent, no doubt, is to shield some children from pressures they cannot handle, and to "normalize" the situation of those who might be able to hold their own. That these actions are triggered by an impending school transition illustrates how organization considerations structure the sorting process.

Finally, outflow continues from city schools during the middle school years. One of the largest outflows overlaps the transition to middle school, with 64 children leaving between the fifth and sixth years. This is 10% of those still in city schools in the fall of Year 5 (64 of 614). Included in this group are two of the four Year 5 sixth graders, the only accelerated youngsters in the cohort at that point.

Middle schools have larger catchment areas than elementary schools and so often lack the sense of community that characterizes the latter. Many parents worry about having their children travel long distances outside the neighborhood, and white parents in particular are often concerned about sending their children to a school with a larger minority enrollment. For these reasons, a jump in out-transfers around the time of the middle school transition is not surprising. But departures continue, and by the end of Year 8 the BSS enrollment in city schools is down to 470. This is 144 less than the Year 5 total, a loss of almost a fourth in the middle school years. Looking back to first grade, the cumulative attrition is just under 40%. As we will see, this loss is distinctively nonrandom.

Just over half (238) of the 470 youngsters still in city schools at this point are at grade level. Thirty-six percent (169 of 470) are behind one or more grades, and 13% (61) are in special education. Of the original 775 who began first grade in the fall of 1982, only 30% (238 of 775) have moved "smoothly" through the system, staying on schedule for 8 years in the same school district.

Educational sorting in relief: first grade retainees and Year 8 seventh graders

Figure 2.1 confirms the numerous retentions, but more important, it also reveals the extraordinary complexity of the process. Retention happens in a larger context of administrative sorting, as the figure reveals (additional aspects of administrative sorting are taken up in Chapter 8).

There are 127 first grade repeaters identified in Figure 2.1 (the 126 students who are in first grade in Year 2, plus one of the two students assigned to special education in Year 1). Only 34 of the 127, or just over a fourth, had smooth promotion histories after repeating the year. These 34 were promoted in each of Years 3 through 8 and were never assigned to special education classes. Another 16 also were promoted each year, but received special education "pullout" instruction in math and/or reading sometime along the way. Together these youngsters make up about 40% of the first grade repeaters. The other 60% encountered many additional complications.

Forty-nine, or more than a third of the total, were retained a second time, and three had triple retentions. Fifty-eight first grade retainees were assigned to special education classes at some point, and four of these were placed in special education schools. Indeed, 30 of the 49 double retainees were placed in special education classes, and another 7 received pullout services from regular classrooms. Hence, 76% of double retainees received some special education services, 61% in separate classes. So, too, did 56% of the other first grade retainees, 20% receiving pullout services and 36% in special education classes. By way of comparison, only 9% (40 of 458) of the never-retained youngsters received special education services at any time in the 8-year period, and most of these (35 of the 40) involved pull-out instruction from regular classes. Only five never-retained children were assigned to special education classes. Altogether, then, 81 of the 127 first grade retainees, or 64%, received some special education services during these 8 years. Erratic grade-level progressions further complicated retainees' promotion histories: 17 experienced mid-year promotions, 12 experienced double promotions, one was put back a grade during the school year, and another one was put back a grade over a summer break. By the beginning of Year 8, only 9 of the 127 (or 10% of the 90 who remained in city schools the entire time) ended up at grade level.[9] Children who are moved into special education classes also tend to stay there. Thirty-eight of the 42 first grade retainees who were placed in special education classes and who stayed in city schools all 8 years still were in special education at the end of Year 8.

The situation of seventh graders at the beginning of Year 8 affords another perspective on the sorting experience. There are 179 such youngsters. (Only 142 show up in the main body of Figure 2.1. The remaining 37 entered special education classes before the start of Year 8.) Though all are a year off schedule, only 22 of the 179, or 12%, are repeating seventh grade. The vast majority are in seventh grade a year late because of earlier – often much earlier – events. For 55 of these 179, their Year 8 standing is the legacy of having been held back in first grade; 42 others repeated second grade; and another 59 were held back in grades 3 through 6. In addition to the 37 who were placed in special education classes, 61 spent some time in pull-out special education programs, and 19 had been held back twice (along with a "skip" at some point, that kept them from falling 2 years behind).

Review of pathways through the first 8 years of school

The promotion histories of first grade retainees and of Year 8 seventh graders illustrate the complexity of children's movement through the primary and middle school grades. These "sorting" interventions have the effect of throwing children off time, and often off track. It is important that such "disorderly" promotion histories are the rule rather than the exception in the experience of the BSS cohort; *only a minority of the cohort moves smoothly through the grade structure in this 8-year period.* Research that samples students at a given grade level, like the NELS–88 project (or similar studies keyed to high school grade levels) needs to be mindful of the complicated school careers that resulted in the particular mix of children that finds itself in the same place at the same time. In most studies, this complicated history is hidden from view.

The special education decision is rare until retention has been tried, but when used it has a special finality about it. Few children transfer out of special education. When they do, it generally is toward the end of middle school, probably in anticipation of high school. The frequency of "skips" among former retainees also picks up in these years, probably for the same reason.

Finally, Figure 2.1 shows that many children leave the city system. We have concentrated thus far on sorting *within* schools – falling behind through retention, or getting off track by assignment to special education. However, sorting *between school systems* has implications too. It is important to consider how this exodus of youngsters from the BCPS complicates the picture.

School transfers and sample attrition

By the end of Year 8, 468 of the original 775 members of the BSS cohort – only 60% – remain in city schools. Retainees, however, do not leave as often as others do. Only 37 first grade retainees transferred out

Table 2.1. *Tally of school moves on an annual basis: within the Baltimore city system and outside the system*

	Year 1	Year 2	Year 3	Year 4	Year 5
No. in BCPS in the fall	767	745	693	631	605
Stayers (through the following fall)[a]	663	616	547	520	524
Within-year transfers	64	68	65	57	50
Between-year (summer) transfers[a]	34	31	41	35	—
Transfers outside city system	22	52	62	26	37
Total moves	120	151	168	118	87
Percentage that move[b]	13.6	17.3	21.1	17.6	13.4

[a]Except in Year 5, where moves are tracked only through the spring.
[b]Percentage who move in a given year is calculated as 1 − (No. of stayers/No. in BCPS).

during this period, an exit rate of 29%. In comparison, 52% of the 458 children with no retentions moved out. This suggests that departures from the city system are not random.

School transfers during the primary and middle school years are rarely studied, but they likely complicate children's academic adjustment, especially during the early primary grades. As just noted, 40% of the original BSS cohort left the city school system during the 8 years covered in this volume. Many more transferred between city schools in the same interval, some several times.

This story of "children in motion" is told in detail elsewhere (Alexander, Entwisle, and Dauber 1994). Table 2.1, reproduced from that report, covers the first 5 years of the cohort's schooling (which in most city schools constitute the elementary years), distinguishing among within-year transfers, summer transfers, and transfers out of the BCPS.[10] "Stayers" are children who remained in the same school from one fall to the next.

The total volume of school relocations, summarized in the last row, shows that between 13.4% and 21.1% of youngsters in city schools at the beginning of a given year will transfer between schools during that year. Of children who remained in city schools the entire time, 21.5% registered one transfer, 13.4% two transfers, and 5.6% three or more transfers. Hence, about 40% of these youngsters relocated at least once *within* the city system. Another 26% (199) of the original cohort left city schools during this 5-year period (scc Table 2.1, row 5), and so are known to have moved at least once. We calculate that two-thirds of the cohort changed schools during the elementary years.

There are two quite distinct migration streams: whites and higher SES children tend to leave the city system; African-Americans and lower SES children tend to move within it. The contrasts are dramatic: 71% of the Exiters (i.e., children who left the system) were white, while 79% of those with two or more transfers within the system were African-American (the percentage of African-American students in the original cohort was 55). Similarly, though a large fraction (46%) of the Exiters qualified for subsidized meals at school (which puts them near or below the federal poverty level), multiple movers within the system were much more often on subsidy (88%). Over time, then, the city enrollment in the cohort is increasingly made up of poor and minority students, and within the BCPS these youngsters are the most mobile.

Over the 5-year period covered in Table 2.1, the cohort collectively attended 112 different schools *just within the city system,* and an unknown additional number of schools outside the BCPS. For the first 2 years of the BSS project we were able to track only students who remained in the original 20 schools. Beginning in the fourth year we began tracking all youngsters still in the BCPS, so our coverage of children who stayed in Baltimore public schools is reasonably complete.[11]

The situation of children who left the city system is more complicated. Of the 775 youngsters who constitute the "core" analysis sample for this volume, 307, or 40%, were out of BCPS schools by the fall of 1990 ("Year 8" in terms of our study design). Information on these youngsters' retention status is available only for the period they were in city schools. Based on these data from the BCPS, 21% of the Exiters, compared with 53% of the Stayers, are identified as retainees. This is a large difference; but undoubtedly some of the Exiters were retained in schools outside the city after they transferred there. As noted, though, children who left the city schools were disproportionately white, relatively well-to-do, and had good readiness skills; for these reasons they would be expected to have lower rates of retention.

To what extent does our abbreviated coverage of Exiters' school rec-ords understate their retentions? If many were missed, this would exaggerate the difference in retention rates between Stayers and Exiters. As a check, we have looked to see how well BCPS school record data on retention accord with retrospective self-reports obtained for 636 youngsters in interviews conducted in the spring of 1991 (Year 10). For 92% of the 636, the two sources agree on retention status, but 4.6% ($N = 29$) report no retention when school records indicate otherwise, and 3.5% ($N = 22$) say they had been held back at some point when BCPS records show no retention. The discrepancies are a small fraction of the total[12] and practically offsetting in the aggregate, but the 22 self-identified repeaters could be retentions missed after children left the BCPS, which is our main concern. However, when we look just at those who left the BCPS at some point and did not return (178 of the 636, or 28%; another 41 moved in and out of city schools over the years), agreement with school reports, which cover promotions only while the students were in city schools, is also 92%. Twelve of the 178 say they had been held back when our records show no retention, so their percentage is a bit higher than the figure overall (6.7% vs. 3.5%); but only a handful of students is involved, and three others (1.7%) say they had not been held back when school records identify them as repeaters. There's no sure way of knowing which reports are the more accurate; school records are not always reliable, but neither are recall and self-reports, especially when potentially sensitive issues are involved. All in all, it appears we have not missed many retentions. This is reassuring, but we also need to consider whether children who left the BCPS differ in other ways that might distort comparisons between retainees and never-retained youngsters. For most Exiters we lack report card marks and test scores in the upper grades. It is important that we have a sense of how this might alter the picture.

Table 2.2 presents comparisons of Exiters and Stayers on some key measures: personal and social demographic characteristics and school performance from early in first grade. The entire sample is covered in the top panel, which reports summary descriptive statistics separately for retainees and for never-retained youngsters. Girls, for example, constitute 56.6% of the never-retained group, versus only 42.9% of the retainees. The second panel describes the Stayers – those who remained in city schools for the entire 8 years. These are the children who are available for most of the analyses performed in later chapters. We want to know how the Stayers compare to the full sample, since the full sample would be the "preferred" group for conducting the analysis.

The third panel reports data for the Exiters. Comparing panels 2 and 3 shows that the Exiters and Stayers look quite different. Two-thirds of the Stayers are African-American, three-fourths receive subsidized meals at school, and the average Stayer parent (both mother and father) is a high school dropout. The Exiters, in contrast, are much more advantaged: 70% are white, only about half get reduced price meals, and the average Exiter parent has some college. These are strikingly different social profiles.

Exiters also had somewhat better readiness skills as beginning first graders, as shown in the rightmost columns.[13] Exiters average a bit above Stayers on all four academic measures, but the differences seem more modest than those involving social demographic characteristics. The 8-point difference on the CAT quantitative subtest is about a fourth of the sample's standard deviation on the test, while the 5-point difference on the verbal subtest corresponds to just over 10% of the test's standard deviation.

Differences in first grade report card marks also favor Exiters. Marks are assigned on a 4-point scale, with "4" corresponding to "excellent" and "1" corresponding to "unsatisfactory." In math, both averages are a bit above satisfactory (2.1 for Stayers; 2.4 for Exiters), while they fall out on either side of satisfactory in reading (1.8 vs. 2.0).

Comparisons by retention status involving these demographic and performance measures are also presented in Table 2.2. In these comparisons, retainees are children held back at any point through the seventh grade. As already noted, in the full sample, boys constitute a higher percentage of the retained subsample than of the never-retained subsample. Similarly, we see that retainees include a higher percentage of minority youngsters, that retainees' parents on average have less education, that retainees much more often receive reduced-price meals at school, and that their performance averages fall well below those of never-retained children on all four measures. These differences are summarized in the fourth row of the "full sample" panel.

The corresponding data calculated for Stayers only are reported in the second panel. Sample sizes are provided in parentheses, and as can be seen there is a large drop when Stayers are selected out for separate consideration. Gender and race are known for everyone, so changes on these items reflect sample attrition that is due specifically to movement out of the BCPS.[14] There are 486 Stayers, which is down almost 40%

Table 2.2. Comparison of full sample, Stayers, and Exiters on background characteristics and early academic performance measures at point of school entry[a]

	Percent female	Percent African-American	Average mother's education	Average father's education	Percent no meal subsidy	Average CAT-M score	Average CAT-R score	Average math mark	Average reading mark
Full sample	50.1	54.4	11.6	12.1	33.1	293.1	281.2	2.2	1.9
	(775)	(775)	(731)	(489)	(699)	(684)	(666)	(695)	(695)
1. Never retained	56.6	48.5	12.4	12.8	47.0	304.6	290.8	2.6	2.2
	(458)	(458)	(431)	(306)	(389)	(408)	(396)	(418)	(418)
2. Retained	42.9	63.1	10.6	10.9	15.5	276.1	267.1	1.8	1.5
	(317)	(317)	(300)	(183)	(310)	(276)	(270)	(277)	(277)
3. Difference (1 − 2)	13.7	14.6	1.8	1.9	31.5	28.5	23.7	0.8	0.7
Stayers	50.8	68.5	11.3	11.6	24.6	290.2	279.3	2.1	1.8
	(486)	(486)	(456)	(326)	(483)	(443)	(432)	(446)	(446)
1. Never retained	60.9	68.3	12.2	12.3	38.8	304.6	292.5	2.6	2.2
	(230)	(230)	(214)	(169)	(227)	(215)	(208)	(218)	(218)
2. Retained	41.8	68.8	10.5	10.8	12.1	276.6	267.0	1.8	1.5
	(256)	(256)	(242)	(157)	(256)	(228)	(224)	(228)	(228)
3. Difference (1 − 2)	19.1	0.5	1.7	1.5	26.7	28.0	25.5	0.8	0.7

Exiters	51.2	30.1	12.3	13.1	51.9	298.5	284.6	2.4	2.0
	(289)	(289)	(275)	(163)	(216)	(241)	(234)	(249)	(249)
1. Never retained	52.2	28.5	12.6	13.4	58.6	304.7	288.8	2.6	2.2
	(228)	(228)	(217)	(137)	(162)	(193)	(188)	(200)	(200)
2. Retained	47.5	39.3	11.1	11.6	31.5	273.5	267.7	1.8	1.4
	(61)	(61)	(58)	(26)	(54)	(48)	(46)	(49)	(49)
3. Difference (1 − 2)	4.7	10.8	1.5	1.8	25.1	31.2	21.1	0.8	0.8

Note: Numbers in parentheses are sample sizes.

[a]All four performance measures are from the fall or first quarter of first grade.

from the full sample. The loss is greater among never-retained young-sters, where the case base drops from 458 to 230, or by just about half. In comparison, 80% (256) of the 317 retainees in the full sample still are in city schools through Year 8.

Averages for the various measures are often very different in the full sample than in the subsample of Stayers. However, most differences between retained and never-retained students seen for the full sample also are seen for Stayers. This holds especially for the academic com-parisons. For example, in the full sample, never-retained children's first-quarter reading marks on average are 0.7 marking units above those of retainees, exactly the same difference as in the subsample of Stayers. The averages are higher in the full sample than in the Stayer subsample, but the relative advantage of never-retained over retained students is identi-cal. The difference involving math marks is identical too, and the CAT subtest comparisons are both very close. These points of comparability are critically important for our purposes, because they indicate that selec-tive sample loss will not likely distort school performance comparisons between retainees and never-retained youngsters.

Comparisons involving personal and social demographic factors in some instances do differ, though, especially for race/ethnicity. In the full sample, 63.1% of retainees are African-American, versus only 48.5% of the never-retained group (altogether 54.4% of the full sample is African-American). The difference of almost 15% signals a large overrepresenta-tion of African-American youngsters among retainees. In contrast, among the Stayers there is near parity; some 68% of both retained and never-retained students are African-American. Hence, if we looked only at the Stayer subsample we could conclude there is no racial imbalance in retentions. The 68% figure is close to the percentage of African-Americans among retainees in the full sample, so it is the never-retained subsample whose racial composition changes most when Exiters are ex-cluded. It has a much higher percentage of minority youngsters, indicat-ing that Exiters are drawn disproportionately from the pool of never-retained whites.

In contrast, comparisons involving socioeconomic distinctions (e.g., parents' education and family income level) reveal only minor differences. For example, though the "spread" between retained and never-retained students in the percentage of those not receiving meal subsidies is a bit smaller among Stayers than in the full sample (i.e., 26.7

vs. 31.5), the two figures are in the same range. Retainees come from poorer families.

The comparison for mother's education is quite close (a difference of 1.8 years between retained and never-retained students in the full sample vs. 1.7 years among the Stayers), but there is a larger discrepancy for father's education. Data coverage for father's education is especially sparse, though, so the gap between the 1.9-year figure favoring never-retained students in the full sample and the 1.5-year figure in the sub-sample of Stayers should be discounted somewhat.

The difference seen when comparing gender composition (13.7% difference in the full sample; 19.1% difference among Stayers) is not great either. Conclusions in general terms would be the same regardless of whether the analyses were performed on the full sample or on the subsample of Stayers: both show boys overrepresented among retainees.

Hence, even though there are indications of social selection along several other dimensions, race/ethnicity stands out as the most striking difference between the Exiters and the Stayers. When whites leave city schools, as they do in large numbers, many other qualities go with them, including their relatively high SES standing and good readiness skills. Other dimensions of social selection are minor in comparison, and, most critically, we see virtually no bias or distortion on academic indicators. This is fortunate because we are especially interested in making sound academic comparisons. In the analyses presented later, because of the comparability of most indicators, children are included whenever data are available for them, whether they are Stayers or Exiters.

3

Characteristics and competencies of repeaters: who is held back?

Chapter 2 pulled back the curtain a bit on the retention story by revealing the complexity of children's educational pathways over the elementary and middle school years. We now have a sense of what is happening. In this chapter we see to whom it is happening. What makes retainees different from children who move smoothly through the grade structure, and what distinguishes different kinds of retainees from one another? One comparison is between first grade repeaters and those held back later. First grade retention may be distinctive because of the stresses that revolve around entry into school. First graders must learn what kinds of behaviors are acceptable, adjust to the school routine, and begin serious academic work. Children retained later in school have had at least a year of satisfactory performance, so they presumably had a smoother transition experience. We also compare retainees who stay on track after repeating a year with children held back twice and/or assigned to special education classes. Children held back twice and those moved into special education are probably having an especially difficult time at school, although this remains to be seen.

Who is held back?

We first ask what sets retainees apart from never-retained youngsters in terms of three broad areas. Data on demographics and family background give a social profile of repeaters. Test scores and report card marks from the fall of first grade give an academic profile. Academic problems at the very beginning of school are the backdrop to retention. They reflect skill deficiencies brought in from outside school; for children raised in poverty, as many of the BSS youngsters are, such problems are likely to be both common and severe. Nonacademic problems also warrant attention. Conduct marks from first grade report cards, children's classroom behavior as rated by their first grade homeroom teachers, diagnostic evaluations made by both kindergarten and first grade teachers, their popularity with other children as perceived by teachers, and first grade absenteeism are used to build a school adjustment profile of repeaters. Comparisons for all three areas are reported in Table 3.1.

Repeaters versus promoted youngsters: demographic profiles

Of the 775 youngsters whose promotion histories while in the BCPS are reasonably complete, 317 were retained at least once through seventh grade; 458 were not.[1] The top panel of Table 3.1 gives the demographics and family circumstances of these youngsters. This information comes from school records (gender, race/ethnicity, and eligibility for reduced-price meals at school), and from parents. Information on living arrangements and on number of siblings comes from 743 parent interviews conducted over several months beginning in the summer before the children started first grade, and continuing into the early fall of that year. Data about the parents' educational level combines information from this first interview with that from several later ones.[2]

The table is split into five columns. The first describes characteristics of the entire cohort. The second and third columns provide data for repeaters and promoted youngsters separately, and the fourth and fifth columns show the difference between averages of the two groups in terms of original scale units and standard deviation units, respectively.[3]

The sample is nearly evenly divided between males and females (51% female), but the percentage of males in the retained group is higher: 57%, as compared with 43% of the never-retained students. Similarly, 63% of retained students are African-American, though African-Americans make up only 54% of the entire sample.[4] These differences involving gender and racial/ethnic composition, both highly significant, are just under 0.3 standard deviations, and so would be considered relatively large.

Differences revolving around family socioeconomic status are larger still. Eligibility for reduced-price meals at school identifies low-income

Table 3.1. *Demographic, academic, and school adjustment profiles of retained and never-retained students*

				Retained vs. never-retained	
	All children[a]	Retained[b]	Never retained[c]	Average difference	Difference in S.D. units
Demographic comparisons					
Proportion male	.49	.57	.43	.14**	0.27
	(0.50)	(0.50)	(0.50)		
Proportion African-American	.54	.63	.48	.15**	0.29
	(0.50)	(0.48)	(0.50)		
Proportion receiving lunch subsidy	.67	.85	.53	-.32**	0.67
	(0.47)	(0.36)	(0.50)		
Average mother's education (years)	11.67	10.61	12.40	-1.79**	0.70
	(2.56)	(2.19)	(2.54)		
Average father's education (years)	12.10	10.90	12.82	-1.92**	0.72
	(2.68)	(1.90)	(2.82)		
Proportion in two-parent family	.53	.42	.61	-.19**	0.39
	(0.50)	(0.49)	(0.49)		
Average number of siblings	1.45	1.62	1.33	0.28**	0.21
	(1.38)	(1.51)	(1.27)		
Academic comparisons					
Average reading mark, first quarter 1982	1.88	1.45	2.17	-0.72**	1.03
	(0.70)	(0.55)	(0.65)		
Average math mark, first quarter 1982	2.25	1.75	2.57	-0.82**	0.98
	(0.84)	(0.71)	(0.76)		

Average CAT-R score, fall 1982	281.16	267.09	290.76	−23.67**	0.58
	(40.62)	(33.75)	(42.13)		
Average CAT-M score, fall 1982	293.11	276.05	304.65	−28.60**	0.90
	(31.72)	(24.00)	(31.13)		
School adjustment comparisons					
Average number of absences	13.22	16.19	11.22	4.97**	0.44
	(11.35)	(13.60)	(9.02)		
Average Cooperation–Compliance score	20.72	19.33	21.67	−2.34**	0.59
	(3.98)	(4.71)	(3.05)		
Average Interest–Participation score	21.98	18.74	24.18	−5.44**	1.00
	(5.43)	(5.07)	(4.49)		
Average Attention Span–Restlessness score	20.70	18.48	22.21	−3.72**	0.92
	(4.03)	(4.57)	(2.75)		
Average conduct mark, fall 1982	1.75	1.66	1.81	−0.16**	0.37
	(0.43)	(0.48)	(0.39)		
MSTOI proportion at risk	.28	.49	.13	.36**	0.79
	(0.45)	(0.50)	(0.34)		
Average peer popularity	3.52	3.09	3.81	−0.72**	.64
	(1.13)	(1.08)	(1.07)		

Note: Numbers in parentheses are standard deviations.

[a]Sample coverage on all children, except for father's education ($N = 489$) and MSTOI ($N = 559$) varies from 775 to 666.

[b]Sample coverage on retained children, except for father's education ($N = 183$) and MSTOI ($N = 230$) varies from 317 to 270.

[c]Sample coverage on never-retained children, except for father's education ($N = 306$) and MSTOI ($N = 329$) varies from 458 to 389.

**signifies differences significant at the 0.01 level.

families. As of the summer of 1984, a child in a family of four with a yearly income of $12,870 or less would receive free meals, while an income of less than $18,315 would allow a reduced fee. These represent 1.3 and 1.85 times federal poverty guidelines, respectively. Fifty-three percent of never-retained students, compared with 85% of the retained sample, qualified for some subsidy. This difference between promoted and retained youngsters amounts to two-thirds of a standard deviation.

Differences involving parents' educational background are also large. Retainees' mothers and fathers both average almost 2 years less schooling than do promoted youngsters' parents. The 2-year gap is about 0.7 standard deviations in each instance. Beyond being large, these differences also straddle an important educational divide: the "typical" retainee parent is a high school dropout, while the typical parent of a promoted youngster has at least finished high school. Twenty-five percent of the parents of never-retained children are dropouts, compared with 48% of the retained students' fathers and 56% of their mothers (not in tables).

Since more education is generally associated with higher earnings, this parent-education gap is another sign that never-retained students come from more economically advantaged homes. It also probably means that never-retained students' parents understand the educational system better and are better able to provide support and resources at home that reinforce the school's agenda (for an overview of differences across socio-economic and racial/ethnic lines in family practices relevant to school readiness, see Hess and Holloway 1984, as well as Slaughter and Epps 1987). The educational "boost" that more-educated parents can provide for their children could be particularly helpful for students having difficulty handling the first grade curriculum.

The never-retained group has the more favorable profile in terms of family type as well. Sixty-one percent of them are in two-parent families (with either natural or stepparents) as against 42% of retained students. Residence in a single-parent household is another demographic factor known to put children at risk academically (e.g., Hetherington, Camara, and Featherman 1983). Promoted youngsters also have fewer siblings, although this difference is not as large as the others. Both groups average between one and two siblings (on the relationship of family size to school performance, see Blake 1989).

All in all, the family circumstances and personal characteristics of retained and promoted children are quite different. Girls and whites are most likely to make it through seventh grade without being held back. These children also come from families that are better-off economically, where the parents are at least high school graduates, where two parents are present, and where there are relatively fewer other children competing for family resources and the parents' attention.

The retained group presents a very different picture. The majority of them are male, African-American, and receive reduced-price meals at school. Their parents typically lack even high school diplomas; most students are in single-parent households, and they have more siblings. Altogether they reflect the characteristic sociodemographic profile for retainees seen in numerous studies (e.g., Bianchi 1984; NCES 1990).

Repeaters versus promoted youngsters: academic profiles

We next consider children's academic standing at the start of first grade using report card marks and test scores. Here too, differences between retained and promoted youngsters are large and significant. Four marks are used in city schools in the primary grades: "unsatisfactory," "satisfactory," "good," and "excellent." We have assigned these values of "1," "2," "3," and "4," respectively. The marking data used in this chapter are from the very first marking period in first grade.

The data on marks (second panel, Table 3.1) suggest a shaky academic start for all the BSS youngsters, both retained and promoted. The math average overall is just above satisfactory (2.25); reading marks average 1.88, just below satisfactory. Nearly everyone has room for improvement, but some children are worse off than others. In both math (1.75) and reading (1.45) retainees' initial marks average well below satisfactory, while promoted children have marks midway between satisfactory and good in math (2.57), and their reading average (2.17) is above satisfactory. The math difference between retained and promoted averages amounts to 0.8 marking units; the reading difference is 0.7 units. The last column shows that both of these differences are close to a full standard deviation, and so would be considered quite large.

Retainees also trail far behind in terms of their initial achievement-test scores. The BCPS administered the California Achievement Test battery twice annually, fall and spring, from 1982 (when the BSS children were just beginning first grade) through the spring of 1988.[5] The averages reported in Table 3.1 are from fall 1982. We focus on two subtests from the CAT battery: the Reading Comprehension subtest and the Math Concepts and Applications subtest, "CAT-R" and "CAT-M." Reading and math dominate the curriculum in the primary grades, and these two areas are included in all versions of the CAT battery designed for administration in Years 1 through 8, allowing us to consider achievement trends in the same areas over this entire period. Other CAT subtests do not provide this continuous coverage.[6]

The Reading Comprehension subtest consists of 20 items in the first and second grade versions, 27 items in the third grade version, and 40 items in all later versions. The Math Concepts and Applications test starts out with 36 items, increases to 40 items in second grade, and contains 45 items thereafter.[7] Our displays report "scale scores." These are vertically calibrated using a common metric across all versions of the test, allowing for meaningful comparisons of scores across grade levels.

Comparing retained to never-retained students (Table 3.1) the average difference for both CAT subtests is more than 20 points. When considered in terms of standard deviation units, the CAT-M difference is almost a full standard deviation, on a par with the differences in report card marks, while the CAT-R comparison favors promoted youngsters by just under 0.6 standard deviations. Three of the four academic differences – report card marks in both areas and scores on the CAT-M – exceed all the differences described involving personal and social demographic characteristics. Elsewhere (Dauber, Alexander, and Entwisle 1993) we have examined how these factors affect the likelihood of retention jointly. That assessment, too, finds the academic predictors considerably more important than demographic factors.[8]

The large differences in test performance are striking, especially since they rate children's performance at the beginning of first grade, before anyone has had much experience in school. Marks and test scores thus point to the same conclusion: children who will be retained sometime in elementary or middle school are far behind academically at the start of school. Their first marks indicate that they are having trouble with the curriculum, and their test scores at the beginning of first grade show serious deficiencies in terms of readiness skills. These comparisons show that future retainees are already at an academic disadvantage, compared with their classmates, from the very beginning of their formal schooling.

Repeaters versus promoted youngsters: school adjustment profiles

Children's school adjustment in nonacademic areas is reflected in their deportment, attendance, and popularity with other students. Children who are frequently absent, have problems with other children, or don't conform easily to the behavioral demands of the classroom are at a disadvantage in school compared with their "well behaving" peers. Such problems signal a poor fit between students and the school environment. The last comparisons in Table 3.1 show whether retainees are also especially prone to nonacademic problems.

Absences in first grade show that never-retained students miss more than 11 days of school on average, but that retainees average almost 16 absences. The 5-day difference in absences between retained and never-retained youngsters exceeds 0.4 standard deviations.

The next three comparisons involve aspects of classroom adjustment as rated by homeroom teachers in the spring of first grade. The three scales are derived from a 14-item inventory adapted from the 1976–77 National Survey of Children. The construction and psychometric properties of the three scales are described in Alexander, Entwisle, and Dauber (1993).[9]

The Cooperation–Compliance scale includes four items that rate students' conformity with rules and acceptable classroom behavior: (1) how they get along with others (whether they fight and tease), (2) whether they lie, (3) whether they lose their temper, or (4) whether they are polite and helpful. Available categories for teachers to rate these behaviors ranged from "exactly like [this student]" to "not at all like," coded from 1 to 6, with high scores used for more positive qualities. The scale thus has a possible range of 4 to 24. Although most children are evaluated favorably on this scale (the average for the total group is higher than 20), there is a significant difference between retained and never-retained children amounting to more than 2 points, or almost 0.6 standard deviations. Repeaters thus are judged less cooperative by their first grade teachers *before* they are retained.

The Interest–Participation scale includes five items that rate students' involvement in, and enthusiasm for, classroom activities, by whether they are (1) enthusiastic, (2) cheerful, (3) creative, (4) loners, or (5) afraid of new situations. These items have clear implications for how students approach their studies. The Interest–Participation scale is significantly related both to first grade standardized test scores and to reading and math marks (Alexander, Entwisle, and Dauber 1993). Students who are more outgoing, cheerful, and inquisitive have superior classroom performance.

In this area, too, students generally are rated favorably by their teachers. The average for the total group is nearly 22 out of a possible 30. Nevertheless, a difference of more than 5 points separates retained and never-retained students, with retainees a full standard deviation below their never-retained peers.

The final classroom adjustment scale, Attention Span–Restlessness, is made up of four items that measure (1) concentration, (2) nervousness, (3) maturity, and (4) restlessness. A child rated low on this scale would likely have difficulty keeping pace with the curriculum because of poor concentration or fidgetiness. Children who score higher on this scale also tend to do better on the CAT tests and get higher report card marks (Alexander, Entwisle, and Dauber 1993). Retained and promoted young-sters differ in their Attention Span–Restlessness ratings by almost 4 points, just under a full standard deviation.

These large differences across all three classroom behavior ratings indicate that prior to their being held back, repeaters are viewed by their teachers as not fitting in well with the school routine. They seemingly are not as comfortable with the behavioral expectations that define the student role.[10] These three aspects of children's classroom behavior are fairly stable during early elementary school, and our earlier study (Alexander, Entwisle, and Dauber 1993) indicates that the Interest–Participation and Attention Span–Restlessness scales have continuing relevance for academic performance through at least the fourth year of school, which is as far as that article pursued the matter.

Conduct marks from report cards, also tallied in Table 3.1, yield a cruder but administratively more important measure of children's class-room deportment. Conduct is rated simply as "satisfactory" (coded 2) or "needs improvement" (coded 1). Retained students again are rated lower (0.16 units) than the nonretainees, by 0.37 standard deviations.

Another adjustment measure reported in Table 3.1 is from the 27-item Maryland Systematic Teacher Observation Inventory (MSTOI),[11] a diagnostic inventory formerly used by the Maryland State Department of Education in the early grades. The MSTOI has teachers evaluate pupils' school adjustment in five areas (psychomotor, sensory/perception, language, cognition, affect/motivation), with from 5 to 11 items in each area. "Finishes tasks late" is an example from the affective area. Whether the child "can tell about a picture while looking at it" is an item from the cognition area. Items are scored on a 5-point scale ranging from "always" to "never."

Besides subscale scores and a total score, there is an at-risk code for youngsters whose total score exceeds a predetermined threshold. Children deemed at risk receive a score of 1; others are scored 0. We use the at-risk designation to judge the MSTOI's effectiveness in anticipating early school failure.[12] MSTOI scores are available for 554 youngsters, with most (458) coming from kindergarten teachers. The rest are from first grade teachers.[13]

Retained students are more often identified as being at risk for school problems: 49% versus only 13% of the never-retained students. When only kindergarten teachers' ratings are used, 42% of retainees are identified as "at risk" versus 11% of never-retained youngsters. Though the percentages in both instances are down some from the figures reported in Table 3.1, the trend is the same. Indeed, these comparisons are perhaps even more striking in that they reflect teachers' impressions from before first grade. Many students who later will be retained thus are identified early on as likely to have difficulty in school.

The final measure in Table 3.1 is the homeroom teacher's rating of children's popularity among classmates. In the spring of the first grade, teachers rated students on a 5-point scale ranging from "least popular" (coded 1) to "most popular" (coded 5). Again, retained students lag behind their never-retained peers, with to-be-retained students rated less popular. The difference is about 0.6 standard deviations.

Overview

What does the overall pattern look like? Retained and never-retained students differ in many ways, with the demographic differences seen in Table 3.1 joined by wide disparities in academic performance and in nonacademic factors important for good school adjustment. The distinctive demographic profile of retainees is important, with minority youths, children from lower SES backgrounds, and boys being held back more often.[14] However, much more pronounced than any aspect of

demographics is selection on the basis of academics and school adjustment, a finding consistent with Reynolds's (1992) results for a sample of
inner-city Chicago youths (all African-American). Retained students fare
poorly on *all* measures of early academic standing. In addition, these
children's classroom conduct, "style," and relations with other pupils are
rated much less favorably by teachers. They are more often absent from
school and are seen early on – even in kindergarten – as potential problem cases (the at-risk MSTOI designation). All these differences are in
evidence before even one retention decision has been made.

Future retainees thus begin school badly disadvantaged. This isn't the
children's fault, of course, and it is hardly surprising considering the
outside stresses that bear upon both the school system and the children it
serves. It is, nevertheless, part of the backdrop to retention. These
youngsters' academic skills when they begin school fall far short of what
is expected, and so they have trouble keeping up with the curriculum.
Their social skills and behavior set up further interference. Rather than
slipping comfortably or successfully into the "student role," these children are just slipping. The problems that eventually lead to their being
held back are foreshadowed in serious adjustment and academic problems from before the first day of school.

First grade repeaters versus later repeaters

The previous section establishes that retained and never-retained students differ in many ways. Now we will see whether different groups of
retainees have distinctive profiles, beginning in this section with distinctions between retainees held back in first grade and those held back at
higher grades (grades 2 through 7).[15] Table 3.2 provides the relevant
comparisons. Differences involving social demographics all are minor (all
nonsignificant). The absence of pronounced "social selection" for early
retention is impressive – there are no differences by gender, race / ethnicity, or economic level, and those involving mother's education and
family composition are all much smaller than differences seen when
comparing all retainees with never-retained children. Minority and economically disadvantaged youngsters thus do not appear to be held back
before others, even though their overall rates of retention are higher.[16]

The clear case is that children singled out earliest are the ones struggling most. Children who will be retained at the end of first grade have
average first-quarter marks in math and reading that are barely above

unsatisfactory (at 1.3 and 1.1, respectively). Indeed, 71% of these young-sters get initial grades of "unsatisfactory" in math, and 90% are rated unsatisfactory in reading.

Later retainees, although performing marginally at this point, are still well above the level of first grade repeaters. Their math average is just above satisfactory (2.03), and their reading average (1.67) is midway between satisfactory and unsatisfactory. The differences in average marks between early and later retainees exceed half a marking unit on a 4-point scale. These are large disparities, both exceeding a full standard devia-tion. *Every* first grade retainee earned a mark of unsatisfactory in reading at the end of the first year (Chapter 6). Here we see that their first-quarter marks were very low as well.

The test score story is much the same: later retainees outperform first grade retainees on both CAT tests, and again the differences are large. The 16-point difference in Reading Comprehension is about 0.5 stan-dard deviations, while the 19-point difference in Math Concepts amounts to 0.8 standard deviations.

All retainees get off to a shaky start academically, but the children held back earliest are the ones struggling most. First grade repeaters' aca-demic performance is already conspicuously bad on the very first evalua-tions made of them. Later retainees are having their problems in first grade too, but it seems they do well enough to be promoted. The sched-uling of these youngsters' retentions thus reflects the severity of their early academic problems, with those held back first lagging farthest behind at the start.

Equally striking, and perhaps more surprising, is that the same pattern holds for the indicators of behavioral adjustment. Again, first grade retainees stand out. Except for differences in conduct marks and days absent, their averages lag far behind those of children who won't be held back until second grade or later. The profile of first grade retainees thus is one of broad-based difficulty. Not only are they seemingly over their heads academically, but they also appear uncomfortable with the school routine and with the social demands of schooling: first grade retainees are rated as less popular with their peers and are viewed as behaving in ways that may make it harder for them to respond to the demands of the classroom. These problems, together with their academic difficulties, lead them to be identified much more often by the MSTOI as requiring monitoring for future problems.[17]

We are especially struck by how teachers see these youngsters. First

Table 3.2. *Demographic, academic, and school adjustment profiles of first grade retainees and second through seventh grade retainees*[a]

	All retainees[a]	Grade 1 retainees[b]	Combined grade 2–7 retainees[c]	Difference between grade 1 and grade 2–7	Difference as a proportion of S.D.
Demographic comparisons					
Proportion male	.57	.57	.57	.00	0.00
	(0.50)	(0.50)	(0.50)		
Proportion African–American	.63	.63	.63	.00	0.00
	(0.48)	(0.49)	(0.48)		
Proportion receiving lunch subsidy	.85	.84	.85	.01	0.02
	(0.36)	(0.37)	(0.36)		
Average mother's education (years)	10.61	10.77	10.50	0.27	0.12
	(2.19)	(2.12)	(2.24)		
Average father's education (years)	10.90	10.91	10.89	0.02	0.01
	(1.90)	(1.84)	(1.94)		
Proportion in two-parent family	.42	.37	.45	−.08	0.17
	(0.49)	(0.49)	(0.50)		
Average number of siblings	1.62	1.79	1.50	0.29	0.19
	(1.51)	(1.80)	(1.27)		
Academic comparisons					
Average reading mark, first quarter 1982	1.45	1.10	1.67	−0.57**	1.04
	(0.55)	(0.31)	(0.56)		
Average math mark, first quarter 1982	1.75	1.30	2.03	−0.73**	1.03
	(0.71)	(0.48)	(0.67)		

Average CAT-R score, fall 1982	267.09 (33.75)	257.01 (34.18)	273.60 (31.91)	-16.59**	0.49
Average CAT-M score, fall 1982	276.05 (24.00)	264.09 (20.49)	283.62 (23.00)	-19.53**	0.81
School adjustment comparisons					
Average number of absences	16.19 (13.60)	18.20 (15.93)	14.93 (11.78)	3.27	0.24
Average Cooperation–Compliance score	19.33 (4.71)	18.52 (5.15)	19.86 (4.34)	-1.34*	0.29
Average Interest–Participation score	18.74 (5.07)	16.34 (4.61)	20.33 (4.74)	-3.99**	0.79
Average Attention Span–Restlessness score	18.48 (4.57)	16.00 (4.54)	20.13 (3.78)	-4.14**	0.90
Average conduct mark, fall 1982	1.66 (0.48)	1.61 (0.49)	1.69 (0.47)	-0.08	0.16
MSTOI proportion at risk	.49 (0.50)	.72 (0.45)	.34 (0.48)	-.38**	0.76
Average peer popularity	3.09 (1.08)	2.61 (1.05)	3.39 (0.99)	-0.78**	0.72

Note: Numbers in parentheses are standard deviations.

[a]Sample coverage on all retainees, except for father's education ($N = 183$) and MSTOI ($N = 230$) varies from 317 to 270.

[b]Sample coverage on first grade retainees, except for father's education ($N = 69$) and MSTOI ($N = 89$) varies from 127 to 105.

[c]Sample coverage on combined second through seventh grade retainees, except for father's education ($N = 114$) and MSTOI ($N = 141$) varies from 190 to 163.

**signifies differences significant at the 0.01 level; * differences significant at the 0.05 level.

grade repeaters are rated less cooperative and much less invested in classroom activities. They also are more restless and more easily distracted. For example, on the Interest–Participation and the Attention Span–Restlessness scales, they average close to 16, while other retainees average around 20, and promoted children get averages of 24 and 22, respectively. This puts first grade retainees almost 2 standard deviations behind never-retained youngsters on classroom behaviors generally recognized as reflecting good school adjustment.

First grade retainees' profiles thus reflect problems on many fronts. Although similar to later retainees in demographic characteristics, they lag far behind on measures of academic performance and on other qualities important for school adjustment. These youngsters begin school with very poor academic skills, and they do not improve enough over the year to prevent their retention.[18]

Later retainees do better academically than first grade retainees at the beginning of first grade, but still are performing below the level of their never-retained peers. The school adjustment indicators give the same impression, with second through seventh grade retainees looking better than first grade repeaters but not scoring as well as never-retained youngsters. Thus, in the comparisons made to this point, whether involving academic performance or school adjustment, first grade retainees fare worst, followed by the later retainees, with the never-retained students always faring best.

Single repeaters versus multiple repeaters and special education children

In this section we consider how children whose administrative problems compound over time differ from those who manage to make orderly progress after being held back. Most (58%, that is, 184 of 317) retainees stay on track after completing their repeated year – they are not retained again or placed in special education. We saw in Chapter 2, though, that children retained in first grade are especially likely to experience these further interventions, and the reasons for this now seem clear – in terms of academics *and* adjustment, these youngsters are much worse off than other repeaters at the start of school. Consistent with this, only 39% (50 of 127) of first grade retainees manage to avoid a second retention and/or assignment to special education.

Demographic characteristics of single retainees and those with double retentions or special education are not very different (Table 3.3). No differences reach even 0.2 standard deviations.[19] Differences involving academics are much larger. Students who will be held back a second time and/or be assigned to special education earn lower marks than other retainees at the beginning of first grade. Children in the multiple-intervention group average close to unsatisfactory on their first-quarter reading mark, and between unsatisfactory and satisfactory in math. The single retainees average nearly a third of a marking unit above the multiple-problem group in reading, and almost half a marking unit higher in math. In fact, single retainees' first-quarter math mark average is almost satisfactory. Both of the mark differences between single retainees and others exceed 0.5 standard deviations – large differences in early school performance among children who are performing poorly altogether.

Multiple-treatment youngsters also have lower test averages in the fall of first grade: 10 points lower on the Math Concepts subtest and 12 points lower on the Reading Comprehension subtest. At around 0.4 standard deviations, these too are large differences.

Finally, multiple repeaters and retainees who are put in special education give evidence of poorer early school adjustment. These youngsters are viewed by their first grade teachers as less cooperative, less engaged in their schoolwork, and more fidgety.[20] They are also viewed as less popular with their peers, and more often are identified in the MSTOI ratings as being at risk.

Conclusions

Repeaters are distinguished from never-retained children in many ways that bear on their academic prospects; also, different "classes" of retainees can be distinguished from one another on the basis of problems discernible at the very start of school.

Family demographic characteristics, early marks and test scores, and factors of school adjustment in first grade show highly patterned differences before any students have been retained. The differences seen during first grade are striking, especially those that involve academic factors and poor school adjustment. Differences in these areas generally are larger than those in children's personal and social demographic

Table 3.3. *Demographic, academic, and school adjustment profiles of students retained only once, and those with a second retention or special education*[a]

	All retainees[a]	Retained once[b]	Retained twice or special ed.[c]	Difference between retained once and retained twice or special ed.	Difference as a proportion of S.D.
Demographic comparisons					
Proportion male	.57	.54	.62	−.08	0.16
	(0.50)	(0.50)	(0.49)		
Proportion African-American	.63	.60	.68	−.08	0.16
	(0.48)	(0.49)	(0.47)		
Proportion receiving lunch subsidy	.85	.84	.85	.01	0.02
	(0.36)	(0.37)	(0.36)		
Average mother's education (years)	10.61	10.75	10.41	0.34	0.16
	(2.19)	(2.36)	(1.93)		
Average father's education (years)	10.90	11.05	10.74	0.31	0.16
	(1.90)	(2.03)	(1.75)		
Proportion in two-parent family	.42	.40	.44	−.04	0.08
	(0.49)	(0.49)	(0.50)		
Average number of siblings	1.62	1.53	1.73	−0.19	0.13
	(1.51)	(1.49)	(1.54)		
Academic comparisons					
Average reading mark, first quarter 1982	1.45	1.59	1.27	0.32**	0.58
	(0.55)	(0.59)	(0.45)		
Average math mark, first quarter 1982	1.75	1.94	1.50	0.44**	0.62
	(0.71)	(0.71)	(0.61)		

Average CAT-R score, fall 1982	267.09 (33.75)	272.24 (33.55)	260.04 (32.88)	12.19**	0.36
Average CAT-M score, fall 1982	276.05 (24.00)	280.11 (23.92)	270.11 (22.95)	10.00**	0.42
School adjustment comparisons					
Average number of absences	16.19 (13.60)	15.54 (12.46)	17.09 (15.03)	−1.56	0.11
Average Cooperation–Compliance score	19.33 (4.71)	20.03 (4.36)	18.36 (5.02)	1.66**	0.35
Average Interest–Participation score	18.74 (5.07)	20.04 (4.96)	16.94 (4.68)	3.10**	0.61
Average Attention Span–Restlessness score	18.48 (4.57)	19.72 (3.95)	16.78 (4.82)	2.94**	0.64
Average conduct mark, fall 1982	1.66 (0.48)	1.69 (0.46)	1.61 (0.49)	0.08	0.16
MSTOI proportion at risk	.49 (0.50)	.43 (0.50)	.57 (0.50)	.14*	0.28
Average peer popularity	3.09 (1.08)	3.37 (1.03)	2.70 (1.03)	0.67**	0.62

Note: Numbers in parentheses are standard deviations.

[a] Sample coverage on all retainees, except for father's education ($N = 183$) and MSTOI ($N = 230$), varies from 317 to 270.

[b] Sample coverage on once-retained children, except for father's education ($N = 94$) and MSTOI ($N = 133$), varies from 184 to 156.

[c] Sample coverage on twice-retained and special education children, except for father's education ($N = 89$) and MSTOI ($N = 91$) varies from 133 to 112.

**signifies differences significant at the 0.01 level; *differences significant at the 0.05 level.

characteristics, yet they have received scant attention in the retention literature. Whereas the ascriptive profile of repeaters is well established, academic differences that predate retention tend to be slighted, and the broad spectrum of adjustment problems documented here has received virtually no attention.

The logic underlying children's differential treatment by schools is vividly drawn in these contrasting histories: distinctive retention profiles mirror distinctive problem profiles. Retainees as a group have serious problems meeting the standards and expectations that await them at school, and this, presumably, is why they are held back. Those whose problems are most "severe" are held back soonest, are held back a second time, and are more likely than other repeaters to wind up in special education.

These descriptive profiles reveal a side of this "unjustifiable, discriminatory, noxious policy" (Abidin et al. 1971) that often gets short shrift. These youngsters need help badly, and the help that retention provides is an extra year (or two) to catch up. Whether they in fact do catch up remains to be seen. Having plotted out children's pathways through the elementary and middle school years (Chapter 2) and seen in this chapter who is held back, we are now ready to explore retention's consequences. We begin in the next three chapters with effects in the academic realm.

4

Monitoring academic performance: test scores before and after retention

Academic consequences of retention are evaluated first using test scores as the criterion (Chapters 4 and 5) and then report card marks (Chapter 6). Whether repeating helps or harms children academically is perhaps the single most pressing question in weighing the pros and cons of retention, yet, as we saw in Chapter 1, the issue is very much open. Despite the many studies, good research on how retention affects children's school performance is sparse. In Chapters 4, 5, and 6 retainees' postretention performance will be evaluated against: (1) their own performance profile before retention; (2) the performance of other youngsters whose early academic record was about the same as theirs but who were not held back (the strategy of "matched controls"); (3) the performance of all never-retained children after adjusting statistically for characteristics other than retention that might contribute to differences between the groups; and (4) the performance of other children who will be held back after the comparison is made.

This last approach is uncommon, but could be especially revealing. We can, for example, compare the second grade progress of children who were held back in first grade with that of children who were not retained until third grade. Although children who will not be retained until third grade have higher first grade test scores than first grade repeaters, Chapter 3 shows that they are still more similar to first grade repeaters in terms of academic and adjustment problems than are children who move smoothly through the primary grades.

Because of these similarities, yet-to-be-retained children's second grade performance is probably a better yardstick than the performance of never-to-be-retained children for judging whether first grade retainees are doing better, worse, or about the same as expected. For example, if first and third grade repeaters are both doing poorly in Year 2 relative to second graders with smooth promotion histories, then something other than retention is likely behind first grade repeaters' academic difficulties. Along with other benchmarks, looking at yet-to-be-retained children's performance should give a clearer picture of retention's consequences than either "matched control" or over-time comparisons of isolated groups of retainees.

The data on children's school performance cover 8 years. Since retainees spend 2 years in the repeated grade, we can plot performance profiles through seventh grade for practically everyone (double retainees are the main exception). The number of retainees is largest in the first 3 years: 127 first-time repeaters in the first year, 68 in the second, and 47 in the third. Since coverage of performance trends *after* retention is longest for these early retainees, profiles will be presented separately for them. Fourth through seventh grade retainees will be grouped together for analysis.

Two comparison groups of never-retained youngsters will also be included in the various comparisons. The first is all never-retained children; the second is a subset of these nonretainees who did poorly in the spring of first grade on the CAT subtests. These children ($N = 106$) have not been held back through the eighth grade, but their verbal and quantitative CAT scores from the spring of their first year are within 1 standard deviation above or below the averages of all retainees. They are a group of promoted children who early in their school careers were performing at about the same level on standardized tests as most of the retainees. The criterion of scoring within 1 standard deviation of retainees' averages on both CAT subtests encompasses about a fourth of the never-retained subsample.[1] Their CAT-R average is 326, compared with 312 for retainees and 371 for other never-retained youngsters; their CAT-M average is 327, versus 319 for repeaters and 366 for other nonrepeaters. Scores for the "poor performing" comparison group thus are much closer to those of retainees than they are to the scores of other never-retained children.

Evaluating the later performance of retainees against that of never-retained youngsters with comparable early academic skills involves the logic of "matched controls," a common strategy in other retention studies. Here we match (roughly) on early test performance, and in later

analyses adjust statistically for other characteristics that distinguish retainees from nonretainees, including measures of family economic level,
race / ethnicity, gender, and so on.

This chapter presents detailed comparisons of children's performance
on CAT tests through the first 8 years of school. It describes test score
gains, or improvement, to see whether retainees' progress keeps pace
with the various comparison groups. In the next chapter we perform
statistical analyses on these test data to clarify the effects of retention.

Retainees' CAT gains going through the repeated grade

A detailed picture of the year–by–year test score trajectories for retained
and never-retained children is given in Table 4.A1 in the appendix to this
chapter. The data reviewed here on grade-level gains and on cumulative
gains across grade levels highlight similarities and differences in developmental patterns between children who have been retained and those who
have not. Figures 4.1 and 4.2 and Table 4.1 report grade level gains for
grades 1, 2, and 3 separately, and for grades 4 through 7 combined.[2]

Table 4.1 includes all the figures necessary to plot Figures 4.1 and 4.2,
so the reader can refer to it for details that might be hard to decipher in
the figures. The table also reports cumulative gains for never-retained
youngsters in grades 5 through 8. In these same years, retainees were
going through grades 4 through 7. The 1-year "offset" allows same-age
comparisons of retainees' and promoted youngsters' gains.

Figures 4.1 and 4.2 show how youngsters who repeated a grade compare to those who passed that grade on the first try, including those who
might have repeated some other grade. Except for retainees in the repeated grade, the height of the bars for grades 1, 2, and 3 represents the
fall-to-spring 1-year gain. For retained pupils in their repeated grade the
bar represents their 2-year total gain for that grade, splitting it into a
"first year" component (fall to spring of the failed year, below the horizontal divide), and a "second year" component (spring of the failed year
to spring of the repeated year, above the horizontal divide). The split
within the 2-year period permits same-grade and same-age comparisons
in the same display.[3]

In every instance save one,[4] retainees' gains during their failed year fall
short of the gains by any other group that year, including children held
back at other grade levels. The shortfall relative to never-retained young-

Table 4.1. *Fall to spring CAT-R and Cat-M gains over first grade, second grade, third grade, fourth through seventh grades combined, and for never-retained pupils, fifth through eighth grades combined*

	1st grade gain[a]	2d grade gain[a]	3d grade gain[a]	4th–7th grade gain	5th–8th grade gain[b]
CAT-R gains					
Year of retention					
1st grade	31.5/57.7	31.6	28.4	85.2	—
	(104)/(70)	(82)	(94)	(57)	
2d grade	40.5	23.4/44.3	29.2	82.9	—
	(59)	(55)/(48)	(48)	(38)	
3d grade	57.8	39.1	16.9/45.0	76.7	—
	(37)	(44)	(35)/(33)	(30)	
4th–7th grade	68.5	45.1	39.6	112.0	—
	(62)	(70)	(64)	(48)	
Never-retained pupils					
All never retained	70.9	47.4	34.3	107.8	99.2
	(387)	(382)	(299)	(201)	(215)
Poor-performing	56.0	56.4	34.5	99.3	93.2
comparison group	(92)	(88)	(72)	(44)	(52)
CAT-M gains					
Year of retention					
1st grade	35.9/40.2	28.3	32.9	72.6	—
	(102)/(69)	(83)	(93)	(55)	
2d grade	45.0	35.1/33.9	35.3	69.6	—
	(58)	(58)/(49)	(49)	(38)	
3d grade	51.9	41.5	32.1/43.3	75.7	—
	(38)	(45)	(35)/(34)	(30)	
4th–7th grade	51.3	47.1	41.2	110.7	—
	(65)	(71)	(64)	(44)	
Never-retained pupils					
All never retained	52.2	44.3	38.9	119.2	102.6
	(396)	(380)	(299)	(200)	(214)
Poor-performing	45.9	46.1	36.9	108.8	90.6
comparison group	(93)	(86)	(72)	(44)	(52)

Note: Numbers in parentheses are sample sizes.

[a] For first, second, and third grade retainees, two gain scores are reported in the year of retention. These separate the 2-year repeated grade gain into its first-year component (fall to spring) and its second-year component (spring to spring). The total 2-year grade-level gain would be the sum of these figures.

[b] Fifth through eighth grade gains are not computed for repeaters.

CAT-R Gains

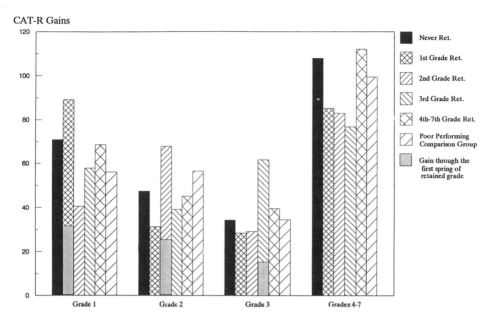

Figure 4.1. Gains on the CAT reading-comprehension test in grades 1 through 7 for first, second, and third grade retainees, for fourth through seventh grade retainees, for all never-retained pupils, and for the poor-performing comparison group. For retained pupils in the year of retention, the first-year component of the grade-level gain is shown below the horizontal divide, the second-year component above the divide.

sters is especially large. Consider improvement in reading comprehension (Figure 4.1). First grade repeaters' scores improve, on average, about 32 points, well below both the 70-plus–point gain registered by all never-retained children and the 56-point gain achieved by the poor-performing comparison group. In comparison, second grade repeaters' scores improved that year by 40 points, and third grade and fourth to seventh grade retainees' gains actually exceeded those of the poor performers. A similar shortfall is seen for first grade retainees on the CAT-M, and the pattern is repeated for second grade retainees in second grade and for third grade retainees in third grade, although for third grade retainees, the shortfall on the Math Concepts test is quite small in several comparisons.

Yet-to-be-retained youngsters in grades other than their failed grade

CAT-M Gains

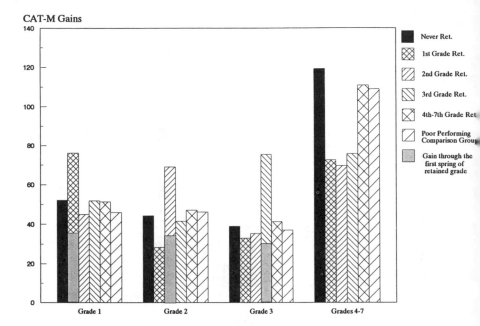

Figure 4.2. Gains on the CAT math-concepts test in grades 1 through 7 for first, second, and third grade retainees, for fourth through seventh grade retainees, for all never-retained pupils, and for the poor-performing comparison group. For retained pupils in the year of retention, the first-year component of the grade-level gain is shown below the horizontal divide, the second-year component above the divide.

also generally gain more than retainees in that grade, but they usually gain less than the never-to-be-retained.[5] Yet-to-be-retained youngsters begin slipping back most noticeably in the year prior to the year they will fail (second grade repeaters in first grade; third grade repeaters in second grade), so the steep falloff registered in the failed year in most instances continues a progressive slide. Retainees thus stand out from all other groups in the year they fail as falling especially far behind in cognitive skill development.

The second time through the grade, though, the picture changes. In some instances retainees make large gains that year, especially on the CAT-R. These are the bar segments above the horizontal divide in Figure 4.1. The 58-point increase registered by first grade retainees and the 45-

point increase registered by third grade retainees during their respective repeated years are both well above their failed-year gains (which were 32 and 17 points, respectively). Second grade retainees' improvement of 44 points also seems large, but fully a third of this advance (16.7 points) was registered over the summer months and so does not reflect repeated-year progress.[6]

These figures for the first and third grade retainees represent impressive strides, and not just when compared with their own meager advances during the year they failed. Their gains on the second try are close to the 1-year gains registered by at least one of the never-retained comparison groups for the same grade even after allowing for summer improvement. Only second grade repeaters fall short in all comparisons.

The pattern for the CAT-M is not quite as favorable for repeaters, but the preretention picture parallels that for the CAT-R. The first time through the grade, youngsters who will later be retained generally lag somewhat behind the others. Also, with the exception of second grade retainees, they gain more upon retaking the grade than they did the first time through.[7] Third grade repeaters' gain in the repeated year, reported in Table 4.1 (43.3 points), exceeds the gains registered by all other groups in third grade; even after subtracting out the summer component (about 10 points) their 33-point school year gain is still close to that of the comparison group in the same period. However, first and second grade retainees' repeated-year gains in most instances fall short of the advances made by others, so the comparisons here are not consistently favorable.

Even leaving aside gains made in the summer – because they may represent practice effects with the test – it is important to note that these 2-year grade-level gains are cumulative, and reflect repeaters' assessed competence when they eventually move along to the next grade. First grade repeaters, for example, improved their CAT-M performance by a total of 76 points over first grade (35.9 + 40.2). The first grade gains for all other groups ranged between 45 and 52 points. Second grade repeaters' 2-year second grade CAT-M gain of 69 points similarly exceeds the 1-year second grade gains of all other groups, as does the 75-point third grade gain of third grade repeaters when compared with all other groups' gains in third grade.

These 2-year versus 1-year comparisons favor retained-year children on the CAT-R as well. Since 2 years of progress is being compared with 1 year, this excess gain is perhaps not surprising, but it does imply that after repeating a grade, retainees are not as far behind as when they were held back. This excess gain thus gives the impression that real progress has been made.[8]

What prompts children to make up lost ground in the repeated year is unknown, because we have little information on whether they merely repeated the same material or had some kind of special help.[9] Nevertheless, retention by itself would alter children's school experience in important ways even if unaccompanied by special remediation efforts. During the repeated year, retainees will be more familiar with the curriculum and with school routines; they will be bigger, older, and possibly more mature than their classmates, which may be especially important in the primary grades; they also usually take the same standardized tests they took the previous fall, and so may profit from test-wiseness.[10] Repeating the year gives children a second chance to learn skills they failed to master the first time through, and the pattern of test score gains seen here suggests that repeating the year helps children make up at least some of what they missed. But does it help them keep up once they are back on track? This question is considered in the next section.

CAT gains after retention: year by year

The main question about test score gains after retention is whether progress registered in the repeated year persists. For first and second grade repeaters, Figures 4.1 and 4.2 plot progress annually through third grade. From fourth grade on, after the first, second, and third grade repeaters have moved back into the normal grade sequence, we report cumulative totals for everyone through the end of seventh grade.

Annual gains in most instances decline over the years for everyone because generally the rate of children's cognitive growth declines with age (Jencks 1985). Never-retained children, for example, drop from an average CAT-R gain of 71 points over first grade, to 47 points over second grade, to 34 points over third grade. Indeed, the growth rate continues to slow in the course of the entire 8 years, as the cumulative fourth through seventh grade increase of 108 points implies an annual average of only about 27 points. Similarly, an orderly drop in CAT-M gains among the never-retained can be seen in the year-by-year comparisons, which fall from 52 points to 39, and in the annual average for grades 4 through 7, which drops further, to just under 30 points.

This trend tells us, among other things, that simply seeing a tapering off of annual gains among retainees after retention doesn't necessarily reflect negatively on retention per se, because progress for all children slows over the years. The pattern for retainees, however, is a bit more complicated, and in revealing ways. In particular, the single-year gains of yet-to-be-retained youngsters in every instance exceed the single-year gains registered by retainees after they have moved back into the normal grade sequence. For example, third grade retainees gain 39 points on the CAT-R in second grade, and fourth through seventh grade retainees gain 45 points and 40 points in second and third grade, respectively. These *preretention* gains all exceed the *postretention* gains registered by first grade repeaters in second grade (31 points) and by first and second grade repeaters in third grade (28 points and 29 points). An identical pattern is seen for CAT-M gains.

We have already seen that the pace of test score improvement falls off for everyone moving from lower grades to higher ones. The poor performance of retainees after being held back is consistent with this. Nevertheless, their annual gains after retention consistently fall short of those registered by comparable youngsters – those who have yet to be retained – at the same grade level. The falloff in the pace of their improvement after retention thus appears to be especially pronounced, suggesting some postretention "backsliding."[11]

The cumulative gains over grades 4 through 7 displayed in Figures 4.1 and 4.2 support this conclusion. All three early retainee groups lag behind during this period, which overlaps the end of elementary school and the first 2 years of middle school. On the CAT-M the average gains for both never-retained groups are considerably more than 100 points; on the CAT-R the full never-retained sample also improves in this range, while the subsample of poor performers falls just short (registering an average gain of 99.3 points). In comparison, the largest increase on either subtest posted by first through third grade retainees is the 85-point gain seen for first grade repeaters on the CAT-R. The others range down to 70 points (for second grade repeaters on the CAT-M).

The *more favorable* of these comparisons has first grade repeaters' overall improvement over grades 4 though 7 falling almost 23 points short of the improvement registered by all never-retained youngsters, and remaining some 14 points shy of the poor performers' upward progress. These deficits correspond to 0.45 and 0.28 pooled sample standard deviations, respectively (the standard deviation of the distribution of gains being 50.4 points and 49.2 for the two comparisons). The *less favorable* comparisons have second grade repeaters' gains lagging some 50 points behind those of the full sample of never-retained children and almost 40 points behind those of the poor performers. The first lag exceeds a full standard deviation difference (which is 47.1 points); the second lag is more than 0.90 standard deviations (the standard deviation being 42.2 points for the poor performers and retainees). Both lags reflect exceedingly large gaps.

The tallies reported in the rightmost columns of Table 4.1 indicate whether the retainees' shortfall in gains just reviewed is exaggerated because of the 1-year "offset" required to line up same-grade comparisons. Since improvement tends to trail off for everyone over time, the same-grade format could put retainees at a disadvantage. Their gains from grades 4 through 7 begin and end a year later than the corresponding grade-level gains for children with smooth promotion histories, so even if nothing else were happening to them during this interval, they likely would appear to be making below-average progress.

Indeed, these concerns are valid because the same-age figures reported for never-retained youngsters in the last columns of Table 4.1 are smaller than the corresponding same-grade figures. The same-grade figures cover grades 4 through 7, while the same-age figures cover grades 5 through 8 (when retainees are in grades 4 through 7). Three of the four entries in the last column indicate gains of less than 100 points, and the other is only 102.6 (for all never-retained youth on the CAT-M). Only one of the four figures for grades 4 through 7 is this low. The difference between corresponding same-grade–same-age gains goes from 18 points (among poor performers on the CAT-M) to 6 points (also among poor performers, on the CAT-R).

These differences are far from trivial, so same-age comparisons between retained and never-retained youngsters do tend to cast retention in a somewhat more favorable light. But even using this approach, retainees do not keep pace. They lag behind, from about 33 points on the CAT-M (involving second grade repeaters vs. all those never retained) to 8 points on the CAT-R (involving first grade repeaters vs. poor performers).

Most of the same-age comparisons are closer to the larger figure than the smaller one, so even using this more favorable basis of comparison we still would conclude that retainees fall farther and farther behind never-retained youngsters for as long as we can monitor their progress. First grade retainees are tracked for 6 years beyond their repeated grade, and third grade retainees for 4 years afterward. These are uncommonly long intervals for an evaluation of effects of retention, and any lasting benefits of retention almost certainly would be apparent within the time spans observed.

A note on children held back at higher grade levels

Thus far we have said little about children held back in the fourth through seventh grades because too few of them repeat any single grade to examine them separately; also, for the combined group, the period of followup after retention is too short to say much about the consequences of retention. Nevertheless, at the start of school they were performing below the level of children who later would have smooth promotion histories (although not below the level of "poor performers" with smooth promotion histories), so it seems wise to include them as yet another comparison group.

When their gains are lined up against those of children held back earlier, the comparisons consistently favor later retainees. In fact, even comparisons with the never-retained usually favor the late retainees. In all but one instance their grade-level gains (including those over the interval of grades 4 through 7) surpass those registered by the poor performers, and are even close to, or occasionally above, the figures for all never-retained children. The one possible exception is the 8+ point difference (Table 4.1) on the CAT-M over grades 4 through 7 (119 − 111 = 8), which gives the edge to promoted children; but even this is reversed when using the same-age total for grades 5 through 8 (103 points) as the basis of comparison.

The 4 through 7 interval used here does not reveal what is happening to these youngsters during the 2-year cycle of their repeated grades, but even lacking this detail it is safe to conclude that the situation of later retainees is radically different from that of their counterparts held back earlier. In the early grades they progress at about the same pace as other promoted youngsters. Their outcomes in the period that frames their problem years are also favorable (at least in the aggregate); and to the extent that we can comment on what happens to them after retention, that assessment is positive as well. On this basis it is hard to say that retention either helps or harms children held back at higher grade levels: they seem to be doing satisfactorily all along, before, during, and after retention. However, more detailed comparisons for fourth, fifth, sixth, and seventh grade repeaters separately also show in most instances a dip in the failed year and recovery in the repeated grade. This is obscured when the groups are combined, but they too tend to follow the characteristic retention pattern. What is most immediately relevant in these comparisons is that early retainees are no more successful in keeping pace with later retainees than in keeping pace with never-retained youngsters. The favorable profile for later retainees thus affords yet another standard against which early retention can be judged, and again the comparison is unfavorable.

Cumulative test score gains from the failed year

The gains across grades 4 through 7 give a picture of how well retainees fare after getting back onto the regular promotion schedule. That they had difficulty is certain, but we also saw indications of progress in the repeated grade. There thus are countervailing trends at work. Figures 4.3 and 4.4, which display cumulative gains for everyone from the fall of first, second, and third grade retainees' failed year to the end of seventh grade (the exact figures are reported in Table 4.2), show where retainees end up. These calculations encompass the period of decline in the failed year, the repeated year "rebound," and the postretention tapering off.

Tallying progress across the three major phases of the retention experience should give a fair reading of how the experience, in its totality, affects academic development. We are mainly interested in how youngsters who have been held back in a given year – first grade repeaters in first grade, second grade repeaters in second grade, and so forth – fare against all others. Entries in the first column of Table 4.2 are of interest for another reason, though. Because they use the fall of first grade retainees' failed year as a baseline, they represent cumulative gains over the entire interval of our study – from the start of school to the end of seventh grade. Never-retained youngsters advance most over these years (272 points on the CAT-R; 253 points on the CAT-M); first grade retainees least (224 points on the CAT-R; 202 points on the CAT-M). The difference of about 50 points in each area leaves first grade repeaters

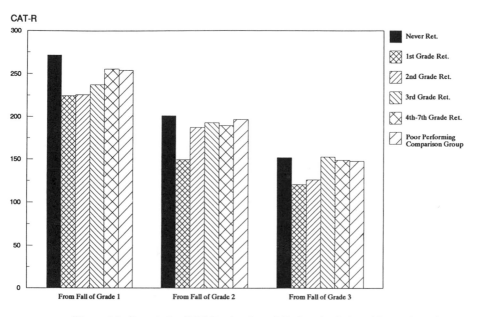

Figure 4.3. Cumulative CAT-R gains from fall of grades 1, 2, and 3 to spring of grade 7.

trailing far behind.[12] The comparison group of poor performers and the children retained at higher grade levels show the next-biggest gains, with the two being quite close on the CAT-R (254 vs. 256). Retainees in grades 4 through 7 lag behind on the CAT-M, however, as their improvement on it (233 points) is closer to third grade retainees' (229 points) than to the poor performers' (244 points).

The other retainee groups all register smaller gains than the never-retained group. Second grade repeaters are not much ahead of first grade repeaters in either area, and both groups fall short of the advances made by third grade retainees. These are small differences in some instances, but still, over these 7 years the ranking of test score gains parallels the scheduling of retention, just as we saw before for the ranking of entry-level scores (see Table 4.A1 in the appendix to this chapter). On the specific question of whether retention helps repeaters, we can see no positive indications for first grade retainees, whose cumulative gains lag far behind almost everyone else's.

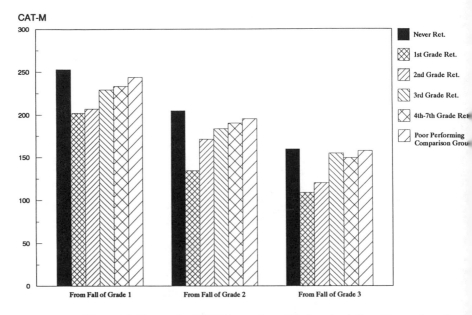

Figure 4.4. Cumulative CAT-M gains from fall of grades 1, 2, and 3 to spring of grade 7.

The situation is much the same for second grade repeaters, whose gains from the autumn of second grade fall short of all others' save those of first grade repeaters. However, their shortfall is generally less than that seen for first grade repeaters, and even less than they themselves had registered over the entire interval (seen in the previous column). For example, on the CAT-R, second grade repeaters' cumulative gain from the fall of first grade fell shy of the low performers' gain by some 28 points. In comparison, the difference when computed from the fall of second grade is just under 10 points, so when never-retained youngsters' large first-year gains are set aside, the comparison for second grade repeaters looks more favorable. They still do not keep pace, but they are not far behind either.

The comparisons reported in the third column, which use third grade repeaters' year of failure as the baseline, are more favorable still. Their cumulative CAT-R gain from the fall of the third grade to the end of the

Table 4.2. *Cumulative CAT gains from fall of grades 1, 2, and 3 to spring of grade 7 for retained groups, never-retained pupils, and the poor-performing comparison group*

	CAT-R			CAT-M		
	From fall 1st grade[a]	From fall 2d grade[a]	From fall 3d grade[a]	From fall 1st grade[a]	From fall 2d grade[a]	From fall 3d grade[a]
Year of retention						
1st grade	**224.4**	149.1	120.4	**202.1**	134.4	108.6
	(53)	(52)	(53)	**(49)**	(48)	(50)
2d grade	225.6	**187.0**	126.0	207.1	**171.1**	120.0
	(35)	**(34)**	(36)	(36)	**(35)**	(35)
3d grade	237.1	192.7	**152.5**	229.1	183.4	**154.4**
	(26)	(31)	**(28)**	(25)	(31)	**(29)**
4th–7th grade	255.5	189.3	148.7	233.1	190.1	149.0
	(44)	(51)	(50)	(44)	(48)	(46)
Never-retained pupils						
All never-retained	271.8	200.8	151.7	252.9	204.8	159.4
	(204)	(222)	(215)	(208)	(220)	(214)
Poor-performing comparison group	253.9	196.5	147.5	243.5	195.2	157.2
	(46)	(51)	(50)	(47)	(51)	(50)

Note: Numbers in parentheses are sample sizes.
[a]Gains for youngsters retained in the baseline grade are in boldface. Because of their repeated year, all retainees require a year longer than never-retained pupils to reach the end of seventh grade, so gains are computed over different intervals for retained and never-retained youngsters.

seventh – 152 points – exceeds all others. Though the margin in most cases is modest, third grade repeaters keep pace not only with the poor performers and with children who will be held back after third grade, but also with the full sample of never-retained youngsters. This parity seems noteworthy.

Third grade retainees' advance in the quantitative area is not so dramatic, but they come close to keeping pace, lagging just 3 points behind the low performers and 5 points behind all never-retained children.

Considering the tremendous gaps seen in most other comparisons, these modest differences seem small, and raise the possibility that retention might actually accomplish some lasting good for third grade repeaters.

The many detailed comparisons made thus far show that the issues connected with retention can be exceedingly complex, and require considerable detective work. The information in Table 4.3 on pre- and postretention gains complicates matters still more.

Gains before and after retention

Children's progress before retention provides yet another frame of reference for structuring comparisons. The preretention record for first grade repeaters involves only their failed year. Their gains in that initial year can be evaluated against their 1-year gains during the repeated year (first panel, Table 4.3). The first entry (32) is simply the increase in their CAT-R average from fall to spring of first grade. The second entry (54) is the increase from fall to spring of their second time through the grade. Unlike the intervals used in Figure 4.1 and Table 4.1, change here is monitored over 1 academic year both prior to and after retention, so the gains are directly comparable. The third column expresses the postretention gain as a proportion of the preretention gain, so we can see which of the two was larger. More informative, though, are the comparisons across groups, which indicate whether the change in retainees' rate of progress after retention is greater than, less than, or about the same as other children's in the same period. Are they slowing down more or less than children who were never held back, or who were held back in other years?

Since the entries for first grade retainees overlap only the 2-year "dip and recovery" of their repeated grade, the gains themselves do not reveal anything new; practically the same figures appear in Table 4.1.[13] First grade repeaters made below-average gains in the first year and above-average gains the second. Correspondingly, they have the lowest figure in the first column and, at least for the CAT-R, one of the highest figures in the second. But the figures in the third column place these gains in relative perspective, so that even a lower-than-average gain, like the first grade repeaters' CAT-M increase after retention (lower part of Table 4.3), signals rather good progress.

First grade retainees' increase of 38 points on the CAT-M in the second year is less than that of all other retainee groups except one, but since first grade repeaters gained relatively little the first time through the grade, for them a gain of 38 points is a large advance. In fact, being 1.05 times their increase from the previous year, this gain is relatively the largest improvement for any group. The poor performers, whose second-year gain was about the same as their first-year gain, come next, with a post- to preretention ratio of 1.00. All the other groups gained less in the second year than in the first, so their ratios all fall below 1.0. At 0.78, second grade repeaters trail off most severely, but the second year for them is their year of failure, so this deficit is not surprising.

First grade repeaters made especially large strides on the CAT-R in the second year. Not only did they gain more than all others that year, but most others actually fell far off from the pace they had registered the previous year. The first grade repeaters' ratio of 1.73 is the largest in the entire table, and is more than double most of the other ratios in this panel.

Although they are not new, the way the comparisons are structured in Table 4.3 puts the results for first graders in a new light. They reveal differences in the relative pace of improvement, and from this vantage point retainees appear to be making good strides. Comparisons in the next panel line up gains for 2 years pre- and postretention: from the fall of first grade through the spring of second grade for the preretention interval; and from the fall of Year 3 (when second grade retainees are repeating second grade) through the spring of Year 4 for the postretention interval. These intervals bracket the retention experience for second grade repeaters.

Since precisely the same interval is used pre- and postretention, the gains are directly comparable. On the CAT-R, second grade repeaters made the smallest postretention gains of any group (52 points), which we ordinarily would take as a negative indication. But the others made much larger strides in Years 1 and 2 than in Years 3 and 4, so their progress actually slowed more than that of the second grade retainees in this same period. In fact, the 0.84 entry for second grade repeaters in the third column indicates that they come closest of any group to maintaining their previous rate of gain. The next highest proportion is 0.74 for third grade retainees, with all the rest ranging between 0.67 and 0.69. These figures show second grade retainees did well on the CAT-R for 2 years after

Table 4.3. *1-year, 2-year, and 3-year CAT gains, defined around first, second, and third grade retainees' failed year*

	1-year gains through and after Year 1			2-year gains through and after Year 2			3-year gains through and after Year 3		
	Pre[a]	Post[b]	Post/Pre[c]	Pre[a]	Post[b]	Post/Pre[c]	Pre[a]	Post[b]	Post/Pre[c]
CAT-R									
Year of retention									
1st grade	**31.5**	**54.5**	**1.73**	89.2	60.5	0.68	99.7	86.1	0.86
	(104)	(71)		(70)	(82)		(84)	(74)	
2d grade	40.5	23.4	0.58	**62.3**	**52.3**	**0.84**	103.4	91.5	0.88
	(59)	(55)		(55)	**(43)**		(49)	(46)	
3d grade	57.8	39.1	0.68	82.8	61.2	0.74	**95.8**	**98.6**	**1.03**
	(37)	(44)		(37)	(33)		**(30)**	**(30)**	
4th–7th grade	68.5	45.1	0.66	106.6	73.5	0.69	136.5	80.2	0.59
	(62)	(70)		(63)	(62)		(56)	(61)	
Never-retained pupils									
All never-retained	70.9	47.4	0.67	121.3	81.5	0.67	157.4	89.4	0.57
	(387)	(382)		(350)	(284)		(274)	(222)	
Poor-performing comparison group	56.0	56.4	1.01	113.0	75.7	0.67	145.1	84.0	0.58
	(92)	(88)		(81)	(70)		(64)	(48)	

CAT-M

Year of retention									
1st grade	**35.9**	**37.6**	**1.05**	76.1	56.6	0.74	95.8	77.1	0.80
	(102)	**(69)**		(69)	(82)		(84)	(73)	
2d grade	45.0	35.1	0.78	**72.0**	**51.7**	**0.72**	103.8	96.1	0.93
	(58)	(58)		**(57)**	**(43)**		(50)	(47)	
3d grade	51.9	41.5	0.80	86.4	75.3	0.87	**102.3**	**91.1**	**0.89**
	(38)	(45)		(37)	(34)		**(29)**	**(30)**	
4th–7th grade	51.3	47.1	0.92	93.7	73.0	0.78	120.6	79.8	0.66
	(65)	(71)		(67)	(62)		(59)	(59)	
Never-retained pupils									
All never-retained	52.2	44.3	0.85	93.8	77.2	0.82	133.4	93.7	0.70
	(396)	(380)		(354)	(283)		(283)	(221)	
Poor-performing comparison group	45.9	46.1	1.00	97.1	80.1	0.82	127.5	83.8	0.66
	(93)	(86)		(76)	(70)		(65)	(48)	

Note: Numbers in parentheses are sample sizes. Boldface entries identify the retainee reference group for each panel.

[a] The "Pre" entries are from the fall of first grade through the spring of the retainee reference group's failed year. For that panel's reference group, they represent cumulative gains preretention.

[b] The "Post" entries use the fall of the repeated year for that panel's reference group as the baseline, with the gains being computed postretention for as many years as are covered in the preretention interval.

[c] The "Post/Pre" entries are simply the ratio of postretention gains to preretention gains for each panel's reference group. For other groups the calculations give the ratio of gains over the corresponding intervals.

retention. The picture is clouded, however, because their ratio for the CAT-M is the lowest (0.72).

For third grade repeaters the signals are more consistently positive. For them, we can look at test performance for 3 years prior to their retention, from the fall of first grade through the spring of third grade. Correspondingly, the postretention interval also extends 3 years: from the fall of Year 4, which is the fall of their repeated year, to the spring of Year 6. On the CAT-R, their gain of 99 points is the largest of any group. Moreover, they are the only group whose 3-year gains from Year 4 through Year 6 exceed their gains over the 3 previous years (1.03 in the third column). Most of the other ratios, including those for both never-retained groups, are much smaller. In fact, the ratios for all three retainee groups exceed those for the never-retained, so the never-retained children's pace slows the most noticeably at the upper grade levels.

On the CAT-M, third grade repeaters' postretention/preretention ratio (0.89) is not the highest (second grade repeaters show 0.93), but is among the highest. Here again, the ratios for never-retained children fall below all the rest, and so repeat the pattern in the 2-year intervals defined around second grade repeaters' retention experience. Never-retained children apparently get a "jump start" in the early grades that puts them so far ahead that retainees are never able to catch up; but retention, at least after the first grade, seems to give children a boost. They do better afterward than before, and so come closer to maintaining a consistent rate of academic progress through the elementary years[14] than do children with smooth promotion histories. Everyone's rate of progress slows, but that of the never-retained children slows more than does that of retainees.

Prospective retainees trail behind badly right from the start, and struggle especially in the year they are held back. Table 4.3 indicates that time spent in repeating a grade helps these youngsters somewhat, and this pattern is intuitively appealing. Retention may not be the best or the most effective way to help these youngsters, but it looks better than simply passing them along. Repeating the grade allows them to master skills that they missed the first time through, and thus they are better prepared when they move on to the next grade. Nevertheless, any "boost" they get still leaves them far behind, because their rates of growth do not accelerate. For the most part they use the year as a period of catching up.

Overview of performance trends

To conclude this section, Table 4.4 presents some figures that show where the several retainee groups stand relative to the never-retained students when they begin school, in the spring of their failed year (their "low point"), in the spring of their repeated year (their "high point"), and at the end of seventh grade, which is as far as our coverage extends in this volume. How retainees fare at these reference points gives some sense of the "natural history" of the retention experience, which is characterized by early, severe academic problems that worsen until the decision is made to hold the child back. Some improvement follows, both absolutely in the repeated year and, as just seen, relatively for years afterwards. Nevertheless, usually retainees are in a relatively worse position at the end than at the start.

The entries in Table 4.4 are differences in test score averages between retained and never-retained youngsters. Since there is more variability in test performance in the later than in the earlier years, the differences are also expressed as proportions of the test score standard deviation for the reference period. This scale conversion can be important because a difference of, say, 10 points is of more concern if scores ranged between values of 0 and 50 than if they ranged between 0 and 500; 10 points is a much larger relative gap in the first instance than in the second. Referencing raw score differences to the variation in scores adjusts for the increasing spread over time in the range of test scores, and so allows for more meaningful comparisons.

The pattern of signs in Table 4.4 confirms our overall impression. Most signs are negative, which means that retainees are not doing as well as the never-retained or poor performers. But six positive signs appear for comparisons with the poor performers – youngsters who also began school with relatively low scores – and these are probably the more relevant comparisons. The first column in each testing area shows the now-familiar pecking order. Retainees lag behind badly at the start of school, the more so the sooner they will be held back. But second and third grade repeaters score close to the level of the poor performers. All three retained groups trail far behind the never-retained youngsters in both areas. Against the full sample, the shortfall is larger on the CAT-M, ranging between 0.75 and 1.28 standard deviations, but gaps on the CAT-R are appreciable too (between 0.44 and 0.83 standard deviations).

Table 4.4. *Differences between retainee and never-retained CAT–R and CAT–M averages at the start of first grade, the end of each retainee group's failed year, the end of each retainee group's repeated year, and the end of seventh grade*

	CAT-R				CAT-M			
	Fall 1st grade	Spring failed year[a]	Spring repeated year[b]	Spring 7th grade	Fall 1st grade	Spring failed year[a]	Spring repeated year[b]	Spring 7th grade
Retained vs. never-retained								
1st grade retainees	(−)33.8 [0.83]	(−)72.7 [1.90]	(−)18.7 [0.49]	(−)82.1 [1.21]	(−)40.5 [1.28]	(−)57.1 [1.77]	(−)16.8 [0.52]	(−)92.7 [1.44]
2d grade retainees	(−)21.2 [0.52]	(−)78.6 [1.82]	(−)37.4 [0.87]	(−)65.1 [0.96]	(−)26.2 [0.83]	(−)43.8 [1.27]	(−)12.8 [0.37]	(−)72.9 [1.13]
3d grade retainees	(−)18.1 [0.44]	(−)80.4 [1.51]	(−)37.3 [0.70]	(−)53.2 [0.78]	(−)24.0 [0.75]	(−)57.8 [1.33]	(−)14.9 [0.34]	(−)50.0 [0.78]
Retained vs. poor-performing comparison group								
1st grade retainees	(−)13.6 [0.33]	(−)39.3 [1.02]	(+)15.1 [0.39]	(−)50.3 [0.74]	(−)17.7 [0.56]	(−)28.3 [0.88]	(+)12.0 [0.37]	(−)66.1 [1.03]
2d grade retainees	(−)1.0 [0.02]	(−)55.2 [1.28]	(−)14.0 [0.32]	(−)33.4 [0.49]	(−)3.4 [0.11]	(−)30.7 [0.89]	(+)0.3 [0.01]	(−)46.3 [0.72]
3d grade retainees	(+)2.3 [0.06]	(−)51.2 [0.96]	(+)8.1 [0.15]	(−)21.4 [0.31]	(−)1.2 [0.04]	(−)28.8 [0.66]	(+)14.1 [0.32]	(−)23.4 [0.36]

Note: A negative sign in parentheses indicates difference favors never-retained; a positive sign favors the retainee group; figures in brackets express the difference as a fraction of the total sample CAT standard deviation for the grade level at issue.

[a] Failed-year differences are calculated for first grade retainees at the end of Year 1, for second grade retainees at the end of Year 2, and for third grade retainees at the end of Year 3.

[b] Repeated-year differences are calculated for first grade retainees at the end of Year 2, for second grade retainees at the end of Year 3, and for third grade retainees at the end of Year 4.

By the spring of their failed year all three retainee groups have fallen even farther behind those never retained. Compared with the full sample, all lag behind by well over 1 standard deviation, and even when evaluated against the poor performers, the differences are about 1 standard deviation. The failed year marks a very low point for all.

On the other hand, if the retainees can ever be said to "shine" academically, it would be when they finish their repeated year (third column). When compared with the low performers, five of the six entries are positively signed, meaning that retainees' scores actually are the higher of the two. They still lag behind all never-retained children, but their standing is much improved relative to just a year earlier, in the spring of their failed year, and in most instances even relative to where they stood at the start of school.

If performance from that point in their school careers could be sustained, we would probably count retention a resounding success. Unfortunately, however, it doesn't work that way: at the end of seventh grade all the retainee groups again lag behind. But even here the picture is not altogether unfavorable. Except for first-grade retainees, repeaters are not behind by as many CAT points as they were in the spring of their failed year, and when the differences are expressed in standard deviation units even first grade repeaters are relatively better off (see the comparison with all never-retained youngsters).

The retention picture more fully considered

The conclusion that there are lasting benefits of retention for retainees at higher grade levels has to be tentative at this point because a number of complications could confound trend comparisons. The sample loss over time and the differences between special education children, double repeaters, and others are examined in this section. Other complications are taken up in Chapter 5, which uses statistical methods to adjust for characteristics of retainees that might make their later testing patterns different from those of promoted children's for reasons having nothing at all to do with retention.

The spread of youngsters through the grade structure, into special education classes, and out of the city school system are complexities that pose challenges for our analysis. For most of the years under study we were unable to secure survey and school record data (including test scores) for youngsters who left the city school system. Even for those who remained in the system, there are often holes in data coverage. Missing test data are a special concern in tracking cognitive performance before and after retention.

The Beginning School Study was designed to be representative (within the stratifying criteria of our research design) of youngsters who began first grade in the fall of 1982 in the BCPS. This important feature of our study could be compromised by selective sample attrition and data loss. Chapter 2 showed that youngsters who left Baltimore schools in the course of the study were disproportionately white and well-to-do. Accordingly, what look like changes in performance trajectories could instead reflect differences in sample composition in the BCPS over time. For example, our conclusion that test score gains diminish over time, and that gains do not slow as much for retainees as for others, actually could be due to losses from attrition. Since never-retained youngsters are more likely to exit the city system than retained children, all comparisons across the retained/never-retained divide also could be affected by differential sample loss. The consequences of such distortions could be serious, and other complications not addressed in the main body of Chapter 4 could further cloud interpretation. For example, because first grade repeaters lag so far behind the others, they are later moved into special education classes and held back a second time in large numbers. The situation of special education children is especially complicated. To mention just a few of the things that set them apart, for most or all of the day they are separated from other children in the school, their curriculum is different from the standard one, their classes are ungraded, and the marking distinctions used on their report cards differ in important ways from those used on regular report cards.

First grade retainees seem to fare especially poorly later on, but we need to know whether this deficit means retention in first grade itself is problematic, or whether it only appears so because first grade repeaters' difficulties are so severe. The comparisons made thus far do not address such possibilities, nor do they adjust for the timing of the second retention visited upon double repeaters. The same-grade comparisons, in consequence, are not properly aligned at the upper grade levels, and this mismatch, too, could affect the seeming advantage or disadvantage associated with retention.

Finally, thus far we have used the performance of retainees held back in grades 4 through 7 mainly as another standard against which to evaluate the performance of children held back earlier. This is sensible from one point of view, but during the critical early period these not-yet-retained youngsters actually would be part of the regularly promoted comparison group that retainees are expected to be keeping up with. So, too, for that matter, would second grade repeaters in the first year and third grade repeaters in the first 2 years. In any event, we have mainly used a "never retained" comparison group rather than a "not retained" comparison group. Since the latter would contain more poor-performing children than the former, this approach could tilt comparisons in favor of promotion. So here again, a largely procedural matter could have substantive implications.

All these issues – selective sample attrition and missing test scores, the situations of special education children and of double retainees, and our treatment of children held back at the higher grade levels – are sources of concern. Accordingly, several supplemental analyses were performed to judge their implications:

1. Exiters are excluded throughout so we can see whether their presence in some parts of the analysis and not in others alters the picture.
2. Children who were ever assigned to special education classes are excluded. This could affect the composition of both the retained and the never-retained subsamples, but mainly the retained ones, and especially the sample of first grade repeaters (58 of 90 – that is, 64% – of the retained special education pupils were first grade repeaters).
3. All fourth through seventh grade retainees are assigned to the never-retained comparison group and also to the poor-performing comparison group if their test scores from the spring of Year 1 meet the criteria for membership. The first, second, and third grade retention groups are not affected by this reassignment.
4. Double retainees are excluded.
5. The 2-year "offset" is implemented for double retainees from the time of their second retention until the end of sixth grade. No seventh grade comparisons are possible for double repeaters when this is done, though, because they do not finish seventh grade until at least the ninth year, which is outside the time frame of this analysis.
6. A final analysis implements several of these procedural changes at the same time. Even though the number of retainees available for analysis after making several such exclusions is quite small, it is useful to see whether the implications of these checks cumulate.

All the comparisons reported in the main body of this chapter have been redone with these various exclusions and rearrangements of the data. Selected grade level averages from all these checks, presented in Table 4.A2 in the appendix to this chapter, show that never-retained children's averages are affected very little by any of these procedural checks, including the loss of Exiters at higher grade levels. The grade-level averages further indicate that among retainees the exclusion of special education students has the greatest impact; retainees' averages sometimes are much higher when special education children are excluded. Since test score gains have been our main focus, it is especially important to examine how special education affects gains comparisons. This examination (Table 4.5) also covers gains comparisons when several of these checks are done together in order to afford a sense of their overall impact.

For comparison purposes, Table 4.5 repeats promoted children's gains from Tables 4.1 and 4.3. The corresponding figures for the main retainee groups are also reproduced here. Two sets of new figures then are reported for retainees: the first excludes special education children from the calculations, and the second excludes special education youngsters, double repeaters, and Exiters. This second set of figures indicates what happens to the comparisons when we look just at children who remained in Baltimore City schools for the entire period of the study, and when the complications surrounding special education and double retention are set aside.

For each retainee group and its comparison groups, Table 4.5 reports cumulative gains from the fall of the retained year to the end of seventh grade (as in Table 4.2) and gains for as many years after retention as are available for before retention (i.e., 1 year in the case of first grade retainees, 2 years for second grade retainees, and 3 years for third grade retainees). These are the kinds of calculations reported in Table 4.3. We also present the ratio of each group's postretention gain to its preretention gain in order to detect whether retention is pivotal in altering the pace of test score improvement. For never-retained youngsters, these same comparisons show the pace of progress over the same time periods, allowing us to judge how retention might enter in.

The first column of figures in Table 4.5 tallies gains from the fall of retainees' failed year to the end of grade 7. The gain for all first grade retainees over this interval was 224 on the CAT-R and 202 on the CAT-M. When repeaters with additional problems (special education, double repeaters, or Exiters) are left out, gains go up on the order of 10 to 15 points, and so are closer to the never-retained gains (272 points). Retainees without other problems still fall far short of those never retained, but the gap for them is smaller, and this is important.

The figures for second and third grade retainees are even more striking, at least on the CAT-R. Just as with first grade repeaters, when special education pupils and multiple problem cases are left out, their gains go up appreciably. In fact, the new figures are about equal to the gains registered by the never-retained samples. For second grade repeaters the CAT-R gain rises from 187 to 200 when all three exclusions are made. This gain exceeds the comparison group's gain over this interval (at 197) and puts second grade retainees equal to the full never-retained sample (at 201).

Table 4.5 shows third grade repeaters who do not have added problems ahead of both never-retained groups on the CAT-R. Indeed, even the modest increases seen for the CAT-M – just 2 to 3 points – have the effect of pulling third grade repeaters very close to the never-retained groups. They are even with the comparison group and only 2 to 3 points shy of the full sample.

On balance, then, the picture for repeaters' cumulative gains from the year of retention forward is favorable when considering just youngsters who manage to stay on track after retention, that is, those for whom retention might be the source of their problems. On the other hand, when gains over fixed intervals from before and after retention are compared, as in the postretention/preretention columns of Table 4.5, the comparisons are not so consistently favorable. The ratio of gains from after retention to those from before retention in some instances go down, not up, after special education children and others are left out. This is because the increase in averages resulting from the various exclusions sometimes are larger in the preretention than in the postretention interval.

The procedural exclusions thus are of consequence all along the way, and need to be taken into account. The tracking of test scores before retention can have nothing to do with the effects of retention, and simply looking at what happens afterward – even when considering differences between retained and never-retained groups – will not always give a reliable reading of how retention affects performance trajectories.

Although in the main these revised calculations are consistent with the earlier ones, the perspective afforded by these postretention/pre-

Table 4.5. *Comparisons of cumulative gains from the fall of first, second, and third grade retainees' failed year, and gains pre- and postretention when special education children are excluded and when several exclusions are implemented together*

	1st grade retainee comparisons				2d grade retainee comparisons				3d grade retainee comparisons			
	Gains from fall 1st grade to end 7th grade[a]	1-year gains through and after Year 1[b]			Gains from fall 2d grade to end 7th grade[a]	2-year gains through and after year 2[b]			Gains from fall 3d grade to end 7th grade[a]	3-year gains through and after year 3[b]		
		Pre	Post	Post/Pre		Pre	Post	Post/Pre		Pre	Post	Post/Pre
CAT-R												
Original retainee figures	224.4 (53)	31.5 (104)	54.5 (71)	1.73	187.0 (34)	62.3 (55)	52.3 (43)	0.84	152.5 (28)	95.8 (30)	98.6 (30)	1.03
Retainee figures excluding special education	239.4 (39)	38.8 (60)	58.9 (43)	1.52	197.4 (26)	63.5 (40)	47.2 (33)	0.74	159.0 (24)	102.4 (25)	100.4 (29)	0.98
Retainee figures with all three exclusions[c]	236.9 (25)	40.6 (27)	44.5 (20)	1.10	200.3 (21)	60.2 (25)	57.9 (25)	0.96	166.8 (18)	114.5 (14)	101.5 (19)	0.89
Original never-retained figures	271.8 (204)	70.9 (387)	47.4 (382)	0.67	200.8 (222)	121.3 (350)	81.5 (284)	0.67	151.7 (215)	157.4 (274)	89.4 (222)	0.57
Original comparison-group figures	253.9 (46)	56.0 (92)	56.4 (88)	1.01	196.5 (51)	113.0 (81)	75.7 (70)	0.67	147.5 (50)	145.1 (64)	84.0 (48)	0.58

CAT-M

Original retainee figures	202.1 (49)	35.9 (102)	37.6 (69)	1.05	171.1 (35)	72.0 (57)	51.7 (43)	0.72	154.4 (29)	102.3 (29)	91.1 (30)	0.89
Retainee figures excluding special education	211.6 (36)	39.1 (60)	45.0 (42)	1.15	172.1 (28)	73.5 (42)	54.2 (33)	0.74	156.4 (24)	106.6 (25)	91.0 (29)	0.85
Retainee figures with all three exclusions[c]	215.3 (23)	39.4 (27)	43.7 (20)	1.11	167.3 (23)	80.7 (27)	60.0 (25)	0.74	157.3 (19)	110.9 (15)	94.1 (19)	0.85
Original never-retained figures	252.9 (208)	52.2 (396)	44.3 (380)	0.85	204.8 (220)	93.8 (354)	77.2 (283)	0.82	159.4 (214)	133.4 (283)	93.7 (221)	0.70
Original comparison-group figures	243.5 (47)	45.9 (93)	46.1 (86)	1.00	195.2 (51)	97.1 (76)	80.1 (70)	0.82	157.2 (50)	127.5 (65)	83.8 (48)	0.66

Note: Numbers in parentheses are sample sizes.

[a]The "original" gain figures come from Table 4.2.

[b]The "original" "Pre," "Post," and "Post/Pre" figures come from Table 4.3.

[c]For these calculations, Exiters (those who left the BCPS), special education pupils, and double retainees are all excluded.

retention ratios is important. Despite their higher postretention scores and greater postretention gains, youngsters retained only once who are never put into special education classes are not always more successful than are all retainees in holding to their preretention pace of test score improvement. Rather, on the CAT-R for first and third grade repeaters, and on the CAT-M for third grade repeaters, these ratios are about the same or lower than those for the more inclusive retainee groups. Only among second grade retainees (on both the CAT-R and the CAT-M) and among first grade retainees (on the CAT-M) are the new calculations more favorable than the originals.

These various checks have accomplished several things. For one, they help allay concern that the loss of Exiters over the years distorts comparisons between retainees and those never retained (Table 4.A2). The comparisons are virtually identical whether Exiters are included or excluded. Sample attrition, being substantial and highly selective for social factors (e.g., race/ethnicity), poses the single greatest procedural threat to a reliable picture of retention's role. That its consequences turn out to be so minor is reassuring.

Other checks, in contrast, sometimes produced large changes. For retainees with uncomplicated promotion histories after being held back, the gaps between the retained and the never-retained are much smaller than when all repeaters are used in the comparisons, and cumulative gains over the higher grade levels most often favored repeaters rather than promoted youngsters. Some of the difference between test scores for those retained and never retained in the overall sample thus reflects the peculiar problems of special education and double-retainee children, which is an important clarification.

On the other hand, examination of the pace of progress before and after retention for retainees with smooth postretention promotion records reveals that the comparisons were not very different from those when all retainees were involved. Hence, the indications here that were favorable to retainees seem to apply pretty much across the board, to all classes of repeaters.

All the analyses show that retention fails to bring repeaters up to the standard of those never retained. However, much of the shortfall in retainees' performance relative to that of those never retained *predates* retention, so simply comparing testing levels at various points along the line is not sufficient. For gains from the retained year forward, the comparisons sometimes look different. First grade retainees still fall behind in gains, but in many instances second and third grade repeaters' gains come close to keeping pace with, or even exceeding, the gains registered by never-retained children.

In addition, in most instances retainees in the postretention period were *more successful* in maintaining their pace of upward movement than were never-retained youngsters in the same years. They still usually gained less, but everyone's gains tended to trail off over time, and those of retainees generally did not taper off as much, relative to their earlier pace, as did those of the never-retained children. Indeed, in some instances they did not trail off at all. It is important that retention seems to help retainees keep pace over the years when others drop back.

This is a detailed, complicated picture already, yet there still are issues that need to be addressed. The most critical need is to take into account other influences on test performance that might be confounded with retention/nonretention. We would expect, for example, that if being from a low-income home hinders school performance, it would do so all along the way. Unless such influences are allowed for, the details just reviewed could be misleading because these other factors could enlarge or shrink the gap between the retained and those never retained. Retainees are more likely to be from low-income families, more of them are boys, they are more often African-American, and so on; these factors affect the course of later schooling, quite apart from retention. We need to separate performance differences that follow from these sorts of considerations from the effects of retention per se. This separation is accomplished in the next chapter, using statistical means to adjust for such possible complicating factors.

Appendix

The following tables provide details alluded to in the main body of this chapter. Table 4.A1 reports CAT-R and CAT-M averages for the several retention and comparison groups from the fall of first grade and the spring of grades 1 through 7. Table 4.A2 reports the CAT-R and CAT-M averages that were computed to check on attrition bias and the consequences of other procedural decisions (see the section titled "The retention picture more fully considered").

Table 4.A1. CAT-R and CAT-M averages for retained groups, never-retained pupils, and the poor-performing comparison group[a]

	Fall of 1st grade[a]	End of 1st grade[b]	End of 2d grade[b]	End of 3d grade[b]	End of 4th grade	End of 5th grade	End of 6th grade	End of 7th grade
CAT-R: reading comprehension average								
Year of retention								
1st grade	257.0	287.1/341.1	358.7	384.7	409.3	440.9	439.7	481.7
	(106)	(118)/(76)	(93)	(97)	(98)	(86)	(77)	(58)
2d grade	269.6	311.5	333.6/374.8	399.9	431.8	454.9	471.3	498.6
	(61)	(65)	(60)/(56)	(50)	(57)	(52)	(48)	(40)
3d grade	272.7	325.6	356.9	369.0/412.1	441.8	478.3	486.1	510.6
	(38)	(43)	(44)	(37)/(35)	(39)	(36)	(34)	(31)
4th–7th grade	277.9	346.0	388.6	448.4	459.6	492.8	502.8	529.3
	(65)	(72)	(72)	(63)	(65)	(72)	(61)	(53)
Never-retained pupils								
All never-retained	290.8	359.8	412.2	449.4	496.0	522.6	542.7	563.8
	(396)	(428)	(389)	(304)	(290)	(291)	(249)	(224)
Poor-performing comparison group	270.6	326.4	388.8	420.2	461.4	481.6	512.6	532.0
	(92)	(106)	(91)	(72)	(70)	(71)	(58)	(52)

CAT-M: Math concepts
average

Year of retention								
1st grade	264.1	299.0/339.3	358.9	385.5	412.2	431.3	444.7	465.8
	(107)	(113)/(74)	(97)	(97)	(96)	(86)	(75)	(56)
2d grade	278.4	320.8	350.6/381.6	402.3	432.1	461.6	470.7	485.6
	(62)	(63)	(56)/(56)	(50)	(56)	(51)	(46)	(40)
3d grade	280.6	332.1	368.4	382.4/425.3	445.1	486.3	491.9	508.5
	(38)	(44)	(45)	(36)/(35)	(39)	(36)	(34)	(31)
4th–7th grade	290.1	341.2	385.3	412.4	451.1	484.8	496.6	519.9
	(69)	(71)	(72)	(64)	(64)	(72)	(58)	(49)
Never-retained pupils								
All never-retained	304.6	356.1	394.4	440.2	478.5	511.7	533.3	558.5
	(406)	(425)	(385)	(304)	(289)	(290)	(248)	(223)
Poor-performing comparison group	281.8	327.3	381.3	411.2	454.3	482.2	505.0	531.9
	(93)	(106)	(88)	(72)	(70)	(71)	(58)	(52)

Note: Numbers in parentheses indicate sample size.

[a] All entries except the first are from the spring of the year. The first entry is from the fall of everyone's first grade, in 1982.

[b] For first, second, and third grade retainees, two end-of-grade averages are reported in the year of retention. The first is from the first time through the grade; the second is from the repeated year.

Table 4.A2. Same-grade test averages, excluding Exiters, special education students, with fourth through seventh grade retainees classified as never-retained, excluding double retainees, and with the 2-year same-grade offset implemented for double retainees

	CAT-R					CAT-M				
	Fall of 1st grade	End of 1st grade	End of 2d grade	End of 3d grade	End of 7th grade	Fall of 1st grade	End of 1st grade	End of 2d grade	End of 3d grade	End of 7th grade
1st grade retainees										
1. Full sample	257.0	341.1	358.7	384.7	481.7	264.1	339.3	358.9	385.5	465.8
	(106)	(76)	(93)	(97)	(58)	(107)	(74)	(97)	(97)	(56)
2. Excluding Exiters	256.5	339.9	358.0	382.6	481.7	265.0	338.8	355.5	383.6	465.8
	(81)	(62)	(74)	(78)	(58)	(80)	(60)	(75)	(78)	(56)
3. Excluding special education pupils	259.4	355.9	369.2	410.8	498.7	266.5	350.5	369.4	406.8	480.6
	(61)	(45)	(55)	(54)	(39)	(61)	(44)	(55)	(53)	(37)
4. Excluding twice-retained pupils	260.7	348.7	368.1	396.2	496.7	265.8	345.8	365.0	396.1	474.5
	(67)	(45)	(55)	(56)	(31)	(69)	(44)	(54)	(56)	(30)
5. With 2-year offset for twice-retained pupils	257.0	341.1	361.1	391.6	496.7	264.1	339.0	361.2	394.2	474.5
	(106)	(76)	(94)	(96)	(31)	(107)	(74)	(95)	(94)	(30)
6. 2, 3, and 4 together	265.8	363.6	374.0	416.0	504.6	273.0	358.6	370.3	416.7	489.8
	(27)	(22)	(25)	(25)	(25)	(27)	(22)	(25)	(24)	(23)

2d grade retainees

1. Full sample	269.6	311.5	374.8	399.9	498.6	278.4	320.8	381.6	402.3	485.6
	(61)	(65)	(56)	(50)	(40)	(62)	(63)	(56)	(50)	(40)
2. Excluding Exiters	269.2	312.5	378.1	399.8	498.6	277.6	316.9	380.6	401.7	485.6
	(47)	(50)	(48)	(44)	(40)	(48)	(48)	(48)	(44)	(40)
3. Excluding special education pupils	272.4	308.9	379.3	407.2	505.6	275.6	319.8	387.2	410.3	488.9
	(41)	(45)	(38)	(35)	(29)	(42)	(43)	(38)	(35)	(30)
4. Excluding twice-retained pupils	271.4	315.0	382.2	410.2	508.3	274.9	326.6	382.3	409.1	484.3
	(44)	(48)	(40)	(37)	(30)	(45)	(46)	(40)	(37)	(31)
5. With 2-year offset for twice-retained pupils	269.6	311.5	374.6	402.5	508.3	278.4	320.8	380.1	406.6	484.3
	(61)	(65)	(56)	(52)	(30)	(62)	(63)	(56)	(52)	(31)
6. 2, 3, and 4 together	272.7	312.4	388.0	416.4	509.5	273.7	320.3	387.3	415.7	485.4
	(26)	(29)	(27)	(27)	(24)	(27)	(27)	(27)	(27)	(25)

(continued)

Table 4.A2 (continued)

	CAT-R					CAT-M				
	Fall of 1st grade	End of 1st grade	End of 2d grade	End of 3d grade	End of 7th grade	Fall of 1st grade	End of 1st grade	End of 2d grade	End of 3d grade	End of 7th grade
3d grade retainees										
1. Full sample	272.7	325.6	356.9	412.1	510.6	280.6	332.1	368.4	425.4	508.5
	(38)	(43)	(44)	(35)	(31)	(38)	(44)	(45)	(45)	(31)
2. Excluding Exiters	269.5	326.5	355.8	417.7	510.6	278.5	330.5	361.3	429.3	508.5
	(29)	(33)	(35)	(29)	(31)	(29)	(34)	(35)	(29)	(31)
3. Excluding special education pupils	272.3	330.8	357.1	416.8	520.8	280.4	333.0	369.2	431.9	514.9
	(32)	(37)	(39)	(29)	(26)	(33)	(38)	(40)	(29)	(26)
4. Excluding twice-retained pupils	275.5	326.6	357.9	413.2	514.3	280.2	332.4	366.8	426.0	511.3
	(28)	(34)	(34)	(29)	(24)	(29)	(34)	(35)	(29)	(24)
5. With 2-year offset for twice-retained pupils	272.7	325.6	356.9	412.1	514.3	280.6	332.1	368.4	425.3	511.3
	(38)	(43)	(44)	(35)	(24)	(38)	(44)	(45)	(35)	(24)
6. 2, 3, and 4 together	268.4	338.0	358.1	428.9	525.2	277.5	330.2	359.1	436.4	517.4
	(16)	(21)	(22)	(19)	(20)	(18)	(21)	(22)	(19)	(20)
Never-retained										
1. Full sample	290.8	359.8	412.2	449.4	563.8	304.6	356.1	394.4	440.2	558.5
	(396)	(428)	(389)	(304)	(224)	(406)	(425)	(385)	(304)	(223)
2. Excluding Exiters	291.5	358.9	411.9	445.0	561.8	304.0	354.0	397.6	437.6	557.1
	(200)	(214)	(215)	(204)	(214)	(207)	(214)	(215)	(204)	(213)

3. Excluding special education pupils	291.0 (392)	360.5 (423)	412.9 (385)	450.3 (301)	564.5 (222)	305.1 (403)	356.7 (420)	400.8 (381)	441.3 (301)	559.7 (221)
4. With 4–7 retained as never-retained	288.9 (461)	357.8 (500)	408.5 (461)	443.9 (368)	557.2 (277)	302.5 (477)	354.0 (496)	397.2 (457)	435.4 (368)	551.5 (272)
5. 2, 3, and 4 together	292.4 (198)	359.7 (211)	411.9 (213)	445.7 (202)	562.5 (212)	304.6 (204)	354.6 (211)	398.0 (213)	438.5 (202)	558.3 (211)
Poor-performing comparison group										
1. Full sample	270.6 (92)	326.4 (106)	388.8 (91)	420.2 (72)	532.0 (52)	281.8 (93)	327.3 (106)	381.3 (88)	411.2 (72)	531.9 (52)
2. Excluding Exiters	278.0 (48)	325.4 (54)	389.3 (52)	420.8 (49)	531.2 (51)	284.8 (49)	328.0 (54)	382.9 (52)	412.5 (49)	532.3 (51)
3. Excluding special education pupils	270.1 (91)	326.5 (105)	390.3 (90)	421.5 (71)	532.0 (52)	281.7 (92)	327.6 (105)	382.1 (87)	412.7 (71)	531.9 (52)
4. With 4–7 retained as never-retained	269.9 (113)	326.5 (131)	388.3 (116)	419.6 (96)	529.0 (75)	281.1 (115)	326.5 (131)	379.7 (113)	411.1 (96)	524.9 (75)
5. 2, 3, and 4 together	278.0 (48)	325.4 (54)	389.3 (52)	420.8 (49)	531.2 (51)	284.8 (49)	328.0 (54)	382.9 (52)	412.5 (49)	532.3 (51)

Note: Numbers in parentheses are sample sizes.

5

How retention affects performance on standardized tests

The need for controlled comparisons and the multiple-regression approach

To see more clearly how retention actually affects students, it is necessary to take account of other factors that might be confounded with retention. As discussed in Chapter 1, this accounting is sometimes done through "matched controls," an approach used to some extent in Chapter 4. Although this approach is fine in principle, in practice it is hard to eliminate alternative explanations this way. Our poor-performing comparison group, for example, screens on just one confounding factor, so the match is far from perfect. While the two groups are roughly comparable in terms of early testing levels, retainees still could be less well off economically, or more of them could be from father-absent families. An alternative to creating matched groups is to adjust statistically for relevant characteristics. This approach, used in the present chapter, is grounded in the same logic as matching but offers the advantage of being able to take account of, or to "adjust for," more factors at once than is usually practical by selecting out certain children for comparison.

Retainees, as a group, fit the at-risk academic profile: they come disproportionately from low-income families; they have poorly educated parents; they are often of minority status; and they enter school lacking important readiness skills, which is reflected in their low beginning test scores and marks. Children who bear such burdens typically have a difficult time at school whether retained or not, and so in the present context these problems constitute potential "confounding factors." Some of retainees' later academic problems likely have nothing to do with retention, but occur due to risks such as these that are already present.

The demographic factors examined previously in Chapters 2 and 3 will be used again here, along with the child's age in September of first grade. They include race/ethnicity (i.e., African-American vs. white), gender, mother's educational level,[1] family income level (as reflected in eligibility for reduced-price meals at school), number of siblings, and whether or not the youngster was living in a two-parent household at the start of first grade.

We also need to take account of differences involving academic skills or competence that predate retention. Eventual retainees and never-to-be retained youngsters registered large differences in CAT averages on the very first tests (given in the fall of first grade), and their scores continued to move farther apart until the point the retention decision was made. Many of the descriptive comparisons reviewed in Chapter 4 used CAT averages from the fall of the failed year as a baseline because any performance differences up to that point could not be due to retention. Now we want to adjust for those preexisting differences to see whether retainees' later standing is better or worse than would be expected given their prior problems.

The statistical method used to implement these adjustments is multiple regression. This kind of analysis gauges the separate influences of several predictors, like the social demographic measures, on outcomes like test scores. Because it adjusts the average difference in gains on tests between retained and promoted youngsters for any nonequivalence on other predictors, this approach can take into account confounding influences involving both earlier test scores and social demographic factors.

Retention status is indicated by year of retention – first, second, or third grade, or fourth through seventh grade combined. These various retention groups are compared with all never-retained youngsters and the subset of them identified previously as the poor-performing comparison group. The statistical models using these retention classifications estimate the average difference in testing levels between the various retention groups and nonretained youngsters, adjusted for differences due to other predictors in the analysis. These, then, are adjusted estimates of the effects of retention.

The "outcome" measures in this chapter are spring CAT scores, mainly from the postretention period. These will be examined using both the same-age perspective (Tables 5.1, 5.3, and 5.5) and the same-grade perspective (Tables 5.2, 5.4, and 5.6). As has been true throughout, the difference between the two depends on whether performance is aligned chronologically or at grade-level benchmarks. Each pair of tables summarizes the results for one main retainee group, youngsters held back in first grade (Tables 5.1 and 5.2), in second grade (Tables 5.3 and 5.4) or in third grade (Tables 5.5 and 5.6).

In each instance, we begin by looking at test score differences between retainees and never-retained youngsters in the fall of the retainees' failed year/grade, before they are held back. This is a useful benchmark for comparing shortfalls after retention. It is also the preretention differential for which we adjust statistically when considering postretention patterns of later CAT performance. The remaining columns in these tables all present results for spring CAT scores, year by year or grade by grade, for as long as performance is tracked. In the same-age comparison, tracking is through the end of Year 8; in the same-grade comparison, it is through the end of seventh grade. These postretention CAT scores are the outcome measures.

Several regressions are used to explain spring test score differences. In the first panel, the only predictor is retention, so the CAT differences estimated here are not adjusted for any other factors. These initial estimates describe retainees' standing relative to never-retained youngsters on the particular test at issue. In the second panel, CAT performance from the fall of the failed year/grade and the entire set of personal and social demographic controls are added to the analysis, so these estimates are adjusted for both prior performance *and* demographic factors. Comparing these second estimates to the first entries in a column shows the effects of the statistical adjustments. The last panel introduces additional adjustments for differences in CAT performance that are associated specifically with special education assignment and double retention. Double retention, special education assignment, and both together are separated from retention alone.[2] Table entries for this last stage of the analysis estimate the CAT shortfall of "regular" retainees – those who have not been held back a second time or been put into special education classes – compared with promoted youngsters.[3]

First grade retainees: CAT shortfall at the start

Tables 5.1 and 5.2 compare first grade-retainees' CAT performance with that of never-retained youngsters. The first column gives test performance from the fall of the repeaters' failed year, which for first grade retainees is the fall of first grade (1982). Subsequent columns report adjusted test score differences from the spring of the year, beginning in the spring of the failed year (i.e., the first time through the failed grade); these extend in Table 5.1 through the end of Year 8, and in Table 5.2 through the end of seventh grade. The comparisons thus go 6 years beyond first grade retainees' repeated year (i.e., 6 years after the 2-year fail–repeat cycle).

The first entry in Table 5.1 (−33.5) indicates that children who will be held back in first grade started that year with CAT-R averages about 34 points below children who would never be held back.[4] This is a large, statistically significant difference. Statistical estimates with double asterisks indicate that a difference as large or larger than the observed one could come about by chance only once in 100 times (1%) if the averages were identical in the population from which this sample is drawn.[5]

At the start of first grade, children who will be held back that year average some 34 CAT-R points below those never retained, but when compared with the low-performing comparison group the difference is much smaller – 13.6 points. In other words, compared with other children with low test scores, the retainees show an additional deficit. Since the 13.6-point spread is significant, the comparison group was not quite comparable initially, which we already knew.[6]

The situation is much the same on the CAT-M, reported in the bottom section of the table. The retained/never-retained differential is 40 CAT-M points when all promoted youngsters are involved, and 17.7 points when just the poor performers are considered. Both differences are significant.

Children who will be held back in first grade thus already lag behind at the start of the year. Their shortfall is relatively large and cannot be a consequence of retention because it predates retention. These preexisting CAT differences are adjusted for in all the remaining analyses.

First grade retainees: same-age and same-grade comparisons for the failed year

In the spring of their first time through first grade, retainees' performance relative to promoted youngsters falls off badly (second column in Table 5.1 for both the CAT-R and the CAT-M). The unadjusted differences amount to about 72 points on the CAT-R and 56 points on

Table 5.1. *Same-age regression-adjusted CAT differences: first grade retainees vs. never-retained students or the poor-performing comparison group*

	Fall of Year 1	Spring of failed year	Spring of repeated year	1 year postret (Year 3)	2 years postret (Year 4)	3 years postret (Year 5)	4 years postret (Year 6)	5 years postret (Year 7)	6 years postret (Year 8)
CAT-R									
With no adjustments[a]									
Ret vs. never-ret	−33.5**	−72.4**	−64.2**	−88.4**	−111.1**	−110.3**	−97.1**	−118.2**	−103.7**
Ret vs. poor-perf comparison group	−13.6**	−39.5**	−47.3**	−58.2**	−73.5**	−68.5**	−63.7**	−81.2**	−69.8**
With fall CAT and demographic adjustments[b]									
Ret vs. never-ret	—	−59.5**	−52.9**	−69.2**	−85.6**	−83.2**	−70.2**	−88.8**	−71.7**
Ret vs. poor-perf comparison group	—	−37.9**	−43.2**	−53.0**	−64.6**	−59.1**	−53.4**	−71.5**	−59.2**
With double-ret and special ed adjustments[c]									
Ret vs. never-ret	—	−49.7**	−42.8**	−53.4**	−57.7**	−50.8**	−34.0**	−55.6**	−46.6**
Ret vs. poor-perf comparison group	—	−27.7**	−31.8**	−37.8**	−38.1**	−28.2**	−16.6	−40.0**	−37.4**
Adj R^2									
Ret vs. never-ret[d]	.09	.46	.49	.52	.56	.52	.46	.54	.45
Ret vs. poor-perf comparison group	.04	.33	.38	.36	.43	.43	.40	.42	.30

CAT-M

With no adjustments[a]									
Ret vs. never-ret	−40.0**	−56.4**	−53.6**	−79.9**	−93.1**	−96.6**	−99.1**	−108.6**	−108.3**
Ret vs. poor-perf comparison group	−17.7**	−28.2**	−40.8**	−50.2**	−66.0**	−65.3**	−67.5**	−77.0**	−80.7**
With fall CAT and demographic adjustments[b]									
Ret vs. never-ret	—	−34.6**	−29.6**	−52.7**	−64.0**	−67.4**	−62.9**	−67.6**	−75.1**
Ret vs. poor-perf comparison group	—	−21.5**	−31.5**	−42.8**	−55.2**	−56.7**	−56.9**	−65.1**	−73.6**
With double-ret and special ed adjustments[c]									
Ret vs. never-ret	—	−28.1**	−23.9**	−39.9**	−38.7**	−43.3**	−28.6**	−40.4**	−58.3**
Ret vs. poor-perf comparison group	—	−15.5**	−25.5**	−30.8**	−32.2**	−34.9**	−26.1**	−41.0**	−57.9**
Adj R^2									
Ret vs. never-ret[d]	.24	.51	.55	.58	.63	.54	.55	.57	.53
Ret vs. poor-perf comparison group	.14	.37	.51	.43	.55	.45	.47	.44	.35

[a]These regressions adjust for differences among the several retainee groups and between retainees and those never retained.

[b]Performed after the fall of Year 1, these regressions adjust additionally for CAT scores from the fall of Year 1 and for demographic factors: race/ethnicity, gender, mother's education, lunch subsidy status (eligible or not), number of siblings, age as of the fall of first grade, and whether or not the child was living in a two-parent household at the start of first grade.

[c]These regressions adjust additionally for differences associated with special education alone, double retention alone, or both. These analyses are not performed in the fall of Year 1.

[d]R^2 statistics are from the most inclusive equation in each column.

**signifies differences significant at the 0.01 level.

113

Table 5.2. *Same-grade regression-adjusted CAT differences: first grade retainees vs. never-retained students or the poor-performing comparison group*

	Fall of 1st grade	End of 1st grade	End of 2d grade	End of 3d grade	End of 4th grade	End of 5th grade	End of 6th grade	End of 7th grade
CAT-R								
With no adjustments[a]								
Ret vs. never-ret	−33.5**	−72.4**/−17.6**	−50.9**	−64.6**	−85.2**	−78.3**	−98.9**	−76.0**
Ret vs. poor-perf comparison group	−13.6**	−39.5**/14.4**	−29.8**	−34.7**	−49.2**	−40.3**	−67.9**	−47.4**
With fall CAT and demographic adjustments[b]								
Ret vs. never-ret	—	−59.5**/−2.9	−38.4**	−42.4**	−60.8**	−51.0**	−73.1**	−46.9**
Ret vs. poor-perf comparison group	—	−37.9**/17.8**	−24.7**	−25.5**	−41.4**	−31.5**	−58.5**	−38.0**
With double-ret and special ed adjustments[c]								
Ret vs. never-ret	—	−49.7**/8.9	−25.9**	−17.0*	−28.6**	−14.7	−41.3**	−27.1**
Ret vs. poor-perf comparison group	—	−27.7**/29.7**	−11.8	−0.6	−11.1	−5.4	−27.1**	−16.4
Adj R^2								
Ret vs. never-ret[d]	.10	.46/.30	.34	.40	.46	.40	.45	.36
Ret vs. poor-perf comparison group	.04	.33/.21	.17	.26	.35	.35	.39	.23

CAT-M

With no adjustments[a]							
Ret vs. never-ret	−40.0**	−56.4**/−15.6**	−38.6**	−54.8**	−65.2**	−77.6**	−85.1**	−85.7**
Ret vs. poor-perf comparison group	−17.7**	−28.2**/12.0**	−21.9**	−25.4**	−39.9**	−49.5**	−56.8**	−62.1**
With fall CAT and demographic adjustments[b]							
Ret vs. never-ret	—	−34.6**/7.3**	−14.9**	−26.7**	−38.6**	−47.9**	−48.6**	−50.1**
Ret vs. poor-perf comparison group	—	−21.5**/19.9**	−13.7**	−15.7**	−31.6**	−39.1**	−46.3**	−56.6**
With double-ret and special ed adjustments[c]							
Ret vs. never-ret	—	−28.1**/17.0**	−6.2	−4.7	−14.1*	−16.3**	−20.4**	−34.0**
Ret vs. poor-perf comparison group	—	−15.5**/28.7**	−5.0	5.3	−8.8	−10.0	−22.0**	−40.5**
Adj R^2[d]							
Ret vs. never-ret	.24	.51/.38	.42	.48	.48	.45	.51	.43
Ret vs. poor-perf comparison group	.14	.37/.26	.29	.38	.36	.41	.39	.27

[a]These regressions adjust for differences among the several retainee groups and between retainees and those never retained.

[b]Performed after the fall of first grade, these regressions adjust additionally for CAT scores from the fall of first grade and for demographic factors: race/ethnicity, gender, mother's education, lunch subsidy status (eligible or not), number of siblings, age as of the fall of first grade, and whether or not the child was living in a two-parent household at the start of first grade.

[c]These regressions adjust additionally for differences associated with special education alone, double retention alone, or both. These analyses are not performed in the fall of first grade.

[d]R^2 statistics are from the most inclusive equation in each column.

**signifies differences significant at the 0.01 level; *differences significant at the 0.05 level.

the CAT-M when all promoted youngsters are used for comparison. The differences are also large when looking at the poor-performer group, so the tapering off during the failed year presents itself again in these regression estimates.

When social demographic factors and CAT scores from the fall of the year are taken into account (second set), the difference between retainees and those never retained drops appreciably, especially on the CAT-M. The original difference of 56 points drops to 35 points in the comparison with all retainees, and from 28 to 22 points in the comparison including the poor performers. Both adjusted differences still reflect substantial gaps between retained and promoted youngsters, but they are smaller than the initial estimates. The adjustments are not nearly so impressive for the CAT-R, but a noteworthy drop still appears in the comparison with all promoted youngsters, and this is important.

The CAT-R changes are more impressive when adjustments are made for special education and double retention in the third set of estimates. The retainees' shortfall drops from 60 points to 50 when compared with all promoted youngsters, and from 38 points to 28 when compared with the poor-performing promoted youngsters. Both gaps are only about 0.7 those seen before any adjustments are made. Comparable reductions are seen in the quantitative area. These large reductions are due to the exceptionally poor performance, relative to other repeaters, of children who later will be assigned to special education classes and/or held back twice. Special education youngsters, for example, average 21 points below the others on the CAT-R, and those who will be held back a second time *and* assigned to special education average 22 points below on the CAT-M (not shown in table).

Whether or not the problems peculiar to double repeaters and special education youngsters should be separated out in this way is arguable, but all the figures indicate that first grade retainees have fallen far off by year's end and that their CAT averages are considerably lower than those of classmates who will move on to second grade. Much of their shortfall reflects the continuation of difficulties already apparent in the test scores for fall of first grade, and problems traceable to demographic risk factors of repeaters.[7] Children who will later experience multiple retentions and/or be placed in special education have fallen especially far behind.

These adjustments thus are quite important, accounting for about one-third of first grade repeaters' CAT shortfall. But the other two-thirds still leaves repeaters far behind, and presumably for reasons beyond those elucidated by the adjustment factors. On the CAT-R repeaters are farther behind than they were at the start of the year (compare entries in the first and second columns). These children simply aren't keeping up, and this no doubt has much to do with the decision to hold them back. But what happens as a result of that decision? We next consider the short-term consequences of retaining the students, evaluated at the end of the re-peated year. The longer-term consequences are taken up later.

First grade retainees: the repeated year

The picture for first grade repeaters after the second time through the grade is mixed (column 3, Table 5.1). Compared with all promoted youngsters, they have made up a little ground. Before adjustments, re-tainees are 64 points lower on the CAT-R and 54 points lower on the CAT-M. These are large differences, but smaller than those registered a year earlier, when the decision was made to hold these children back; at that time, they fell short of promoted youngsters by 72 points on the CAT-R and 56 points on the CAT-M.

When all the adjustments are made, the gap separating the perfor-mance of retainees from those who were promoted is cut by a third in the verbal area and by more than half in the quantitative. More relevant, though, are comparisons across the corresponding adjusted estimates. In these comparisons, retainees' CAT shortfall at the end of the repeated year is less than it had been a year earlier, when they were held back, but not dramatically so. The gap separating retainees' CAT performance from that of those promoted has narrowed from 50 points on the CAT-R to 43 points, and from 28 points on the CAT-M to 24.

These youngsters still trail badly, but they are not as far behind as they were, and this may be important. However, in comparisons with the poor-performing group, first grade repeaters trail farther behind after 2 years in the grade than they had at the end of their failed year. The two comparisons thus suggest contradictory conclusions.[8] The comparisons in Table 5.1 rate retainees' performance upon finishing first grade with that of the promoted children on finishing second grade. This same-age format here yields ambiguous results.

The same-grade format, however (reported in Table 5.2), reflects differently on the experience. The plan of Table 5.2 parallels that of Table 5.1, except CAT scores are compared for children at the same grade. Retainees' second-year scores – for when they are finishing first grade – are compared with promoted youngsters' scores from the previous year, when they, too, were finishing first grade. Upon repeating a grade, retainees are folded in with a new, younger set of classmates. These are the children they will probably be compared with the rest of their school careers, and the same-grade framework approximates how retainees are faring in this new classroom context.

When their end-of-first-grade scores are compared with those of all promoted youngsters, retainees still fall short, but are much better off than in their first time through the grade. On the CAT-R they pull up from 72 points behind to just 18 points behind; on the CAT-M they move up from 56 points back to only 16 points back (compare entries on either side of the vertical divide at the top of the table). These *unadjusted* same-grade comparisons thus have a favorable cast, and when the comparisons are adjusted for risk factors that affect test performance apart from retention, the comparisons become more favorable still. Indeed, when all adjustments are made, retainees actually score *above* promoted youngsters on the CAT-M, by some 17 points. This advantage is a first for retainees. Moreover, retainees' scores surpass the poor-performing comparison group's in every instance, with the spread reaching almost 30 points on both CAT subtests when all statistical adjustments are made.

The same-grade trends thus reflect the dip–recovery retention cycle described in Chapter 4. When first grade repeaters move to second grade, they perform at a level much closer to that of their classmates than before being held back; and after adjustments are made for other factors that damp scores, the retainees actually surpass their classmates. In other words, when we allow for where youngsters started, and for disadvantages like coming from homes close to the poverty level, being held back seems to confer a benefit.

First grade retainees after retention

It takes first grade repeaters 2 years to finish first grade, so their CAT performance from the spring of Year 3 indicates how well they are doing after moving back into the "normal" promotion sequence. Table 5.1 summarizes retainees' progress relative to never-retained youngsters annually through Year 8, which is 6 years after they finished first grade. Because Table 5.2 uses the same-grade format, the comparisons there extend through seventh grade. The two perspectives are entirely consonant: first grade repeaters fall behind again as soon as they get back into the regular promotion sequence, and after just a few years they are far behind.

The Year 8 comparisons in Table 5.1 show that retainees average more than 100 points below all never-retained children on the CAT-R and almost 70 points below the poor-performing comparison group. These enormous differences amount to 1.3 standard deviations and 1.1 standard deviations respectively. Indeed, retainees' relative standing falls off sharply even when adjustments are made for demographic factors and beginning test scores. On the CAT-R they fall from 53 points behind in the spring of their repeated year to 69 points behind a year later. On the CAT-M the drop is from 30 points to 53 points. These are comparisons with all promoted children, but the situation is much the same with the poor performers. All these comparisons put retention in an unfavorable light: in practically every instance the gap in CAT averages is bigger in Years 4 through 8 (or equivalently, in Years 2 through 6, postretention) than it had been a year postretention. The adjusted differences in test score points are large, ranging from the low 70s to the upper 80s on the CAT-R, and from the low 60s to the mid-70s on the CAT-M, when repeaters are compared with all promoted children. Against the poor performers, retainees' averages trail behind 53 points to 72 on the CAT-R and 55 points to 74 on the CAT-M. They remain large in the last panel too; after adjustments have been made for the especially poor performance of special education children and double repeaters, retainees generally are worse off after retention than they had been in the spring of their failed year.

The picture is much the same when retainees' relative standing is evaluated from the same-grade perspective (Table 5.2), although the differences in subsequent years shown in that table are usually smaller than those in Table 5.1. In these comparisons, retainees have one more year of schooling than the promoted youngsters with whom they are being compared, but even with this edge they regress badly after getting back into the regular promotion schedule. Indeed, their advances while repeating first grade pretty much evaporate in just a year. At the end of second grade, first grade retainees place a bit ahead of where they had been at the end of their failed grade (see the figures to the left of the slashes in column 2), but not by much, and even these modest gains do not hold up long. By fourth grade the (unadjusted) gaps separating retainees' performance from that of promoted youngsters are again large.

This holds even after demographic and first grade CAT adjustments are made, although more so for the CAT-M than for the CAT-R. On the CAT-M, for example, retainees fall farther behind grade by grade, so at the end of seventh grade, the 50.1 point disparity compared with all never-retained youngsters, and the 56.6 point disparity compared with the poor performers, are the largest in the second panel. The CAT-R comparisons, though more favorable, still have retainees lagging far behind (in seventh grade by 38 points,[9] and by 46.9 points when compared with all promoted children).

Only in the last set of estimates do we see consistent indications of lasting benefit. These figures are quite important, though, as they are our best estimate of what happens to one-time repeaters – those who make orderly progress after getting back on track. Most same-grade comparisons in the elementary years (through fifth grade) show much smaller differences against both all promoted children and the poor performers than in the spring of the failed year, and most of these are not significant. By sixth and seventh grade, though, repeaters again are behind on the CAT-M, and have slipped some on the CAT-R (although not to where they had been in first grade).

Summary: first grade retainees

Throughout the 6-year postretention period, first grade retainees' scores fall well below what would be expected based on the performance of children with similar sociodemographic characteristics or similar test scores before retention. Not only do they trail badly, but they do so by more after being held back than they had before. Their improved academic performance during the repeated year is not sustained, so over the long term, first grade repeaters have not profited from the retention experience. Aside from some scattered gains in the short term, up through seventh grade, retention cannot be said to have helped first grade repeaters.

Second and third grade repeaters

Analyses similar to those just reviewed for first grade repeaters also were done for second grade retainees (Tables 5.3 and 5.4) and third grade retainees (Tables 5.5 and 5.6). To distinguish the effects of retention from the consequences of children's prior academic experience, our approach looks forward from the fall of the failed grade. All comparisons extend through either Year 8 or seventh grade.

The first columns in these tables indicate that retainees trail far behind at the start of their failed year.[10] Third grade repeaters are a bit farther behind at the start than second grade repeaters are, and both are much farther behind than were first grade retainees in the fall of their failed year (Table 5.1). We saw in Chapter 4 that children held back in second and third grade also lagged behind in the fall of first grade, but not by as much as first grade repeaters. However, in the years before retention they trail off badly, so by the time they are retained, second and third grade repeaters stand far back. None of this reflects the consequences of retention, though. Adjusting for testing patterns only at the time of school entry, as we did for first grade repeaters, would miss this downward track after starting school. The shortfall over first grade for second grade retainees, and over the first and second grades for third grade retainees, would show up as consequences of retention.

Entries in the second column reflect the familiar failed-year pattern (Table 5.3 for second grade repeaters; Table 5.5 for third grade repeaters). Retainees start the year at a disadvantage, and fall even farther behind in the course of it. Second grade repeaters, for example, go from 60 points back in the fall to 82 points back in the spring (Table 5.3). The adjusted figures indicate that these youngsters' spring performance is well below what would be predicted.

All entries in the second column are negative and most are sizable. In these respects the pattern for second and third grade repeaters parallels that for first grade repeaters.[11] Do similar parallels characterize the postretention period? We consider first the same-age picture for second grade retainees (Table 5.3).

Although the unadjusted trends look unfavorable, the situation changes when adjustments are made for demographic characteristics and baseline test level. On the CAT-R, retainees are never as badly off as when they failed second grade (−57 points). Instead, their standing afterward is generally close to what it had been after repeating the grade (−44).[12] Though still far back, they are ahead of where they were in the spring of their failed year. On the CAT-M, the adjusted postretention gaps usually remain larger than the preretention figures, but except for Year 8 they are not much larger.

The favorable picture for second grade retainees is even clearer when

Table 5.3. *Same-age regression–adjusted CAT differences: second grade retainees vs. never–retained students or the poor–performing comparison group*

	Fall of Year 2	End of failed year	Spring of repeated year	1 year postret (Year 4)	2 years postret (Year 5)	3 years postret (Year 6)	4 years postret (Year 7)	5 years postret (Year 8)
CAT-R								
With no adjustments[a]								
Ret vs. never-ret	−60.1**	−82.1**	−75.0**	−93.4**	−89.1**	−86.9**	−89.6**	−96.0**
Ret vs. poor-perf comparison group	−31.2**	−60.7**	−43.7**	−57.4**	−47.3**	−52.7**	−52.0**	−57.8**
With fall CAT and demographic adjustments[b]								
Ret vs. never-ret	—	−57.1**	−43.7**	−48.8**	−47.6**	−46.2**	−48.2**	−50.2**
Ret vs. poor-perf comparison group	—	−49.5**	−34.7**	−40.2**	−33.5**	−39.7**	−40.1**	−46.6**
With double-ret and special ed adjustments[c]								
Ret vs. never-ret	—	−52.0**	−34.7**	−32.9**	−28.7**	−24.8	−28.1*	−35.8**
Ret vs. poor-perf comparison group	—	−43.9**	−26.3**	−25.9**	−16.0	−18.6	−21.5	−34.2**
Adj R^2								
Ret vs. never-ret[d]	.33	.57	.57	.64	.55	.49	.54	.48
Ret vs. poor-perf comparison group	.26	.43	.37	.46	.43	.39	.40	.30

CAT-M

With no adjustments[a]								
Ret vs. never-ret	−43.0**	−51.8**	−58.7**	−74.1**	−78.2**	−69.5**	−85.3**	−99.5**
Ret vs. poor-perf comparison group	−24.7**	−35.6**	−28.4**	−48.5**	−46.9**	−38.6**	−53.0**	−67.3**
With fall CAT and demographic adjustments[b]								
Ret vs. never-ret	—	−23.7**	−27.6**	−35.6**	−41.7**	−30.0**	−38.8**	−59.3**
Ret vs. poor-perf comparison group	—	−18.4**	−16.2**	−28.8**	−30.8**	−18.2	−32.9**	−55.2**
With double-ret and special ed adjustments[c]								
Ret vs. never-ret	—	−20.5**	−19.5**	−19.7**	−26.6**	−5.8	−22.4**	−48.7**
Ret vs. poor-perf comparison group	—	−15.4**	−9.4	−15.7*	−18.5*	−1.0	−20.1**	−46.0**
Adj R^2								
Ret vs. never-ret[d]	.31	.65	.63	.72	.61	.62	.61	.57
Ret vs. poor-perf comparison group	.31	.57	.44	.59	.50	.50	.46	.36

[a]These regressions adjust for differences among the several retainee groups and between retainees and those never retained.

[b]Performed after the fall of Year 2, these regressions adjust additionally for CAT scores from the fall of Year 2 and for demographic factors: race/ethnicity, gender, mother's education, lunch subsidy status (eligible or not), number of siblings, age as of the fall of first grade, and whether or not the child was living in a two-parent household at the start of first grade.

[c]These regressions adjust additionally for differences associated with special education alone, double retention alone, or both. These analyses are not performed in the fall of Year 2.

[d]R^2 statistics are from the most inclusive equation in each column.

**signifies differences significant at the 0.01 level; *differences significant at the 0.05 level.

Table 5.4. *Same-grade regression–adjusted CAT differences: second grade retainees vs. never-retained students or the poor-performing comparison group*

	Fall of 2d grade	Spring of 2d grade	End of 3d grade	End of 4th grade	End of 5th grade	End of 6th grade	End of 7th grade
CAT-R							
With no adjustments[a]							
Ret *vs.* never-ret	−57.8**	−80.0**/−37.6**	−48.0**	−63.0**	−68.4**	−70.6**	−65.9**
Ret *vs.* poor-perf comparison group	−26.8**	−56.8**/−15.2*	−19.1*	−27.0**	−29.3**	−38.9**	−34.5**
With fall CAT and demographic adjustments[b]							
Ret *vs.* never-ret	—	−54.4**/−11.6*	−11.5	−21.9*	−27.4**	−27.7**	−21.4*
Ret *vs.* poor-perf comparison group	—	−45.4**/−3.4	−3.6	−14.1	−15.9	−22.7*	−20.1
With double-ret and special ed adjustments[c]							
Ret *vs.* never-ret	—	−49.0**/−4.4	3.8	−2.4	−5.7	−9.0	−10.1
Ret *vs.* poor-perf comparison group	—	−40.1**/3.3	10.7	3.1	5.3	−4.9	−8.4
Adj R^2							
Ret *vs.* never-ret[d]	.20	.52/.46	.48	.53	.45	.50	.41
Ret *vs.* poor-perf comparison group	.09	.36/.27	.29	.36	.36	.40	.25

CAT-M

With no adjustments[a]						
Ret vs. never-ret	−41.4**	−49.8**/−18.1**	−36.7**	−45.6**	−49.3**	−61.9**	−74.8**
Ret vs. poor-perf comparison group	−21.2**	−31.8**/−0.6	−8.4	−20.6**	−26.5**	−33.0**	−47.8**
With fall CAT and demographic adjustments[b]						
Ret vs. never-ret	—	−22.4**/8.8*	−3.6	−8.0	−12.7	−19.2*	−35.6**
Ret vs. poor-perf comparison group	—	−16.0**/14.1*	7.4	−1.8	−2.7	−11.8	−38.4**
With double-ret and special ed adjustments[c]						
Ret vs. never-ret	—	−19.8**/12.5**	8.4	4.9	4.1	−4.6	−27.3**
Ret vs. poor-perf comparison group	—	−13.8**/17.3**	17.7**	8.9	11.3	−0.9	−30.0**
Adj R^2						
Ret vs. never-ret[d]	.17	.60/.54	.57	.62	.53	.58	.47
Ret vs. poor-perf comparison group	.07	.51/.40	.43	.45	.45	.46	.28

[a]These regressions adjust for differences among the several retainee groups and between retainees and those never retained.

[b]Performed after the fall of second grade, these regressions adjust additionally for CAT scores from the fall of second grade and for demographic factors: race/ethnicity, gender, mother's education, lunch subsidy status (eligible or not), number of siblings, age as of the fall of first grade, and whether or not the child was living in a two-parent household at the start of first grade.

[c]These regressions adjust additionally for differences associated with special education alone, double retention alone, or both. These analyses are not performed in the fall of second grade.

[d]R^2 statistics are from the most inclusive equation in each column.

**signifies differences significant at the 0.01 level; *differences significant at the 0.05 level.

125

Table 5.5. *Same-age regression-adjusted CAT differences: third grade retainees vs. never-retained students or the poor-performing comparison group*

	Fall of Year 3	Spring of failed year	Spring of repeated year	1 year postret (Year 5)	2 years postret (Year 6)	3 years postret (Year 7)	4 years postret (Year 8)
CAT-R							
With no adjustments[a]							
Ret vs. never-ret	−68.0**	−79.8**	−81.0**	−77.8**	−60.0**	−73.3**	−85.9**
Ret vs. poor-perf comparison group	−37.0**	−49.1**	−45.4**	−37.0**	−27.4*	−36.2**	−45.8**
With fall CAT and demographic adjustments[b]							
Ret vs. never-ret	—	−34.7**	−25.1**	−21.3*	−7.9	−17.3	−22.9
Ret vs. poor-perf comparison group	—	−28.6**	−22.4*	−16.6	−9.7	−14.7	−23.8
With double-ret and special ed adjustments[c]							
Ret vs. never-ret	—	−28.4**	−15.9	−13.9	1.1	−9.7	−16.0
Ret vs. poor-perf comparison group	—	−23.3**	−14.9	−10.3	−1.1	−8.4	−18.5
Adj R^2							
Ret vs. never-ret[d]	.41	.66	.67	.60	.53	.58	.54
Ret vs. poor-perf comparison group	.29	.51	.51	.46	.41	.42	.35

126

CAT-M

With no adjustments[a]							
Ret vs. never-ret	−48.6**	−56.4**	−50.3**	−64.1**	−42.3**	−62.7**	−77.1**
Ret vs. poor-perf comparison group	−20.4**	−27.3**	−25.7**	−33.5**	−12.7	−30.4**	−43.1**
With fall CAT and demographic adjustments[b]							
Ret vs. never-ret	—	−13.6**	−6.7	−18.8*	9.2	−7.2	−26.3**
Ret vs. poor-perf comparison group	—	−11.2*	−9.6	−16.5*	7.8	−9.1	−26.7**
With double-ret and special ed adjustments[c]							
Ret vs. never-ret	—	−10.6*	0.4	−12.4	17.1*	−2.9	−21.6
Ret vs. poor-perf comparison group	—	−8.8	−3.6	−11.1	14.3	−5.9	−22.0
Adj R^2							
Ret vs. never-ret[d]	.42	.75	.74	.67	.66	.64	.62
Ret vs. poor-perf comparison group	.30	.60	.63	.53	.56	.51	.41

[a]These regressions adjust for differences among the several retainee groups and between retainees and those never retained.

[b]Performed after the fall of Year 3, these regressions adjust additionally for CAT scores from the fall of Year 3 and for demographic factors: race/ethnicity, gender, mother's education, lunch subsidy status (eligible or not), number of siblings, age as of the fall of first grade, and whether or not the child was living in a two-parent household at the start of first grade.

[c]These regressions adjust additionally for differences associated with special education alone, double retention alone, or both. These analyses are not performed in the fall of Year 3.

[d]R^2 statistics are from the most inclusive equation in each column.

**signifies differences significant at the 0.01 level; *differences significant at the 0.05 level.

Table 5.6. *Same-grade regression–adjusted CAT differences: third grade retainees vs. never–retained students or the poor-performing comparison group*

	Fall of 3d grade	End of 3d grade	End of 4th grade	End of 5th grade	End of 6th grade	End of 7th grade
CAT-R						
With no adjustments[a]						
Ret vs. never–ret	−68.6**	−81.0**/−35.6**	−51.8**	−42.7**	−54.8**	−54.9**
Ret vs. poor–perf comparison group	−37.2**	−50.2**/−7.0	−16.6	−4.7	−23.3	−22.0
With fall CAT and demographic adjustments[b]						
Ret vs. never–ret	—	−31.2**/15.6*	4.7	15.0	0.2	−0.2
Ret vs. poor–perf comparison group	—	−23.7**/21.6**	7.9	17.9	2.4	−2.3
With double–ret and special ed adjustments[c]						
Ret vs. never–ret	—	−24.9**/21.7**	8.4	20.7*	4.3	2.5
Ret vs. poor–perf comparison group	—	−18.1*/27.1**	11.0	23.3*	6.3	1.0
Adj R^2						
Ret vs. never–ret[d]	.26	.62/.60	.61	.52	.52	.46
Ret vs. poor–perf comparison group	.09	.52/.49	.46	.40	.41	.29

128

CAT-M

With no adjustments[a]					
Ret vs. never-ret	-48.9**	-57.4**/-13.3	-31.3**	-23.5*	-39.7**	-51.5**
Ret vs. poor-perf comparison group	-20.5**	-28.1**/14.5*	-6.9	3.5	-10.6	-23.2*
With fall CAT and demographic adjustments[b]						
Ret vs. never-ret	—	-12.7/31.1**	10.9	20.7**	7.8	-3.1
Ret vs. poor-perf comparison group	—	-11.2/31.5**	8.2	20.3**	6.6	-10.1
With double-ret and special ed adjustments[c]						
Ret vs. never-ret	—	-9.7/34.9**	14.4*	25.4**	10.4	0.5
Ret vs. poor-perf comparison group	—	-8.3/35.2**	12.0	24.8**	9.0	-5.9
Adj R^2						
Ret vs. never-ret[d]	.28	.72/.70	.60	.55	.55	.50
Ret vs. poor-perf comparison group	.09	.59/.57	.45	.45	.40	.31

[a]These regressions adjust for differences among the several retainee groups and between retainees and those never retained.

[b]Performed after the fall of third grade, these regressions adjust additionally for CAT scores from the fall of third grade and for demographic factors: race/ethnicity, gender, mother's education, lunch subsidy status (eligible or not), number of siblings, age as of the fall of first grade, and whether or not the child was living in a two-parent household at the start of first grade.

[c]These regressions adjust additionally for differences associated with special education alone, double retention alone, or both. These analyses are not performed in the fall of third grade.

[d]R^2 statistics are from the most inclusive equation in each column.

**signifies differences significant at the 0.01 level; *differences significant at the 0.05 level.

129

the tendency for test scores to increase over time is taken into consideration. Because of this increase, a constant difference in terms of test score points actually signifies relative improvement. For example, the second grade CAT-R difference of 57 points is about 1.2 standard deviations, a very large shortfall. By Year 8 the CAT-R standard deviation for the full sample of promoted and retained youngsters increases from 47.3 to 79.7, so the 50.2-point difference registered then is 0.63 standard deviations. When looked at this way, retainees' progress is more impressive, because in almost every instance the postretention differences reflect improved relative standing for retainees.

Such standing holds as well for same-grade comparisons (Table 5.4). In fact, the fully adjusted figures show second grade repeaters performing either on a par with (CAT-R) or above (CAT-M) their new classmates at the end of their repeated year. Again, though, their relative standing trails off. However, in about half the postretention comparisons in which retainees' averages fall below those of promoted youngsters, the difference is not significant. In the other comparisons, retainees do lag significantly behind, but their scores are closer to the promoted level than before retention (except for seventh grade CAT-M averages). Hence, second grade retainees' relative standing generally *improves* after retention.

For third grade retainees, trends are more favorable still (Tables 5.5 and 5.6). On the CAT-R, none of the adjusted same-age disparities after retention is as large as any of the benchmark disparities (fall of third grade, spring of failed year, or spring of repeated year). Hence, for several years after retention, retainees in these comparisons do better relative to promoted youngsters than before. And again, since scores get more variable over time, retainees actually fare even better in relative terms.

On the CAT-M, the adjusted differences are also small throughout.[13] Indeed, several of the same-age differences are not even significant (spring of the repeated year, Year 6, and Year 7; see Table 5.5).

The same-grade comparisons for third grade repeaters are almost all favorable (Table 5.6). After adjusting for CAT scores and background factors they are significantly *ahead* of their new classmates in the repeated year, and their advantage increases when additional adjustments are made for children's status with respect to special education and double retention.[14] Later, after third grade repeaters move back into the regular promotion sequence, their adjusted CAT averages never fall significantly below those of promoted youngsters.

Retainees still trail far behind when judged by the unadjusted comparisons, and we must not lose sight of this. In the years after retention, however, their serious performance deficits can be traced almost entirely to circumstances other than retention, for example their poor readiness skills when starting school, their slower progress in the early grades, and other risk factors. After statistical procedures allow for this expected shortfall, retainees do about as well as everyone else. Our best guess is that these third grade repeaters have done better in the fourth, fifth, sixth, and seventh grades than had they not been held back; that is, retention very likely has helped them.

Retention and test performance: taking stock

We now return to the question posed at the start of the previous chapter: does retention help children academically or harm them? We have examined the issue from several angles: comparing different groups of retainees with one another, with children not retained, with themselves over time, and with others of the same age or grade level; using statistical adjustments; and using a matched comparison group. We have looked at both verbal and quantitative performance over many years.

The clearest patterns mainly involve the backdrop to retention, not its consequences. For example, yet-to-be-retained children performed far below the standard of never-to-be-retained youngsters from the very start of first grade. Those farthest behind are retained the earliest. First grade repeaters have exceptionally poor initial CAT performance, and later many of these youngsters are moved into special education classes and/or held back a second time.

Youngsters held back in second grade and beyond also enter school with low scores, but not as low as those of first grade repeaters. They are passed along, but over the years fall behind, dropping especially far back in their failed year. We saw this in Chapter 4 by comparing these children's gains through their year of retention (whether second or third) with those of youngsters who move smoothly through the system.

Children who are held back thus start out far behind, and until they are retained lose additional ground relative to their classmates. Assuming that the competencies tapped in these tests are important to the early elementary curriculum (and we assume they are), these children are stumbling badly. Their problems are real and severe, and critics of retention often seem to lose sight of this. These children need help, and retention does seem to help somewhat, especially in the short-term: during their repeated year all retainees make up ground. These advances are most apparent in same-grade comparisons, which simulate the class-room context repeaters experience after retention. For second and third grade repeaters, however, the advances are also seen in same-age com-parisons with their original classmates, now a grade ahead.

If the standard of success is that repeating a grade will halt retainees' downward slide, help them catch up somewhat, help them do better than would be predicted from their prior academic record, and enable them to perform at close to grade level by the time they move up to the next grade, then the indications are consistently positive. By these standards, the "repeated year rebound" reflects favorably on retention.

Unfortunately, the aspect of retainees' experience during the repeated year that leads to this success is not revealed in these comparisons. In Baltimore schools, there are no supplemental programs designed specifi-cally to help repeaters, although some teachers do probably make special efforts for them. Working on the same curriculum for a second time and retaking the tests may help repeaters show what they have actually learned.

Has retention transformed these struggling youngsters into academic stars? Absolutely not; but when allowance is made for their problems before retention, they do better than would be predicted. In fact, our estimates suggest that had it not been for their prior difficulties, in many instances they would perform close to, and occasionally even ahead of, their new classmates. But retainees continue to suffer from their early difficulties, which retention does not erase. Most retainees never catch up once they have fallen behind, but for many the free-fall is slowed, possi-bly even stopped; at least, this appears to be the case for second and third grade repeaters. Short of actually getting them up to the level of their promoted agemates, this seems an impressive showing.

Children who are not too far behind to begin with are the ones helped most by retention. It buys them the time to mobilize their resources and to master some of the skills they apparently did not acquire the first time through the grade. Our comparisons indicate that second and third grade repeaters, once they get back on track, seem to hold their own. Children who are struggling the most – first grade repeaters and those destined for either special education or a second retention – are helped very little. Retention's effectiveness varies inversely with its scheduling, helping first graders least and third graders most. Indeed, even though we have not explored the situation of fourth through seventh grade repeaters in detail, they appeared to be having the least difficulty all along the way.

Since our main conclusions come from regressions that use a moving baseline (i.e., CAT scores from the fall of retainees' failed grade), there is a risk that what looks like differential effectiveness might be due instead to the different intervals covered by the baseline scores. For third grade repeaters, 3 years will have passed versus just 1 year for first grade repeaters. Perhaps most of third grade repeaters' troubles are already behind them by the time they are held back, while most of first grade repeaters' difficulties still lie ahead. This is another potential false signal that could lead to misreading retention's effects, but as far as we can tell, these youngsters' trajectories actually are altered by retention. This was indicated in Chapter 4, where preretention and postretention CAT gains were compared across fixed intervals, and also by the repeated-year gains seen for practically everyone. For each of the tables presented in the text, we also have estimated CAT differences between promoted youngsters and every repeater group. These additional results were not reported for reasons of space, but when the "moving baselines" are used for everyone (e.g., everyone's fall Year 3 scores are used when looking at outcomes in Year 4 and beyond), in practically every comparison retainees held back in the baseline year score closer to promoted youngsters than retainees from earlier years. Even this approach is not conclusive, but it does offer assurance that the moving baseline itself is not the reason first grade repeaters appear to be doing the worst and third grade repeaters the best.

In the concluding chapter, we consider what this complex pattern might imply for educational practice. By then we will also have information related to children's marks and their socioemotional status. Marks are taken up next, in Chapter 6.

6

Teachers' classroom evaluations of repeaters: report card marks in reading and math

In this chapter we look at report card marks in math and reading, the two subjects that dominate the curriculum in the primary grades. These are the building blocks for most other academic subjects, and for that reason probably have special relevance for how children come to think of themselves in their academic roles (a topic taken up in Chapter 7).

Retained children found it impossible to keep up before they were held back, but we saw in the last chapter that their test performance improved during the repeated year, and that in many instances they continued to do better relative to their classmates after retention. These successes are important, but whether children fully appreciate them is dubious. Feedback about test scores is hard to decipher, and often reaches children indirectly or not at all. Report card marks, on the other hand, are readily understood and are much more public than test scores. In elementary school all children take reading and math, and the marking system, as described previously, rates their performance excellent, good, satisfactory, or unsatisfactory (scored 4 through 1). Marks are given to children and sent home to their parents. Children discuss marks among themselves, and youngsters in a class tend to know who is doing well and who is doing poorly. By design, marks provide direct feedback from teachers to children on the quality of their performance, and so successes registered in report card marks very likely carry greater weight with youngsters than improvements in test performance.

Marks are important for what they reflect about children's performance in the classroom, and for the signals they send. With marks, unlike test scores, there are no particular developmental trends to be plotted out[1] and no age-graded benchmarks against which to judge children's standing. Marks are most meaningfully compared at grade level, where

children are being rated against the same curriculum and in the same classroom context; so in this chapter we will consider marking patterns from the same-grade perspective only.

We begin by looking at marking trends from the first grade through the seventh. After reviewing these trends, regression-adjusted estimates are presented to see whether retainees' marks are better or worse after being held back than would be expected from preretention achievement levels and sociodemographic characteristics. As before, we will look at first, second, and third grade retainees separately, comparing their marks with those of (1) all promoted youngsters, (2) the subsample of poor-performing promoted youngsters, and (3) fourth through seventh grade repeaters combined.

Report card marks before and after retention: more indications of success

Table 6.1 lines up same-grade comparisons of report card marks, beginning in the fall of first grade, and at the end of every grade thereafter.[2] In the year of retention, two averages are reported: the first from the initial time through the grade, when students are earmarked for retention, the second when the grade is repeated.[3]

The middle school program is different because all children no longer take the same curriculum, and not all courses run for the full year. In middle school, English is taken as part of the regular curriculum, whereas reading is usually remedial. Some children take only reading, some take only English, and some take both.

One math course is the norm, but its nature varies. Many sixth graders, for example, take remedial math – courses with titles like "Special Education Math," "Supplementary Remedial Math," and the like. Others take the regular sixth grade math program, while still others take advanced courses (e.g., "Advanced Academic Math," "Pre-Algebra," etc.). Here we look just at marks, without regard to whether they are obtained in remedial, regular, or advanced courses, because the marks are the feedback children get from their teachers, and our purpose is to determine whether these signals are positive or negative. In Chapter 8, we examine middle school course-taking patterns to see whether repeaters are tracked differently, an important concern in its own right.

Table 6.1. Average reading and math report card marks from first through seventh grade for retained groups, never-retained pupils, and the poor-performing comparison group

	Fall of 1st grade[a]	End of 1st grade[a]	End of 2d grade[a]	End of 3d grade	End of 4th grade	End of 5th grade	End of 6th grade	End of 7th grade
Average reading mark								
Year of retention								
1st grade	1.1	1.0/1.9	1.9	1.8	1.9	2.1	1.9	1.9
	(106)	(105)/(84)	(105)	(93)	(86)	(90)	(74)	(89)
2d grade	1.5	1.7	1.2/2.2	2.0	1.9	2.2	2.0	2.0
	(61)	(62)	(53)/(60)	(55)	(55)	(50)	(49)	(54)
3d grade	1.6	2.1	1.9	1.3/1.8	1.9	2.0	1.9	2.1
	(42)	(43)	(41)	(40)/(36)	(34)	(34)	(33)	(35)
4th–7th grades	1.9	2.2	2.3	2.0	2.0	2.2	1.9	1.9
	(68)	(68)	(60)	(70)	(64)	(57)	(67)	(68)
Never-retained pupils								
All never-retained	2.2	2.7	2.7	2.7	2.6	2.8	2.6	2.6
	(418)	(414)	(358)	(331)	(295)	(254)	(234)	(234)
Poor-performing comparison group	1.9	2.2	2.2	2.2	2.1	2.3	2.4	2.4
	(98)	(98)	(80)	(78)	(69)	(60)	(54)	(55)

Average math mark

Year of retention

1st grade	1.3	1.3/2.2	1.9	1.9	1.9	2.1	1.8	1.9
	(105)	(104)/(84)	(107)	(92)	(85)	(90)	(74)	(89)
2d grade	1.8	2.0	1.6/2.3	2.1	2.1	2.2	1.7	1.8
	(62)	(62)	(53)/(60)	(55)	(56)	(52)	(49)	(54)
3d grade	2.1	2.6	2.1	1.6/2.3	2.2	2.1	2.2	1.9
	(43)	(43)	(41)	(42)/(36)	(34)	(34)	(33)	(35)
4th–7th grades	2.2	2.5	2.4	2.1	2.1	2.1	1.9	1.6
	(67)	(68)	(60)	(70)	(65)	(61)	(67)	(68)
Never-retained pupils								
All never-retained	2.6	3.0	2.8	2.7	2.6	2.8	2.5	2.3
	(418)	(412)	(358)	(333)	(294)	(255)	(235)	(234)
Poor-performing	2.4	2.6	2.5	2.2	2.2	2.4	2.2	1.9
comparison group	(98)	(98)	(80)	(77)	(69)	(60)	(54)	(55)

Note: All marks are on a scale from 1 (unsatisfactory) to 4 (excellent). All entries except those in the first column are from the final quarter of the year. The first-column entries are from the fall of first grade, in 1982. Numbers in parentheses are sample sizes.
[a] For first, second, and third grade retainees, two end-of-grade averages are reported. The first is from the first time through the grade; the second is from the repeated year.

The marking system in middle school uses percentages, rather than letter grades as in elementary school. We have collapsed these into four categories, scoring 90% through 100% as "4," 80% through 89% as "3," 70% though 79% as "2," and below 70% as "1." This roughly parallels the primary-grade distinctions for excellent, good, satisfactory, and unsatisfactory, allowing us to plot marks all 7 years using a common scale. For middle school we use the last-quarter mark in a given subject. Most of these are from the fourth quarter (at year's end) but for one-semester courses they can be from the second quarter.[4] At the elementary level, fourth-quarter marks are used throughout, so at both levels of schooling we report the teacher's evaluation from the course's final quarter.

Finally, there is the matter of whether to use reading or English marks in middle school. At the elementary level, reading is the focus, so reading marks are also used from middle school when they are available. In Year 6, the first year of middle school for never-retained youngsters, there are 200 children with reading marks; there are 357 in Year 7, and 300 in Year 8. English marks are used when available for children who lack reading marks. This increases our coverage in Year 6 to 293, in Year 7 to 458, and in Year 8 to 470.

The Year 6 figure seems low, but all retainees except those held back in sixth and seventh grade were still in elementary schools in Year 6. When elementary and middle school marks for Year 6 are combined, as they are in our tables, coverage increases to 491.[5]

Retainees' early marks are generally low and correspond with the eventual scheduling of their retentions (Table 6.1). First grade repeaters' marks from the fall of first grade are lowest, more than a full unit behind all never-retained youngsters in both reading and math. Indeed, their average math mark is even a full marking unit behind that of the poor-performing comparison group. The sample-wide standard deviations for reading and math marks are 0.7 and 0.8 respectively, so these disparities all are large.

In every instance retainees in second or third grade have lower first grade averages than all never-retained children, and, with one exception, lower averages than the poor-performing comparison group as well. Their orderliness is striking: the earlier the retention, the greater the gap between retained and never-retained students. This pattern, which duplicates what we saw for initial CAT levels, is another clue that the timing of retention is tied to the severity of children's academic difficulties. All retainees start out behind, but those held back earliest are farthest behind.

In fact, first grade repeaters' marks start out so low there is barely any room for them to fall farther, yet they do fall in reading: every first grade repeater fails reading at year's end. Indeed, their spring reading average of 1.0 and their spring math average of 1.3 are the two lowest entries in Table 6.1 (figures to the right of the slashes in Table 6.1 are from a year later, the spring of the repeated year; these will be discussed shortly).

Unlike first grade retainees, other retainees' marks improve somewhat from fall to spring of the first grade. Second grade repeaters' progress over the year is modest (only a fifth of a marking unit in both instances), but at least they move in the right direction. After first grade, though, their marks also decline, falling to 1.2 in reading and 1.6 in math in the spring of second grade. Both averages leave them below even their poor showing at the start of first grade, and well below the second-year averages of children who are not held back until third grade or later. Much the same pattern is seen for third grade repeaters, and children held back in the fourth through seventh grades also have averages that go up for a couple of years before dropping back. Our format does not pinpoint the year of retention for the combined group, but the group's general trend is consistent with that for the others. Apparently, backsliding triggers the decision to retain: in the year of their retention, repeaters in first, second, and third grades all have averages below every other group.

Over time, then, the marks of children who repeat fall farther and farther behind, and this parallels the testing trends seen in the last chapter. Teachers and administrators, it seems, resort to retention when children's performance slips from bad to worse. Many marginal performers, we see, are moved along for several years before being held back, so it seems the decision is not made lightly.

It is hard to be optimistic about retained children's prospects if what awaits them simply extends this experience through their failed year. Indeed, not much of a recovery would be expected even if from that point forward they managed to parallel the later performance of promoted youngsters, because promoted children's marks also tend to go down over time, and especially in middle school. This general downward trend in children's marks with increasing age is a pattern seen in other studies as well (e.g., Simmons and Blyth 1987). Except for a noticeable jump in fifth grade, promoted children's marks generally do not change much over the elementary grades, about 0.1 marking units from year to year.[6] In middle school, though, marks decline, and not just when compared with the high marks from fifth grade. For all never-retained children in both reading and math, and for the poor performers in math, not a single sixth or seventh grade average is above any spring average from the first through fourth grades. The transition from elementary to middle school challenges children generally, and performance typically dips (Eccles and Midgley 1990; Harvard Education Letter 1992b). What is important for our purposes is that even the most successful pupils – the never-retained youngsters – are struggling at this point.

What are the implications for retainees of the downward drift in marks? Before retention their marks are dropping, as are those of the promoted children. Neither trend suggests that retainees' marks will improve after retention. Improve they do, though, and the progress registered at the end of retainees' repeated year is especially striking (see the figures to the right of the slash marks in columns with double en-tries). By juxtaposing children's failing marks before retention against their marks when they finish the grade for the second time, the repeated year "rebound" comes through dramatically. In math, the three main repeater groups have marks well above satisfactory at the end of their repeated grade, whereas in the previous year their marks hovered midway between unsatisfactory and satisfactory. First-grade repeaters' marks improve on average 0.9 marking units, while second and third grade repeaters' marks improve 0.7 units.

In contrast, the largest spring-to-spring change in marks during these same years for other groups is 0.3 units, and reflects *declines:* fourth through seventh grade retainees' math average drops from 2.4 to 2.1 between second and third grade, and that of the poor performers falls from 2.5 to 2.2 in the same period (see Table 6.1). Thus, retainees' improvement in their repeated years not only is exceptionally large, but also moves against the downward trend seen for most other children.

If retention is supposed to give children a second chance to master materials they missed the first time so they will be better able to keep up when they finally do move on, repeating a year works, or at least helps. Marks improve, and the previous chapter shows that test scores did so as well, so it is unlikely that teachers are simply going easy on repeaters. By the time these children move up to the next grade they are closer to keeping pace with their classmates than before, and their improved marks give them positive feedback about their performance.

This performance during the repeated year reflects favorably on retention; but what happens to these children when they move into a new grade and encounter a new curriculum? Are they better able to keep up because of retention, or are the new challenges too much? The picture is mixed, because retainees' performance does drop off some as they start a new grade. However, since promoted children's marks also fall off in the upper grades, this decline does not necessarily reflect on the lasting effects of retention. In fact, retainees' middle school marks remain close to their marks in the later years of elementary school, while those of their promoted peers do not.[7]

After retainees finish their repeated grade, their marks generally hover around satisfactory for the rest of elementary school. First grade repeaters' marks fall a bit below 2.0, and those of second and third graders average a bit above 2.0. These are lower than their repeated-year marks, but higher than their failed-year marks.

In sixth and seventh grade, retainees' marks are about the same as in elementary school. Their seventh grade averages are around 2.0 in reading (1.9, 2.0, and 2.1 for first, second, and third graders respectively) and slightly lower in math. Neither average is at the level of promoted children's; nevertheless, retainees in middle school often perform at a level closer to that of promoted children than was true before retention, closer even than at the high point of their repeated year.[8] The main exception involves comparisons with the poor-performing promoted group in reading, whose marks improve slightly in middle school.

Overall, then, in terms of either test scores or marks, retainees seem better off after retention. On the negative side, their marks remain marginal (right around satisfactory), they continue to lag behind promoted children, and their performance trails off some after the repeated year. However, retainees' marks improve noticeably during the repeated year, and the tapering off of their marks afterward looks more like that seen for everyone than something peculiar to repeaters. Indeed, in most instances, repeaters' marks don't drop quite as much as those of promoted children, and even after the postretention dip they are still ahead of their preretention position. Whether these positive signs actually reflect "benefits" of retention is taken up in the next section.

Regression-adjusted comparisons of same-grade marks

In this section we adjust marking patterns for prior achievement levels and for children's demographic characteristics. As in Chapter 5, multiple regression is used to implement these adjustments, and our analysis parallels that used before, except that for marks we perform only same-grade regressions. Regression-adjusted differences are reported for first, second, and third grade repeaters separately, again beginning with marks from the fall of the failed year. For first grade repeaters the analysis extends 6 years "postretention"; for third grade repeaters the postretention interval is 4 years.

The entries in Table 6.2 reflect differences between the marks of first grade retainees and those of promoted youngsters, adjusted for the other factors. Comparisons are made with all never-retained children and with the poor performers. Both adjusted and unadjusted differences are given, but we are mainly interested in the comparisons after adjustments are made for test scores from the fall of the failed year, for personal and social demographic characteristics, and for difficulties that might be peculiar to double repeaters and children in special education. These adjusted differences give the clearest reading of how retainees fare.

In both reading and math, retainees' first marks are more than a full unit behind those of all promoted children, and far behind those of the poor-performing never-retained children as well. After all adjustments are made, retainees' entering marks are still from 0.69 to 0.83 marking units back. These disparities are on the order of a full standard deviation,[9] showing that retainees' problems are much more severe than would be predicted from their low entering CAT levels and from their demographic characteristics. Academic difficulties thus are not limited to low-income or minority youngsters. Exactly what is behind their shaky start cannot be determined from Table 6.2, but it clearly goes beyond initial problems settling in, as the marking gap widens from fall to spring. Indeed, at year's end, even retainees' adjusted marks are more than a full unit behind those of promoted youngsters (see entries to the left of the slash mark in the second column).

It is a gloomy picture to this point, but what happens to these youngsters on their second try at first grade? Do their marks improve or does this downward track continue? The unadjusted figures to the right of the slash mark in the "End of first grade" column compare first grade repeaters' marks from the second time through the grade with those of promoted youngsters from the previous year, when they were finishing first grade (i.e., Year 2 marks in the first instance vs. Year 1 marks in the second). Retainees' averages in these four comparisons are from 0.36 to 0.78 marking units back, so they are still having problems in the repeated year. Nevertheless, in each instance their shortfall is much lower than the first time through the grade (fall or spring), and in the adjusted comparisons, three of these differences are too small to be considered reliable; the fourth, at 0.29 marking units, is less than half the (adjusted) gap from when they began school.

First grade repeaters thus come much closer to keeping pace after repeating than before. Nothing here indicates that retainees' marks suffer because the students were held back. Indeed, the opposite is true: at the end of first grade these children perform at about the same level as others after allowance is made for their prior difficulties. This is a much better showing than they made before.

The picture for these youngsters at the end of their repeated grade is virtually unchanged through the rest of elementary school and into middle school. In the unadjusted comparisons, retainees' averages in most years are on the order of 0.6 to 0.7 marking units behind those of all never-retained children (7 of the 12 figures are in this range), and 0.2 to 0.3 marking units behind those of the poor performers (several of which are not significant). Retainees' marks look better still when adjusted for problems that predate retention. In Table 6.2 only half the adjusted comparisons with all promoted youngsters yield differences large enough to be considered reliable, that is, about 0.3 to 0.4 marking units. Against the poor performers, there are even fewer significant differences – only 3 of 12.

The most troublesome thing about the figures for first grade repeaters is that the significant differences are mainly in the middle school years, that is, the sixth and seventh grades (five of the eight middle school differences are significant). These children's middle school marks, although far ahead of where they were before retention, still have slipped a notch from the later years of elementary school. The more challenging middle school curriculum – and the less supportive environment – may take their toll on these children, who otherwise have been doing reason-

Table 6.2. *Same-grade regression–adjusted mark differences: first grade retainees vs. never-retained students or the poor-performing comparison group*

	Fall of 1st grade	End of 1st grade	End of 2d grade	End of 3d grade	End of 4th grade	End of 5th grade	End of 6th grade	End of 7th grade
Reading marks								
With no adjustments[a]								
Ret vs. never-ret	−1.04**	−1.68**/−0.78**	−0.81**	−0.84**	−0.68**	−0.61**	−0.59**	−0.61**
Ret vs. poor-perf comparison group	−0.79**	−1.25**/−0.36**	−0.34**	−0.41**	−0.21	−0.09	−0.34*	−0.39**
With fall CAT and social demographic adjustments[b]								
Ret vs. never-ret	−0.82**	−1.41**/−0.46**	−0.47**	−0.46**	−0.27**	−0.22**	−0.43**	−0.37**
Ret vs. poor-perf comparison group	−0.74**	−1.23**/−0.28**	−0.25*	−0.31**	−0.13	0.01	−0.29*	−0.30*
With double-ret and special ed adjustments[c]								
Ret vs. never-ret	−0.76**	−1.36**/−0.29**	−0.38**	−0.34**	−0.18	−0.23	−0.38**	−0.42**
Ret vs. poor-perf comparison group	−0.69**	−1.18**/−0.13	−0.16	−0.19	−0.04	0.00	−0.24	−0.36*
Adj R^2								
Ret vs. never-ret[d]	.41	.55/.34	.32	.34	.35	.29	.22	.18
Ret vs. poor-perf comparison group	.31	.55/.14	.11	.08	.02	.05	.17	.07

Math marks

With no adjustments[a]

Ret vs. never-ret	−1.25**	−1.67**/−0.71**	−0.85**	−0.77**	−0.64**	−0.65***	−0.61**	−0.39**
Ret vs. poor-perf comparison group	−1.10**	−1.38**/−0.44**	−0.50**	−0.32**	−0.26*	−0.21	−0.32*	−0.01

With fall CAT and demographic adjustments[b]

Ret vs. never-ret	−0.85**	−1.22**/−0.23**	−0.48**	−0.31**	−0.18	−0.23	−0.41**	−0.11
Ret vs. poor-perf comparison group	−0.91**	−1.22**/−0.25*	−0.39**	−0.20	−0.16	−0.18	−0.31**	−0.04

With double-ret and special ed adjustments[c]

Ret vs. never-ret	−0.74**	−1.12**/−0.09	−0.38**	−0.18	−0.07	−0.19	−0.41**	−0.25
Ret vs. poor-perf comparison group	−0.83**	−1.12**/−0.11	−0.33**	−0.08	−0.07	−0.16	−0.32*	−0.09

Adj R^2

Ret vs. never-ret[d]	.42	.57/.36	.24	.26	.22	.19	.19	.15
Ret vs. poor-perf comparison group	.41	.56/.22	.11	.06	.02	.00	.14	.10

[a] These regressions adjust for differences among the several retainee groups and between retainees and those never retained.

[b] These regressions adjust additionally for CAT scores from the fall of first grade and for demographic factors: race/ethnicity, gender, mother's education, lunch subsidy status (eligible or not), number of siblings, age as of the fall of first grade, and whether or not the child was living in a two-parent household at the start of first grade.

[c] These regressions adjust additionally for differences associated with special education alone, double retention alone, and both combined.

[d] R^2 statistics are from the most inclusive equation in each column.

** signifies differences significant at the 0.01 level; * differences significant at the 0.05 level.

ably well since repeating a grade. Impressions here thus are a bit different from those in the previous section, where repeaters' marks appeared to be holding up better than those of most other children in middle school.

The picture for second and third grade repeaters is more favorable still (Tables 6.3 and 6.4). The dip-and-recovery cycle in the failed grade is vivid for these groups as well. In every instance, second and third grade repeaters begin their failed year far behind, and drop back even farther from fall to spring. This dip usually leaves them a full marking unit behind, but the recovery by the end of their repeated year shows them vastly improved. In the most favorable comparisons, they draw even with promoted children (in three of the four unadjusted comparisons with the poor performers), but even in the least favorable comparisons, they are much closer to other children than during the failed year. Moreover, when adjustments are made for prior test scores and the like, not a single one of the repeated-year disparities between retained and promoted youngsters is significant, and six of the eight favor retainees. In contrast, all the unadjusted comparisons from the failed year showed retainees significantly behind promoted children.

The story is much the same beyond the repeated year through seventh grade. Retainees in most instances trail by about 0.5 to 0.7 marking units. These differentials, all significant, reflect a real shortfall; nevertheless, differences are always less than those before retention and generally are not much greater than in the repeated year. Comparisons with the poor performers all show smaller differences and most (15 of 18) are not significant. Two of the significant differences, though, are from sixth grade, and some of the other middle school comparisons, while not significant, are large enough to catch the eye (those in the 0.24 to 0.26 range). As with first grade repeaters, there thus are indications here of difficulties arising again in middle school.

However, after adjustments are made for testing levels from before retention and for other risk factors, second and third grade retainees' marks lag significantly behind in only 2 of 36 comparisons. Their adjusted marks thus are about on a par with those of promoted children all through the postretention period.

For all three retainee groups, then, marks seem to improve in the postretention period, both absolutely and relative to those of their promoted classmates. In Chapter 5 we saw that retainees' test scores were also helped by repeating a grade, so the picture with respect to retention's *academic* consequences is basically positive for both test scores and marks. This conclusion – that retention helps repeaters learn more and do better in school than they would otherwise – flies in the face of much research and commentary on the issue, although it is in accord with most practitioners' intuitions (e.g., Smith and Shepard 1988; Tomchin and Impara 1992). The next chapter examines how retainees react personally to the experience, but before moving on, we want to step back a bit to consider what has been learned to this point, for it appears that being retained is not entirely, and perhaps not even preponderantly, a negative experience.

Retention and school performance: what have we learned?

We now have looked at test scores and marks from many vantage points to see how retention affects them, and have tried in these chapters to point out some of the difficult issues that have to be addressed in securing credible evidence on the issue. Some of the complications, like retainees' academic difficulties before they are held back, or problems arising out of selective sample loss, are obvious. Others, as whether special education children and multiple repeaters are included or excluded from the evaluation, are more subtle. In a typical cohort of youngsters attending public school in cities like Baltimore, a great many children will experience one or another of these "treatments," yet most studies of retention are unclear as to how multiple retentions or special education have been handled. In our judgment, it makes sense to focus on children who are held back for a year and then get back on track, as in the statistical analyses. However, for those who feel that retention should be judged on its consequences for all repeaters, estimates of test score differences and of mark differences – before adjusting for the patterns of performance of special education children and double repeaters – are reported in the second panel of the regression tables. The estimates are not radically different under the two approaches, especially for report card marks.

Using test scores to compare retainees with others also poses challenges. We have used tests only for which ceiling limits are adequate. Tests that are too easy will limit promoted children's performance more than that of retainees, and so distort comparisons between students who

Table 6.3. *Same-grade regression-adjusted mark differences: second grade retainees vs. never-retained students or the poor-performing comparison group*

	Fall of 2d grade	End of 2d grade	End of 3d grade	End of 4th grade	End of 5th grade	End of 6th grade	End of 7th grade
Reading marks							
With no adjustments[a]							
Ret vs. never-ret	−1.18**	−1.44**/−0.52**	−0.68**	−0.78**	−0.53**	−0.53**	−0.48**
Ret vs. poor-perf comparison group	−0.64**	−0.98**/−0.04	−0.23	−0.26*	−0.01	−0.26	−0.26
With fall CAT and demographic adjustments[b]							
Ret vs. never-ret	−0.56**	−0.83**/0.08	−0.13	−0.20	0.00	−0.33*	−0.16
Ret vs. poor-perf comparison group	−0.43**	−0.76**/0.15	−0.10	−0.16	0.08	−0.18	−0.14
With double-ret and special ed adjustments[c]							
Ret vs. never-ret	−0.48**	−0.79**/0.12	−0.07	−0.15	−0.01	−0.29	−0.19
Ret vs. poor-perf comparison group	−0.37**	−0.73**/0.19	−0.04	−0.11	0.08	−0.14	−0.17
Adj R^2							
Ret vs. never-ret[d]	.48	.54/.43	.38	.39	.32	.23	.18
Ret vs. poor-perf comparison group	.20	.33/.16	.08	.02	.02	.17	.06

Math marks

With no adjustments[a]							
Ret *vs.* never-ret	−0.88**	−1.20**/−0.49**	−0.61**	−0.53**	−0.56**	−0.83**	−0.53**
Ret *vs.* poor-perf comparison group	−0.63**	−0.85**/−0.12	−0.15	−0.12	−0.12	−0.50**	−0.12
With fall CAT and demographic adjustments[b]							
Ret *vs.* never-ret	−0.45**	−0.73**/−0.03	−0.10	0.01	−0.08	−0.52**	−0.12
Ret *vs.* poor-perf comparison group	−0.42**	−0.64**/0.06	0.05	0.03	0.01	−0.35*	0.00
With double-ret and special ed adjustments[c]							
Ret *vs.* never-ret	−0.43**	−0.68**/0.01	−0.05	0.04	−0.07	−0.50**	−0.22
Ret *vs.* poor-perf comparison group	−0.42**	−0.62**/0.08	0.09	0.07	0.02	−0.35*	−0.07
Adj R^2							
Ret *vs.* never-ret[d]	.32	.37/.29	.30	.27	.23	.23	.18
Ret *vs.* poor-perf comparison group	.18	.22/.13	.09	.03	.01	.16	.09

[a]These regressions adjust for differences among the several retainee groups and between retainees and those never retained.

[b]These regressions adjust additionally for CAT scores from the fall of second grade and for demographic factors: race/ethnicity, gender, mother's education, lunch subsidy status (eligible or not), number of siblings, age as of the fall of first grade, and whether or not the child was living in a two–parent household at the start of first grade.

[c]These regressions adjust additionally for differences associated with special education alone, double retention alone, and both combined.

[d]R^2 statistics are from the most inclusive equation in each column.

**signifies differences significant at the 0.01 level; *differences significant at the 0.05 level.

149

Table 6.4. *Same-grade regression-adjusted mark differences: third grade retainees vs. never-retained students or the poor-performing comparison group*

	Fall of 3d grade	End of 3d grade	End of 4th grade	End of 5th grade	End of 6th grade	End of 7th grade
Reading marks						
With no adjustments[a]						
Ret vs. never-ret	-1.19**	-1.45**/-0.80**	-0.71**	-0.76**	-0.67**	-0.44*
Ret vs. poor-perf comparison group	-0.77**	-0.95**/-0.36**	-0.22	-0.24	-0.39*	-0.24
With fall CAT and demographic adjustments[b]						
Ret vs. never-ret	-0.65**	-0.79**/-0.14	-0.05	-0.11	-0.41*	-0.16
Ret vs. poor-perf comparison group	-0.56**	-0.76**/-0.17	-0.05	-0.07	-0.29	-0.14
With double-ret and special ed adjustments[c]						
Ret vs. never-ret	-0.63**	-0.78**/-0.15	-0.02	-0.10	-0.28	-0.13
Ret vs. poor-perf comparison group	-0.54**	-0.74**/-0.17	-0.02	-0.05	-0.17	-0.12
Adj R^2						
Ret vs. never-ret[d]	.44	.46/.41	.40	.37	.23	.21
Ret vs. poor-perf comparison group	.23	.21/.12	.04	.06	.17	.06

Math marks

	(1)	(2)	(3)	(4)	(5)	(6)
With no adjustments[a]						
Ret vs. never-ret	−1.02**	−1.13**/−0.32*	−0.38*	−0.62**	−0.29	−0.39*
Ret vs. poor-perf comparison group	−0.50**	−0.64**/0.13	0.01	−0.18	0.01	−0.01
With fall CAT and demographic adjustments[b]						
Ret vs. never-ret	−0.46**	−0.56**/0.24	0.20	−0.07	0.07	0.05
Ret vs. poor-perf comparison group	−0.34**	−0.50**/0.25	0.13	−0.08	0.12	0.16
With double-ret and special ed adjustments[c]						
Ret vs. never-ret	−0.45**	−0.55**/0.25	0.23	−0.03	0.15	0.00
Ret vs. poor-perf comparison group	−0.34**	−0.48**/0.27	0.17	−0.03	0.21	0.13
Adj R^2						
Ret vs. never-ret[d]	.39	.38/.31	.26	.25	.25	.17
Ret vs. poor-perf comparison group	.19	.10/.06	.02	.01	.14	.09

[a]These regressions adjust for differences among the several retainee groups and between retainees and those never retained.

[b]These regressions adjust additionally for CAT scores from the fall of third grade and for demographic factors: race/ethnicity, gender, mother's education, lunch subsidy status (eligible or not), number of siblings, age as of the fall of first grade, and whether or not the child was living in a two-parent household at the start of first grade.

[c]These regressions adjust additionally for differences associated with special education alone, double retention alone, and both combined.

[d]R^2 statistics are from the most inclusive equation in each column.

**significes differences significant at the 0.01 level; *differences significant at the 0.05 level.

have been retained and those who have not. Research that neglects the ceiling issue could be seriously flawed.

Distorting tendencies can go in both directions, though. For example, younger children typically make greater strides than older ones on tests like the CAT. This phenomenon of decelerating gains has nothing to do with retention, yet it would be easy to misread it as a poor showing for retention. It would have been so misread, for example, if we had compared just retainees' gains after retention with those from before. The declining growth rate also affects same-grade comparisons, because in these, older retainees' performance is compared with that of younger children who have been promoted.

There are thus many pitfalls in trying to understand the consequences of retention. Not all have been addressed as fully as we would like; nevertheless, we have managed to avoid ceiling limits, to take account, at least partially, of potential confounding factors like early test scores and demographic characteristics and, at the end of Chapter 4, to get a sense of how problematic missing test scores and sample attrition might be.

Determining what constitutes success is another challenge. For retention to be deemed effective is it necessary that retainees equal the performance level of all promoted youngsters, or if not, then perhaps that of promoted youngsters "like themselves"? Closing the gap may be too much to expect; perhaps narrowing it should be considered a positive showing. But if repeaters are falling farther and farther behind before being held back, even holding the gap unchanged after retention would be an accomplishment. Or perhaps we should expect retainees to make better progress after being held back than they had made before.

Our point is that there are many reasonable standards, and too often commentary on retention fails to define what a reasonable standard is. If the expectation is that retention will bring repeaters up to the level of promoted youngsters and keep them there for the rest of their school careers, then the evidence in these chapters is unequivocal: retention doesn't work. But such a standard is severe because it requires that retention effectively redress all these children's problems, including those traceable to circumstances outside of school. No one thinks retention is the solution to the school difficulties of poor-performing, disadvantaged children, yet this is the standard implied if retainees are supposed to blend unobtrusively into the student body after getting back on track. This is *not* the standard adopted in evaluations of retention that use the strategy of matched controls. Instead, that approach looks to see whether repeaters are able to keep up with other poor-performing youngsters, none of whom may be doing particularly well academically. The criterion is whether they are doing better than expected, which might be far below what we would want for them. The analyses in these three chapters present evidence relevant to all these criteria for judging retention's effectiveness, including the most stringent. The picture for all, save the one requiring parity, is basically positive.

Although retention didn't appear to help first grade repeaters' test performance much in the long run, they were the only exception to an otherwise favorable pattern. During their repeated year, all three retainee groups drew closer than they had been before to the performance level of promoted children, and second and third grade retainees were able to sustain at least part of these gains for as long as we were able to track their progress – through seventh grade in the same-grade comparisons. In no instance did these youngsters actually reach the performance level of promoted children, but they were often close in comparisons with the poor performers, and especially so in the same-grade format. This format affords a useful perspective on retainees' postretention situation, as it gauges their standing relative to the classmates they join after being held back.

The indications were even more favorable when adjustments were made for testing levels prior to retention, and for other risk factors that complicate repeaters' school adjustment. These adjusted comparisons indicate whether retainees' test scores relative to those of promoted children were better or worse than would be expected based on preexisting conditions. Often retainees' scores were not significantly below those of promoted children in these comparisons, and sometimes they were even ahead; but almost always they were closer than they had been before retention. We are not asking whether retention fixes these children's problems. The logic of controlled comparisons is to see whether retainees after retention do better or worse than children like them who have not been held back. These comparisons provide our best evidence about retention's effects, and from them we conclude that it often helps children.

Test scores and marks afford complementary perspectives on retention, and it turns out that how they are affected by retention is complementary too. From test scores we see that repeaters learn more; from marks we see that this enhanced learning shows up and is rewarded in the classroom. The 2-year dip-and-recovery pattern seen for test scores also comes across vividly in retainees' marks. Their performance goes from bad to worse until they are held back. Upon repeating the grade, they improve dramatically in marks. Their marks do not reach those of promoted children, but their averages are much higher than before. What lies behind this altogether favorable showing is a mystery, however, and we wish we understood it better. Teachers no doubt feel uneasy about holding children back twice, especially in the same grade, so it is possible that their standards for repeaters are more lenient. But this is unlikely to be the entire story. For one thing, many youngsters in the BCPS *are* held back twice, so such reservations are far from binding. More important, the testing data confirm that after retention these youngsters know more of what is expected of them, and so it seems likely that their academic performance actually has improved. After the repeated year all three retainee groups come close to keeping pace. Their actual marks are comparatively low, but their adjusted marks are usually either equal to (in the case of all promoted children) or ahead of (in the case of the poor-performing comparison group) those of other children. The mark trends are favorable throughout, even more so than those of test scores.

Retained youngsters never shine academically, but they get by, whereas before retention they had been losing ground. For retention to be helpful does not require that marginal and below-marginal students be transformed into academic superstars; just to keep up with the others is a singular accomplishment for children who previously knew only failure.

Academic consequences of retention are not the only consideration, of course; there is concern, too, about the possible stigma of retention. Even if retention helped children academically, we would still worry if it assaulted their sense of self. But the evidence just reviewed on retention's positive contributions to repeaters' school performance suggests there may be countervailing forces. In school systems like that of Baltimore, where retention rates are high, retainees probably do not attract much attention; there's anonymity as well as strength in numbers. At the same time, these youngsters are getting positive signals from their teachers in the form of improved marks. If these indications of success register with students, then the emotional repercussions of retention could be mitigated, especially over time, after the failure itself has faded into the background.

The pattern of improved marks after retention has at least two implications for the stigma issue:

1. The dramatic improvement in retainees' postretention marks provides positive feedback, and probably reflects real progress in their schoolwork. Such positive signals should give a boost to children whose feedback to that point had been mostly negative.

2. There is no indication of especially harsh grading later on. If teachers harbored bias against repeaters, we would expect marks to be skewed low, but there is no hint of this in marking patterns. Instead, in the repeated year retained children get marks higher than expected on the basis of their test scores, and in subsequent years often hold their own or almost do so. This pattern suggests that repeaters do not suffer by virtue of their identity as "failures." This is hardly conclusive, however, so in the next chapter we examine how the children themselves are holding up.

7

The stigma of retention: effects on children's sense of self, attitudes toward school, and achievement orientations

[handwritten marginalia: "Pushed back 1st grade repeaters larger group"]

This chapter deals with the possible stigmatizing effects of retention. It explores children's reactions to retention through interview data secured directly from them.

[handwritten marginalia: "Neg affects"]

It is important to determine whether practices intended to help children are harmful instead. One such apprehension about retention – that it sets children back academically – has turned out to be mainly unfounded. Rather than setting them back, repeating a grade gives most children's performance a boost (Chapters 4, 5, and 6). Another apprehension is that children are scarred emotionally by retention, which could happen even though they are better off academically.

Retainees are conspicuous. Their failure is public. Parents, classmates, and teachers all know who repeaters are. Teachers and parents may not be as blunt in communicating their feelings as are classmates, but if parents doubt retainees' abilities, or if teachers resent having retainees in their classes, the children may sense these feelings. Most repeaters are held back in grades 1 through 3, when children's sense of self is just taking form (see, e.g., Stipek 1984; Weisz and Cameron 1985). At this life stage, difficulties in relationships with others may carry special weight.

The BSS children were first interviewed early in the fall of first grade, when most were 6 years old. Individual fall and spring interviews were conducted in each of the ensuing 8 school years except Years 3 and 5.[1] Although hardly any questions were posed in these interviews about retention per se, there is information about these youngsters' attitudes toward school, about themselves, and about how well they thought they would do academically. If retention shakes children's self-confidence or colors their thinking, these consequences should be revealed in their ideas about self and school.

The main focus, again, will be on first grade repeaters. They are by far the largest group, they were the youngest when held back, their problems are the most severe, and their situations are the most complicated and disorderly (i.e., they often wind up in special education or are held back a second time). If any children suffer emotionally because of the retention experience, it would likely be first grade repeaters. Also, for first grade repeaters we can make comparisons like those in previous chapters for test scores and marks: the fail–repeat cycle is covered in interviews from Years 1 and 2; interviews from Years 4 and beyond monitor children's later thinking. Second and third grade retainees will be considered as well, but no interviews were conducted in Year 3, so some critical comparisons are not possible for them (Year 3 is the repeated year for second grade repeaters and the failed year for third grade repeaters).

First grade repeaters' thinking in the failed year, the repeated year, and afterward

Academic self-image

Does retention shake children's self-confidence? Repeaters do have negative ideas about themselves, but it turns out these predate retention. A series of figures (7.1 to 7.5) plots first grade repeaters' averages on several attitude measures against those for all promoted children, and against averages for the comparison group of poor performers. (The exact averages are given in Tables 7.A1 through 7.A5 in the appendix at the end of this chapter, where values for second grade repeaters, third grade repeaters, and the combined group of fourth through seventh grade repeaters are also reported.) The plots begin with Year 1 averages. On each measure, first grade retainees' scores are lowest.

Consider the pattern in Figure 7.1, which presents average scores on a scale that ranks children's academic self-image. The scale was administered in the fall (before the end of the first marking period) and spring (between third and fourth report cards) in Years 1, 2, and 4. Beyond Year 4, the scale was given only in the fall. The youngsters were asked how "good" or "bad" they were at reading, writing, arithmetic, learning new things quickly, and being a good student. Response options ranged from very good (5) to very bad (1). The scale was constructed as the sum of children's responses to these five items, so scores can range from 5 to 25.[2]

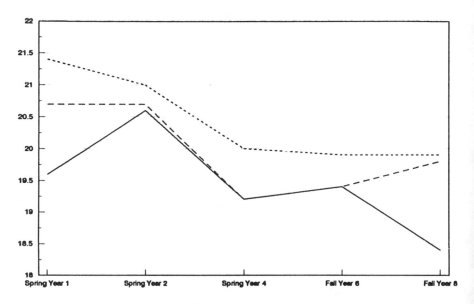

Figure 7.1. Academic self-esteem averages for first grade retainees (——), never-retained pupils (- - -), and the poor-performing comparison group (– –).

Scale averages, presented from the spring of Years 1, 2, and 4, and from the fall of Years 6 and 8,[3] are skewed high overall, with most about 20 points, equivalent to a self-assessment of "good" on each of the five items. Within years (and even between years), most of the differences among groups are not large. In Year 1, the full sample of never-retained children has the highest average, at 21.4, followed by the never-retained poor performers.[4] First grade retainees are lowest. Their 19.6 average is almost 2 points behind the average for never-retained children and more than a full point behind the poor performers' average. A gap of 2 points is about two-thirds of a standard deviation, the largest difference in the table.

We saw before that these early retainees tested poorly, received low report card marks, and had other adjustment problems right from the start of first grade. That their self-assessments from the spring of the first year are so far off the level of other children's suggests that these young-sters are aware of their low standing. But retention is not involved here, because first graders did not receive their notice until year's end. (Second grade repeaters had the next lowest beginning average, and they were not held back until a year later; see Table 7.A1.) It is likely these youngsters realize they are not doing well, and it may well be that classroom dynamics are strongly conditioned by this. These are serious considerations, but they fall outside the scope of the present volume. We are concerned, narrowly, with consequences that follow from the administrative act of having children repeat a grade. Problems that present themselves before then, even if rooted in classroom experience, are the backdrop to retention, not its consequence.

These children's low academic sense of self in first grade – before retention – is a key baseline against which levels of self-assessment after retention can be judged. Most studies of retention do not measure children before retention, and so have no basis on which to establish children's preretention status.

According to this first grade baseline, first grade repeaters' academic self-assessment in Year 2 is higher, not lower. Their academic self-image increases by 1 point from the spring of Year 1 to Year 2, which is the largest increase registered by any group (see Table 7.A1).[5] In contrast, the Year 2 average for the never-retained group is 0.4 points *below* their Year 1 average (the largest drop registered by any group), and that for the comparison group is unchanged. Improvement in repeaters' feelings about themselves in the student role makes no sense if one thinks of retention only as a burden. But these children's marks and test scores improve markedly when they go through the grade for a second time (Chapters 4, 5, nd 6), and this improvement apparently sends a positive signal.

Moreover, favorable signs are not limited only to the self-image. On all the measures examined in this chapter, first grade repeaters' initial averages are lower than those of promoted youngsters (and lower than those of most other repeaters; see the tables in the appendix to this chapter), and in most instances they show the greatest upward movement between Years 1 and 2. This pattern mimics changes in their academic standing.

The remaining columns of Figure 7.1 reveal how retainees fare in Years 4, 6, and 8. First grade repeaters' Year 4 average is well below their average from Year 2. Indeed, their Year 4 average drops below that from first grade, which was initially the lowest of any group. The Year 2 "boost" thus is short-lived, and one might surmise that problems surrounding retention were finally catching up with these children. The experiences of other children over the same interval suggest another interpretation, though, namely that the tapering off seen here is not peculiar to repeaters, but instead reflects a downward trend for all children's self-confidence in the academic area as they get older (for an overview see Eccles and Midgley 1990; Stipek 1984; Wcisz and Cameron 1985; trends with respect to children's self-esteem in the BSS are explored more fully in Pallas et al. 1990). In fact, *every* group's average is lower in Year 4 than in Year 2 (see Table 7.A1, as well as Figure 7.1). Furthermore, the drop seen for first grade repeaters is about midrange, so their decline is not especially pronounced.

Over the longer interval from Year 1 to Year 4, first grade repeaters fall back about 0.4 points, which turns out to be the smallest net decline of any group (second grade repeaters are closest, at 0.5 points). By way of comparison, the never-retained Year 4 average is 1.4 points below their Year 1 average, and the never-retained poor performers are 1.5 points below. First grade repeaters' level of academic self-regard thus holds up better than that of other children.

This positive pattern for repeaters' self-images continues in Year 6 as well, where averages are not much different from Year 4. Year 8, though, reveals a different pattern. First grade repeaters' average is down a full point from Year 6 (18.4 vs. 19.4), while promoted youngsters' averages have either increased some (i.e., the poor performers) or held steady (the full never-retained sample).

This sharp falloff in self-assessments between Years 6 and 8 leaves first grade repeaters 1.2 points behind where they had been in the spring of first grade, their year of failure. Never-retained youngsters are farther back at this point too, though, and some of the other retained groups have dropped off even more than first grade repeaters (third grade retainees, and the combined group of fourth through seventh grade repeaters, for example, are both almost two points back: see Table 7.A1). Nevertheless, first grade retainees' improvement over the intervening years relative to that of promoted youngsters by Year 8 has evaporated.

In reflecting upon these comparisons it is important to keep in mind children's grade placements. In Year 6, first grade repeaters were still in elementary school. Most were in fifth grade; those held back twice were in fourth grade. Their ideas about self at this point were still relatively favorable, at least compared with those of never-retained youngsters, who in Year 6 already were in middle school (which begins in sixth grade). By

Year 8, first grade repeaters were also in middle school (although still one to two grades behind the others), and at that point their self-confidence had slipped badly, relative both to others and to their own thinking from before middle school.[6]

Middle school is 5 years beyond first grade retainees' repeated year, so it seems unreasonable to blame retention for problems that arise so much later. Other research shows that the middle grades transition challenges children generally (Eccles, Lord, and Midgley 1991), and previous chapters have revealed that retainees in particular had difficulty sustaining academic advances from the elementary into the middle school period. The Year 8 drop in academic self-evaluation thus aligns with performance trends reviewed previously and suggests that much of the shoring up that retention accomplishes in elementary school is overwhelmed by the increased pressures and demands children face in middle school. In middle school, too, curricular tracking becomes more formal and rigid, and retainees, as seen in the next chapter, are most often relegated to low-level, remedial courses in the core academic subjects. This is especially true of first grade repeaters. Children may not be harmed by retention academically or socioemotionally, but neither does it equip them to keep up over the long term, especially in middle school.

Expectations for marks in reading and math

Other attitudinal data, beginning with children's expectations for their marks, mirror this general pattern. Expectations for upcoming report card marks are specific and focused reflections of academic self-confidence. Children who *expect* to do better in school generally do (Entwisle and Hayduk 1982).

Figures 7.2 and 7.3 organize mark expectations in reading and math. Children were asked to anticipate the marks they would be getting at year's end in one-on-one interviews conducted each year between the third and fourth marking periods.[7] The coding for expectations is the same as that used with marks. In the elementary grades, marks in academic subjects are excellent, good, satisfactory, and unsatisfactory, coded 4 through 1. The Year 1 averages in Figures 7.2 and 7.3 (and, correspondingly, in Tables 7.A2 and 7.A3) are all above 3, most well above. This corresponds to an average expectation of "good" or better, at a time when marks themselves were averaging midway between satisfactory and good.

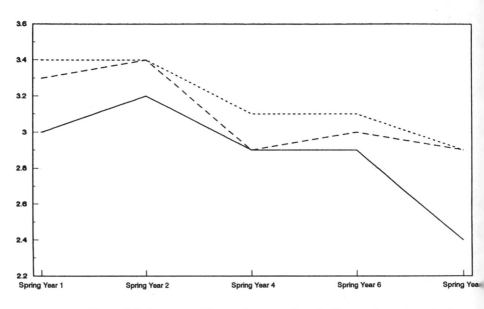

Figure 7.2. Average reading mark expectations for first grade retainees (—), never-retained pupils (- - -), and the poor-performing comparison group (– –).

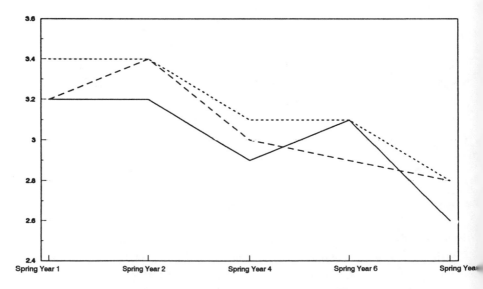

Figure 7.3. Average math mark expectations for first grade retainees (—), never-retained pupils (- - -), and the poor-performing comparison group (– –).

Sample-wide, the average fourth-quarter Year 1 mark was 2.4 in reading, 2.6 in math.

Optimism thus is pervasive throughout the sample, and especially among first grade repeaters, a pattern seen in other studies too (e.g., Entwisle and Hayduk 1978). Even though the first grade retainees have the lowest expected marks in both areas (3.0 in reading and 3.2 in math), their actual performance is lower still; we saw in Chapter 6 that every one of them failed reading, and their marks in math were not much better, with an end-of-year average of 1.3. In comparison, never-retained children averaged 2.7 and 3.0 in reading and math, respectively, so their mark expectations (3.4 in both areas) are a half unit or so too high. The expectation–performance "gap" thus is large for everyone, but more so among repeaters than promoted youngsters.

Whether such elevated expectations are good or bad is not clear (see Alexander, Entwisle, and Bedinger 1994; Entwisle and Hayduk 1978). Of most immediate relevance here, however, is that children's expectations, despite being skewed so high overall, are still colored by classroom experience. First grade repeaters have the lowest expectations, and never-retained children have the highest, paralleling the pattern of their marks. The question, then, is what happens to repeaters' confidence after they have been singled out as failures.

Contrary to what might be predicted, first grade repeaters' performance expectations in Year 2 are not lower. Rather, their expectations either increase (by some 0.2 points in reading) or hold steady (in math). These are not dramatic changes, but the increase in reading exceeds that of both never-retained groups, and though promoted youngsters' math expectations do not fall off during this interval, Table 7.A3 shows modest Year 2 declines among some of the other repeater groups.

Beyond Year 2, expectations trail off for everyone, probably because children become more adept at processing such feedback and begin to realize that their marks do not measure up to their expectations. That performance expectations become increasingly "realistic" over the elementary years has been documented in other studies (for an overview see Stipek 1984). In Years 4 through 8 children's expectations mostly range between satisfactory and good – still high, but considerably closer to their actual marks than in Years 1 and 2. First grade repeaters' expectations drop along with everyone else's, but hold up better than most, at least through Year 6. In both reading and math, for example, their Year 6 averages are the closest of any group to their Year 1 levels. The net decline for them is just 0.1 units (2.9 vs. 3.0) in reading and 0.1 units (3.1 vs. 3.2) in math. For all never-retained children and the poor-performing comparison group youngsters, the corresponding declines are 0.3 units in both areas.[8] None of these differences is large, but they nevertheless indicate that first grade repeaters' expectations are maintained at least as well as everyone else's. This pattern is hard to reconcile with a view of the retention experience as a hovering dark cloud.

Just as with the measure of academic self-regard, however, the Year 8 picture looks quite different. First grade repeaters' expectations drop sharply between Years 6 and 8, by about half a marking unit in both areas, the largest declines registered in this interval, while expectations for never-retained children dip only from 0.1 to 0.3 points. As a result, first grade repeaters' and promoted youngsters' expectations are both about 0.6 marking units behind their respective Year 1 levels, so whatever "advantage" repeaters might have had through Year 6 evaporates in middle school. Again, then, middle school, not the circumstance of re-tention, stands out as the challenge children face that leads to downward trends.

Satisfaction with school

Satisfaction with school is measured by two items, combined in Figure 7.4 into a single scale. Both items come from spring interviews. One item asked whether children found school work "dull" (coded 1) or "interest-ing" (coded 2). The other asked whether they "like school a lot" (coded 3), "think it's just OK" (coded 2) or "don't like it much at all" (coded 1). The measure used in Figure 7.4 is the sum of scores on these two items, so values can range from 2 to 5, with higher values reflecting more favorable sentiment.

All the Year 1 averages are in the 4 range, but first grade repeaters, at 4.1, again start out lowest. Their average is 0.1 units below that of the poor performers and 0.2 units below the full sample of never-retained children. Sample-wide, the standard deviation for this two–item scale is 0.9 units, so the spread in averages across groups is small, and smaller than for the other measures already reviewed.

In Year 2, first grade repeaters' school satisfaction average is just a bit higher (by 0.1 units) than it had been in Year 1, but so too are most of the

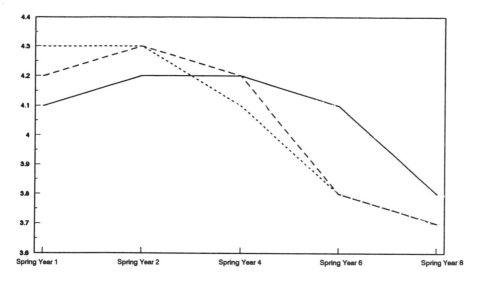

Figure 7.4. School satisfaction averages for first grade retainees (—), never-retained pupils (- - -), and the poor-performing comparison group (– –).

other averages. In Years 4 and 6 just about everyone's liking of school drops, but the decline is smaller among first grade repeaters than others. As a result, in the Year 6 comparisons their average is the *highest*. While the actual changes themselves are modest, the reversal itself is striking; during the later years of elementary school, first grade repeaters wind up liking school more than everyone else, and in comparisons against promoted children the difference increases through Years 4 and 6, even persisting in Year 8.

By Year 8, all the groups have averages below 4, with first grade repeaters falling back 0.3 units between Years 6 and 8. This is the largest decline for them, and again, it overlaps the elementary-to-middle-school transition. But the other groups' liking for school continues to slip too, and by virtue of their earlier, steeper falloff, both promoted groups have Year 8 averages a little lower than do the first grade retainees. In middle school, then, liking of school is about the same regardless of children's retention status.

This is not an especially cheery assessment, as it reflects a pervasive falloff in positive sentiment toward school. This trend is seen in other studies (Blumenfeld, Pintrich, Meece, and Wessels 1982; Epstein and McPartland 1976), so again, it appears that no negative consequences can be attributed to retention as such.

Sense of control

The final measure considered in this chapter is different from the others. Rather than tapping ideas related to school, it ranks children according to their "sense of control" – whether they tend to attribute things that happen to them mainly to outside forces (an external orientation) or to their own actions (an internal one). Referred to as "locus of control" (Rotter 1966), such orientations reflect the child's sense of personal efficacy. Internally oriented persons tend to be more self-directed and proactive in response to challenges, while externally oriented individuals are given more to fatalism, passivity, and resignation, especially in the face of adversity. With respect to schooling and academic considerations, there is some evidence that internally oriented youngsters have an edge over "externals" (see, for example, Coleman et al. 1966; Stipek and Weisz 1981).

The measure used in Figure 7.5 came from parts of two scales designed for use with young children, the Stanford Preschool Internal–External Scale (Mischel, Zeiss, and Zeiss 1974) and the Crandall Intellectual Achievement Responsibility Questionnaire (Crandall, Katkovsky, and Crandall 1965). The Stanford scale is designed to rate children in terms of their general internal–external orientation. There are two versions of it, each consisting of 14 items that measure children's understandings about the sources of events: whether events occur because of the children's own action (internal control) or because of external forces (external control). The questions from the scale used in our interviews are all of the same general format:

> When you are happy, are you happy
> (a) because somebody was nice to you,
>   or
> (b) because you did something fun?

Response (b) is the "internal" response. The original scales are balanced between questions that reflect responsibility for good outcomes as well as bad, but of the six used in our interviews, only the three positive items proved adequate psychometrically.

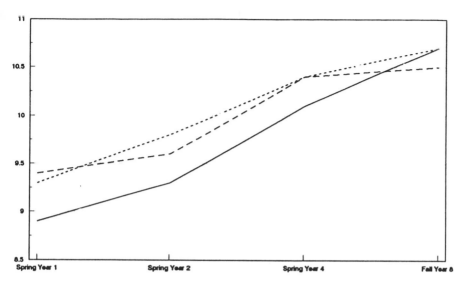

Figure 7.5. Locus-of-control averages for first grade retainees (—), never-retained pupils (- - -), and the poor-performing comparison group (– –).

The Crandall scale rates children in terms of their internal–external orientation in the academic domain specifically. It consists of 34 items, similar in format to the Stanford scale, of which we used three of the positive items also, again because of their superior psychometric properties. Some of the wording was altered in minor ways to make items more intelligible. For example, in the original item "solve" was used rather than "put . . . together."

> If you put a puzzle together quickly, is that
> (a) because it wasn't a very hard puzzle,
>   or
> (b) because you worked on it carefully?

Response (b) is the internal option.

The questions borrowed from the two scales (three items from each) were asked fall and spring in Years 1, 2, and 4, and in the fall of Year 8.[9] Responses to these six items were summed with internal options scored 2 and external ones scored 1. Scale scores thus can range from 6 to 12. Internal reliability coefficients for the scales all are in the vicinity of 0.50, lower than we would prefer, but still serviceable. The averages reported in Figure 7.5 are from spring interviews when available.

As has been true throughout, first grade repeaters start out lowest. Their Year 1 average in Figure 7.5 is 8.9, while those of promoted children are 9.3 and 9.4. This puts first grade repeaters about half a point below never-retained children. Sample-wide, the standard deviation for the locus of control scale is 1.6 points, so first grade repeaters are back about a third of a standard deviation.[10]

Averages in Year 2 are substantially higher than in Year 1, and those of first grade repeaters increase along with everyone else's – by about 0.4 points. Not shown in our displays, though, are some details of first graders' experience that makes their pattern distinctive. Their fall average in the second year, when they were just beginning their repeated grade, was lower, not higher, than it had been the previous spring.[11] Hence, the gain in first grade retainees' feelings of internal control by the end of their repeated year actually represents a turnaround for them, because their sense of control had been going down to that point, by about half a point since the fall of first grade. In contrast, for all the other groups there are only two instances in which averages drop during this interval, and both declines are of just 0.1 point.

The experience of failure thus apparently did compromise children's self-confidence temporarily, but it seems that their academic success during the repeated year helped turn things around. From that point forward their scores track modestly upward, parallel to those of most other groups. In fact, in Year 8, first grade repeaters' average of 10.7 is 0.2 points above the comparison group of poor performers, and is tied with the full never-retained sample. Their Year 8 average is not the highest, but neither is it the lowest.

These favorable indications involving locus of control are consistent with the trends for general academic self-regard, specific performance expectations in reading and math, and general liking of school. Improvement after retention was evident for each measure, and on most this gain either continued, or was at least maintained, into Year 8. The Year 8 comparisons, which signal slippage for several outcomes, likely reflect pressures in middle school and the difficulties all marginal students have in managing those pressures. In the concluding chapter we comment on the need to help children – all children – weather this passage. It seems unlikely, however, that problems originating in the experience of retention would be delayed until Year 8. Rather, retention seems to confer benefits in the attitudinal area generally, just as in the academic area.[12]

Retention and children's thinking: regression-adjusted comparisons

These comparisons present a consistent picture, but simple descriptive trends can be misleading. The concern, as before, is that retained and promoted youngsters can differ a priori in many ways. This phenomenon is evident in the Year 1 comparisons in Figures 7.1 to 7.5, where first grade repeaters *before being held back* ranked at the bottom on all five sense-of-self and attitudinal measures.

Beyond Year 1, preexisting differences, including those grounded in children's early academic difficulties, are confounded with the retention experience; simply comparing averages as we have been doing makes no allowance for this. Just as was done earlier with test scores and marks, initial differences between repeaters and nonrepeaters need to be allowed for. Still, it is unlikely the adjustments will be as consequential here as they were previously. For one thing, repeaters (at least those held back in first grade, who thus far have been our main concern) do not have especially negative or self-critical attitudes after retention, even in the simple trend comparisons. Earlier there were large differences in test scores and marks, and these clearly overstated the negative consequences of retention. Here there are no negative indications to begin with, so instead of guarding against exaggerating retention's effects, the checks here are more to make sure there is an accurate reading of children's initial status.

Also, attitudes are not as stable as test scores or marks over time, nor are they as highly confounded with other potential risk factors involving children's family, personal background, and early skill differences. For example, sample-wide Year 8 CAT-R performance is correlated .19 with race/ethnicity, .40 with mother's education, .39 with the family-income indicator, .38 with CAT-R performance from the spring of first grade, and .50 with CAT-R performance from the fall of first grade. The latter two reflect stability or continuity in performance trends over the entire interval of our study. In comparison, with one exception, correlations for the Year 8 measure of academic self-esteem are much smaller: .19 for race/ethnicity; .10 for mother's education; .07 for the family income indicator; .11 for fall CAT-R; .19 for spring CAT-R; and .12 for the counterpart Year 1 measure.

Almost all the self-esteem correlations are statistically significant, so children's ideas about self indeed are socially patterned, reflect their abilities, and are somewhat stable over time.[13] Still, none of these correlations is especially large, and except for the one involving race/ethnicity, all are much smaller than the corresponding associations involving CAT performance. Our measures of attitudes and personality overlap with ascriptive characteristics much less than performance outcomes do.

A complication in making statistical adjustments for second and third grade repeaters is that there were no pupil interviews in Year 3. This means that for third grade repeaters there is no baseline measure from the failed year with which to compare postretention attitudes, and that for second grade retainees the repeated-year part of the fail–repeat cycle cannot be examined. Even lacking Year 3 data, however, we still have preretention attitude assessments for both second and third grade repeaters (these could be from either Year 1 or 2) and postretention data for them through Year 8.

The statistical analyses use baseline data from the year of retention whenever possible. The moving baseline adjusts for conditions up to the time of retention. As before, when CAT scores and marks were the outcomes, we adjust for demographic factors such as family SES level, gender, and so on, as well as for CAT performance from the fall of the failed year. Preretention attitudes are used as further controls – the first grade measure for first grade repeaters and the second grade measure for second grade repeaters. To this point, the third-year gap causes no particular difficulties. When evaluating outcomes for third grade repeaters, however, Year 3 attitude measures are not available, so measures from Year 2 are used because they are the closest to the event of retention.

Apart from the "Time 1" controls, the statistical procedures in this chapter parallel those used in Chapters 5 and 6. Multiple-regression analysis adjusts for several blocks of control variables including the baseline counterpart of the outcome measure. The statistics reported are metric regression coefficients that estimate average differences between retained and promoted youngsters, other things being equal. Again, comparisons are against all never-retained children and the group of poor pcrformcrs, so six separate analyses are reported. First, second, and third grade repeaters are each evaluated against all promoted youngsters, and against the comparison group of poor-performing promoted children.[14]

Academic self-esteem

Table 7.1 covers academic self-esteem, with separate columns for outcomes in Years 1, 2, 4, 6, and 8. Within years, differences are reported for first, second, and third grade repeaters separately.[15]

The first estimates are from regression equations that yield average-scale score differences between the retention groups, identical to properly weighted differences that could be derived from Table 7.A1. The question here is what happens when these large initial differences are adjusted for children's demographic characteristics and entry-level CAT performance (the second pair of entries), and for the compounding of children's later problems (i.e., double retention and / or special education placement). The adjustments for demographic factors and early test scores shrink the self-esteem gap from about a third to almost a half (Table 7.1). The comparison with poor performers drops below significance, implying that the difference between first grade retainees' and poor performers' self-attitudes *in first grade* can be attributed to initial test score differences and the social mix of children in the two groups. Taking these factors into account, though, does not abolish the gap separating first grade retainees from all promoted youngsters. This margin holds up even when adjustments are made for inclusion of children who eventually will be held back twice or assigned to special education.[16]

Year 2 is when we would expect to see retention's consequences for first grade repeaters, but in the second year none of the comparisons between retained and promoted children is significant. Thus first grade retainees' academic self-image when they are repeating first grade is like that of other children their age (i.e., their original classmates' responses from the same interview cycle).[17] This finding is at odds with the widely held notion that repeaters' sense of self is compromised by the stigma of retention, but is consistent with other recent research (e.g., Pierson and Connell 1992; Reynolds 1992). Possibly their resilience stems from the fact that their teachers were not grading them harshly (for a more thorough discussion of this see Chapter 6).

Prior research on retention, in fact, often reports equivalence for

Table 7.1. Regression-adjusted self-esteem differences: first, second, and third grade retainees vs. never-retained students or the poor-performing comparison group

| | Spring Year 1 | Spring Year 2 | | Spring Year 4 | | | Fall Year 6 | | | Fall Year 8 | | |
	First grade ret	First grade ret	Second grade ret	First grade ret	Second grade ret	Third grade ret	First grade ret	Second grade ret	Third grade ret	First grade ret	Second grade ret	Third grade ret
With no adjustments[b]												
Ret vs. never-ret	-1.79**	-0.45	-0.79*	-0.71*	-0.51	-0.55	-0.42	-0.84	-0.48	-1.42**	-0.91	-0.94
Ret vs. poor-perf comparison group	-1.11**	-0.13	-0.46	-0.01	0.21	0.15	0.10	-0.24	0.06	-1.14**	-0.63	-0.69
With fall CAT and demographic adjustments[c]												
Ret vs. never-ret	-1.14**	-0.06	0.12	-0.32	0.22	0.40	-0.24	-0.41	0.02	-1.31**	-0.65	-0.30
Ret vs. poor-perf comparison group	-0.57	0.19	0.41	0.42	1.09*	1.07*	0.43	0.55	0.73	-0.85	-0.14	0.03
With baseline measure adjustments[d]												
Ret vs. never-ret	—	0.20	—	-0.18	0.19	0.34	-0.08	-0.43	-0.04	-1.24**	-0.67	-0.33
Ret vs. poor-perf comparison group	—	0.32	—	0.49	0.99*	0.98	0.52	0.47	0.65	-0.81	-0.20	-0.02

With double-ret and special ed adjustments[e]												
Ret vs. never-ret	-1.22**	0.42	0.24	-0.26	0.06	0.27	-0.36	-0.66	-0.23	-1.59**	-0.97	-0.50
Ret vs. poor-perf comparison group	-0.47	0.49	0.52	0.60	1.01*	0.97	0.51	0.45	0.58	-0.90	-0.29	-0.08
Adj R^2												
Ret vs. never-ret[f]	.10	.16	.13	.07	.14	.15	.12	.16	.15	.14	.17	.18
Ret vs. poor-perf comparison group	.09	.16	.15	.08	.17	.18	.12	.18	.17	.13	.16	.17

[a] In Year 1 only first grade contrasts are reported; in Year 2 separate analyses are performed for first and second grade repeaters, using the moving baseline controls appropriate for each; from Year 4 through Year 8, separate analyses are performed for first, second, and third grade repeaters, using the moving baseline controls appropriate for each.

[b] These regressions adjust for differences among the several retainee groups and between retainees and those never retained.

[c] These regressions adjust additionally for CAT scores from the fall of the appropriate baseline year and for demographic factors: race/ethnicity, gender, mother's education, lunch subsidy status (eligible or not), number of siblings, age as of the fall of first grade, and whether the child was living in a two-parent household at the start of first grade.

[d] These regressions adjust additionally for self-esteem scores from the appropriate baseline year. For first and second grade repeaters, in the baseline year these are the outcome measures, and are not used as controls (indicated by a dash in table body).

[e] These regressions adjust additionally for differences associated with special education alone, double retention alone, and both combined.

[f] R^2 statistics are for the most inclusive equation in each column.

** Identifies differences significant at the .01 level; * differences significant at the .05 level.

repeaters and promoted children on both academic and attitudinal outcomes (see the literature reviews cited in Chapter 1). This equivalence usually is interpreted as showing that retention doesn't help, but for retainees' attitudes to be no different from those of promoted children is a positive finding: either concerns about stigmatizing effects are exaggerated, or negative effects are offset by other experiences that help sustain children's sense of self. As a result, the net effect is neutral.

In Chapter 1 we pointed out that examining scores only after retention can give a misleading or incomplete picture. The pre- and postretention comparisons in Table 7.1 illustrate this concern. By looking back at retainees' scores before they were held back, we see that the Year 2 pattern of "no difference" actually reflects substantial improvement over Year 1, when repeaters lagged well behind promoted children. These over-time comparisons afford an important perspective because, far from being neutral, retention actually *increases* retainees' self-regard and brings their scores close to the level of other children.

Most differences in Years 4 and 6 also fall short of significance, especially once statistical adjustments are made. In Year 8, though, first grade repeaters again lag behind, and the differences involving all promoted children are not explained by preretention factors. The adjusted difference against the poor performers is also large, but because sample sizes in Year 8 are small, a difference of this magnitude (almost a full point) is not statistically significant. Still, it is suggestive.

The adjusted comparisons in Table 7.1, our best evidence on the existence of stigma, reinforce impressions grounded in the descriptive trends: first grade repeaters' academic sense of self is depressed in first grade, reflecting the difficulties they are having before retention. During the repeated year, their self-confidence improves to bring their attitudes about self to roughly the same level as those of other children. This picture holds through the remaining elementary years. Scores drop off again in Year 8, however, which is the first middle school assessment of repeaters' self-attitudes. Until middle school, retention seems to shore up repeaters' sense of self.

The second panel gives comparisons for second grade repeaters; the third panel gives them for third grade repeaters. These comparisons show few significant differences even before making adjustments, and the adjusted comparisons most often favor repeaters when differences are large enough to be statistically reliable (see entries in the spring Year 4 panel, which show positive differences for comparisons against the promoted poor performers). However, in Year 8 retainees also fall short, a trend again suggesting some middle school slippage.

Other outcomes

This same basic story is retold for the other attitudinal measures: reading and math mark expectations in Tables 7.2 and 7.3; school satisfaction in Table 7.4; and locus of control in Table 7.5. In all these analyses, most of the significant differences involve first grade repeaters, and even these are not especially numerous. Significant differences almost always exist in Year 1, before retention, and then do not appear again until Year 8, when the repeaters are in middle school.[18]

First grade retainees lag behind promoted children on a variety of attitudinal assessments in first grade: reading expectations, math expectations, and locus of control (differences involving the school satisfaction measure are insignificant throughout). Only for locus of control, though, is the comparison with the poor-performing group significant; the other noteworthy differences are in comparisons with all promoted children. This evidence is troubling, not so much as a commentary on retention, but because it reveals how demographic factors and entering testing levels, over which children have no control, can compromise children's self-confidence.

For mark expectations, differences involving first grade repeaters again are significant in Year 8, and generally remain so even after statistical adjustments are made, including that for first grade mark expectations. Hence, the middle school setback is most apparent in the attitude measures that relate to academics (i.e., self-esteem and mark expectations), and among first grade repeaters in particular.

For second and third grade repeaters, there are few comparisons where their scores are significantly more negative than those of promoted youngsters. Indeed, significant positive differences are more numerous, and these begin to appear when the preretention statistical adjustments are phased in. All in all, these results give little reason to think retention imposes an emotional burden on second and third grade repeaters.

As mentioned, our data are most robust for assessing first grade repeaters. For them only, data are available from both the failed year and the repeated year, as well as on into the later grades. This coverage is impor-

Table 7.2. *Regression-adjusted reading expectation differences: first, second, and third grade retainees vs. never-retained students or the poor-performing comparison group*

	Spring Year 1[a]	Spring Year 2		Spring Year 4			Spring Year 6			Spring Year 8		
	First grade ret	First grade ret	Second grade ret	First grade ret	Second grade ret	Third grade ret	First grade ret	Second grade ret	Third grade ret	First grade ret	Second grade ret	Third grade ret
With no adjustments[b]												
Ret vs. never-ret	-0.36**	-0.16	-0.28**	-0.14	-0.21	-0.20	-0.20	-0.22	-0.36*	-0.48**	-0.33*	-0.39*
Ret vs. poor-perf comparison group	-0.22	-0.10	-0.22	0.04	-0.02	-0.02	-0.09	-0.12	-0.24	-0.41**	-0.24	-0.30
With fall CAT and demographic adjustments[c]												
Ret vs. never-ret	-0.23*	-0.09	-0.11	0.04	0.15	0.19	-0.17	-0.15	-0.13	-0.33**	-0.13	-0.18
Ret vs. poor-perf comparison group	-0.13	-0.04	-0.10	0.15	0.23	0.27	-0.04	-0.01	-0.03	-0.28*	-0.08	-0.11
With baseline measure adjustments[d]												
Ret vs. never-ret	—	-0.06	—	0.06	0.17	0.20	-0.15	-0.14	-0.13	-0.33**	-0.12	-0.17
Ret vs. poor-perf comparison group	—	-0.03	—	0.17	0.24	0.27	-0.03	0.00	-0.03	-0.28*	-0.07	-0.11

With double-ret and special ed adjustments[e]

Ret vs. never-ret	−0.18	0.05	−0.04	0.09	0.16	0.21	−0.11	−0.12	−0.11	−0.49**	−0.23	−0.20
Ret vs. poor-perf comparison group	−0.08	0.05	−0.05	0.21	0.24	0.28	0.04	0.03	−0.01	−0.36**	−0.12	−0.10
Adj R²												
Ret vs. never-ret[f]	.07	.10	.10	.08	.13	.13	.06	.06	.09	.18	.20	.20
Ret vs. poor-perf comparison group	.07	.11	.10	.09	.15	.15	.05	.06	.11	.17	.19	.19

[a] In Year 1 only first grade contrasts are reported; in Year 2 separate analyses are performed for first and second grade repeaters, using the moving baseline controls appropriate for each; from Year 4 through Year 8, separate analyses are performed for first, second, and third grade repeaters, using the moving baseline controls appropriate for each.

[b] These regressions adjust for differences among the several retainee groups and between retainees and those never retained.

[c] These regressions adjust additionally for CAT scores from the fall of the appropriate baseline year and for demographic factors: race/ethnicity, gender, mother's education, lunch subsidy status (eligible or not), number of siblings, age as of the fall of first grade, and whether the child was living in a two–parent household at the start of first grade.

[d] These regressions adjust additionally for mark expectations from the appropriate baseline year.

[e] These regressions adjust additionally for differences associated with special education alone, double retention alone, and both combined.

[f] R^2 statistics are for the most inclusive equation in each column.

** Identifies differences significant at the .01 level; * differences significant at the .05 level.

Table 7.3. *Regression-adjusted math mark expectation differences: first, second, and third grade retainees vs. never-retained students or the poor-performing comparison group*

	Spring Year 1[a]	Spring Year 2		Spring Year 4			Spring Year 6			Spring Year 8		
	First grade ret	First grade ret	Second grade ret	First grade ret	Second grade ret	Third grade ret	First grade ret	Second grade ret	Third grade ret	First grade ret	Second grade ret	Third grade ret
With no adjustments[b]												
Ret vs. never-ret	-0.27**	-0.19*	-0.02	-0.24*	-0.17	0.09	0.00	-0.16	-0.04	-0.25*	-0.16	-0.29
Ret vs. poor-perf comparison group	-0.08	-0.24*	-0.07	-0.11	-0.04	0.19	0.15	0.00	0.11	-0.17	-0.08	-0.21
With fall CAT and demographic adjustments[c]												
Ret vs. never-ret	-0.15	-0.17	0.18	0.05	0.18	0.45**	0.11	-0.06	0.20	-0.16	-0.07	-0.11
Ret vs. poor-perf comparison group	0.00	-0.22	0.08	0.07	0.25	0.40*	0.25	0.16	0.30	-0.07	0.05	-0.03
With baseline measure adjustments[d]												
Ret vs. never-ret	—	-0.14	—	0.06	0.15	0.46**	0.12	-0.09	0.21	-0.16	-0.10	-0.09
Ret vs. poor-perf comparison group	—	-0.22	—	0.07	0.24	0.43*	0.25	0.14	0.33*	-0.07	0.04	0.00

With double-ret and special ed adjustments[e]

Ret vs. never-ret	-0.11	-0.14	0.18	-0.02	0.10	0.43*	0.11	-0.09	0.23	-0.33*	-0.21	-0.14
Ret vs. poor-perf comparison group	0.06	-0.23	0.07	0.02	0.22	0.41*	0.27	0.17	0.35*	-0.15	0.00	-0.01
Adj R²												
Ret vs. never-ret[f]	.04	.05	.06	.09	.12	.12	.07	.08	.10	.09	.11	.12
Ret vs. poor-perf comparison group	.05	.06	.06	.10	.14	.14	.09	.11	.15	.09	.10	.12

[a] In Year 1 only first grade contrasts are reported; in Year 2 separate analyses are performed for first and second grade repeaters, using the moving baseline controls appropriate for each; from Year 4 through Year 8, separate analyses are performed for first, second, and third grade repeaters, using the moving baseline controls appropriate for each.

[b] These regressions adjust for differences among the several retainee groups and between retainees and those never retained.

[c] These regressions adjust additionally for CAT scores from the fall of the appropriate baseline year and for demographic factors: race/ethnicity, gender, mother's education, lunch subsidy status (eligible or not), number of siblings, age as of the fall of first grade, and whether the child was living in a two-parent household at the start of first grade.

[d] These regressions adjust additionally for mark expectations from the appropriate baseline year. For first and second grade repeaters, in the baseline year these are the outcome measures, so they are not used as controls (indicated by a dash in the table body).

[e] These regressions adjust additionally for differences associated with special education alone, double retention alone, and both combined.

[f] R^2 statistics are for the most inclusive equation in each column.

**Identifies differences significant at the .01 level; *differences significant at the .05 level.

Table 7.4. *Regression-adjusted school satisfaction differences: first, second, and third grade retainees vs. never-retained students or the poor-performing comparison group*

	Spring Year 1[a]	Spring Year 2		Spring Year 4			Spring Year 6			Spring Year 8		
	First grade ret	First grade ret	Second grade ret	First grade ret	Second grade ret	Third grade ret	First grade ret	Second grade ret	Third grade ret	First grade ret	Second grade ret	Third grade ret
With no adjustments[b]												
Ret vs. never-ret	−0.16	−0.12	−0.09	0.06	0.19	−0.01	0.23	0.15	−0.05	0.12	0.14	0.02
Ret vs. poor-perf comparison group	−0.07	−0.08	−0.05	−0.01	0.11	−0.08	0.26	0.19	0.00	0.06	0.08	−0.04
With fall CAT and demographic adjustments[c]												
Ret vs. never-ret	−0.09	−0.08	0.02	0.00	0.12	−0.10	0.26	0.11	−0.06	0.04	0.01	0.00
Ret vs. poor-perf comparison group	−0.03	−0.07	0.02	−0.03	0.10	−0.14	0.29	0.22	0.03	0.03	0.01	−0.01
With baseline measure adjustments[d]												
Ret vs. never-ret	—	−0.06	—	0.01	0.11	−0.15	0.28*	0.11	−0.09	0.04	0.01	0.00
Ret vs. poor-perf comparison group	—	−0.06	—	−0.02	0.09	−0.18	0.30*	0.22	0.00	0.03	0.01	−0.02

With double-ret and special ed adjustments[e]

Ret vs. never-ret	-0.12	-0.07	0.00	0.04	0.13	-0.12	0.21	0.07	-0.10	-0.02	-0.02	-0.01
Ret vs. poor-perf comparison group	-0.03	-0.07	0.01	-0.01	0.10	-0.17	0.25	0.20	0.00	0.00	-0.01	-0.03
Adj R^2												
Ret vs. never-ret[f]	.03	.10	.04	.08	.10	.10	.06	.05	.05	.05	.05	.05
Ret vs. poor-perf comparison group	.03	.10	.04	.08	.11	.11	.07	.06	.06	.05	.05	.05

[a] In Year 1 only first grade contrasts are reported; in Year 2 separate analyses are performed for first and second grade repeaters, using the moving baseline controls appropriate for each; from Year 4 through Year 8, separate analyses are performed for first, second, and third grade repeaters, using the moving baseline controls appropriate for each.

[b] These regressions adjust for differences among the several retainee groups and between retainees and those never retained.

[c] These regressions adjust additionally for CAT scores from the fall of the appropriate baseline year and for demographic factors: race/ethnicity, gender, mother's education, lunch subsidy status (eligible or not), number of siblings, age as of the fall of first grade, and whether the child was living in a two-parent household at the start of first grade.

[d] These regressions adjust additionally for satisfaction scores from the appropriate baseline year. For first and second grade repeaters, in the baseline year these are the outcome measures, so they are not used as controls (indicated by a dash in the table body).

[e] These regressions adjust additionally for differences associated with special education alone, double retention alone, and both combined.

[f] R^2 statistics are for the most inclusive equation in each column.

*Identifies differences significant at the .05 level.

181

Table 7.5. *Regression-adjusted locus-of-control differences: first, second, and third grade retainees vs. never-retained students or the poor-performing comparison group*

	Spring Year 1[a]	Spring Year 2		Spring Year 4			Fall Year 8		
	First grade ret	First grade ret	Second grade ret	First grade ret	Second grade ret	Third grade ret	First grade ret	Second grade ret	Third grade ret
With no adjustments[b]									
Ret vs. never-ret	−0.45*	−0.45*	−0.33	−0.29	−0.28	−0.23	−0.02	0.29	0.29
Ret vs. poor-perf comparison group	−0.53*	−0.34	−0.21	−0.28	−0.27	−0.23	0.11	0.40	0.41
With full CAT and demographic adjustments[c]									
Ret vs. never-ret	−0.34	−0.23	−0.17	−0.18	−0.30	−0.28	0.03	0.21	0.26
Ret vs. poor-perf comparison group	−0.46	−0.25	−0.22	−0.24	−0.34	−0.31	0.08	0.28	0.32
With baseline measure adjustments[d]									
Ret vs. never-ret	—	−0.09	—	−0.10	−0.25	−0.30	0.01	0.22	0.26
Ret vs. poor-perf comparison group	—	−0.06	—	−0.13	−0.28	−0.38	0.06	0.29	0.31

With double-ret and special ed adjustments[e]

Ret vs. never-ret	-0.38	-0.05	-0.15	0.11	-0.12	-0.25	-0.03	0.19	0.23
Ret vs. poor–perf comparison group	-0.50	-0.04	-0.22	-0.02	-0.20	-0.35	0.03	0.27	0.30

Adj R^2

Ret vs. never-ret[f]	.04	.21	.05	.13	.18	.18	.05	.04	.05
Ret vs. poor–perf comparison group	.04	.22	.07	.13	.18	.19	.06	.06	.06

[a] In Year 1 only first grade contrasts are reported; in Year 2 separate analyses are performed for first and second grade repeaters, using the moving baseline controls appropriate for each; in Years 4 and 8, separate analyses are performed for first, second, and third grade repeaters, using the moving baseline controls appropriate for each.

[b] These regressions adjust for differences among the several retainee groups and between retainees and those never retained.

[c] These regressions adjust additionally for CAT scores from the fall of the appropriate baseline year and for demographic factors: race/ethnicity, gender, mother's education, lunch subsidy status (eligible or not), number of siblings, age as of the fall of first grade, and whether the child was living in a two-parent household at the start of first grade.

[d] These regressions adjust additionally for locus-of-control scores from the appropriate baseline year. For first and second grade repeaters, in the baseline year these are the outcome measures, so they are not used as controls (indicated by a dash in the table body).

[e] These regressions adjust additionally for differences associated with special education alone, double retention alone, and both combined.

[f] R^2 statistics are for the most inclusive equation in each column.

*Identifies differences significant at the .05 level.

tant, because these children's low standing in their failed year, before retention, highlights their improvement in the repeated year.

We earlier argued that first grade repeaters, being the youngest and farthest behind of all the retainee groups, would be most likely to suffer emotionally from the experience. The results seem to bear us out: the only negative indications in these many comparisons involved first graders. These negative signs, however, did not appear until Year 8, and seem to be better explained by the middle school context than by the trauma of retention so far back in the past.

Does retention stigmatize children and harm them emotionally? There is little indication of such in this chapter. Instead, children's attitudes about themselves and about academics improve after retention, especially while repeating the failed grade. This pattern of improvement in children's affective profile dovetails with the signs of improvement from repeating a year seen for marks and test scores in Chapters 4, 5, and 6. It also dovetails with findings in other reports. In a prospective study of Philadelphia first graders with comparison and nonpromoted groups like those in the present study, Finlayson (1977) found that youngsters' self-concepts were higher in their repeated year, and the averages across groups were indistinguishable. Reynolds's study (1992) of inner-city Chicago children also finds positive effects on attitudes, while Pierson and Connell (1992), studying children from upstate New York, found no differences in comparisons between retained and matched-control students involving general self-worth or perceived cognitive competence.[19] Such findings are consistent with reference-group ideas (Goethals 1987; Richer 1976) that images of the self form in relation to comparisons with nearby individuals. Retained pupils, for a year at least, have an advantage over their classmates in terms of chronological age and previous experience with the curriculum, and their performance improves, both relatively and absolutely. All this, it appears, produces positive "spillover" in the attitudinal/affective domain.

Appendix

This appendix provides the tables that correspond to Figures 7.1 to 7.5. The figures display trends just for first grade repeaters and never-retained youngsters. The tables include these groups, as well as second grade, third grade, and fourth through seventh grade repeaters.

Table 7.A1. *Academic self-esteem averages for retained groups, never-retained pupils, and the poor-performing comparison group*

	Spring Year 1	Spring Year 2	Spring Year 4	Fall Year 6	Fall Year 8
Year of retention					
1st grade	19.6	20.6	19.2	19.4	18.4
	(111)	(89)	(101)	(92)	(80)
2d grade	19.9	20.2	19.4	19.1	19.0
	(63)	(53)	(58)	(58)	(54)
3d grade	20.8	20.5	19.4	19.4	18.9
	(41)	(41)	(37)	(36)	(33)
4th–7th grade	20.8	20.9	18.6	18.8	18.9
	(69)	(61)	(67)	(66)	(61)
Never-retained pupils					
All never-retained	21.4	21.0	20.0	19.9	19.9
	(421)	(358)	(295)	(231)	(215)
Poor-performing	20.7	20.7	19.2	19.4	19.8
comparison group	(102)	(80)	(68)	(55)	(51)

Table 7.A2. *Average reading mark expectations for retained groups, never-retained pupils, and the poor-performing comparison group*

	Spring Year 1	Spring Year 2	Spring Year 4	Spring Year 6	Spring Year 8
Year of retention					
1st grade	3.0	3.2	2.9	2.9	2.4
	(114)	(89)	(96)	(89)	(69)
2d grade	3.3	3.1	2.9	2.9	2.6
	(63)	(54)	(54)	(52)	(44)
3d grade	3.3	3.2	2.9	2.7	2.5
	(43)	(42)	(33)	(35)	(31)
4th–7th grade	3.3	3.4	2.8	2.8	2.5
	(70)	(61)	(65)	(59)	(49)
Never-retained pupils					
All never-retained	3.4	3.4	3.1	3.1	2.9
	(428)	(361)	(287)	(228)	(205)
Poor-performing	3.3	3.4	2.9	3.0	2.9
comparison group	(103)	(80)	(67)	(52)	(50)

Table 7.A3. *Average math mark expectations for retained groups, never-retained pupils, and the poor-performing comparison group*

	Spring Year 1	Spring Year 2	Spring Year 4	Spring Year 6	Spring Year 8
Year of retention					
1st grade	3.2	3.2	2.9	3.1	2.6
	(114)	(89)	(96)	(89)	(68)
2d grade	3.4	3.3	3.0	2.9	2.7
	(63)	(54)	(54)	(52)	(44)
3d grade	3.2	3.2	3.2	3.0	2.6
	(43)	(42)	(32)	(35)	(31)
4th–7th grade	3.5	3.4	2.8	2.7	2.5
	(70)	(61)	(65)	(59)	(49)
Never-retained pupils					
All never-retained	3.4	3.4	3.1	3.1	2.8
	(428)	(361)	(287)	(228)	(204)
Poor-performing comparison group	3.2	3.4	3.0	2.9	2.8
	(103)	(80)	(67)	(52)	(50)

Table 7.A4. *School satisfaction averages for retained groups, never-retained pupils, and the poor-performing comparison group*

	Spring Year 1	Spring Year 2	Spring Year 4	Spring Year 6	Spring Year 8
Year of retention					
1st grade	4.1	4.2	4.2	4.1	3.8
	(112)	(89)	(101)	(92)	(69)
2d grade	4.2	4.2	4.3	4.0	3.8
	(63)	(53)	(58)	(54)	(44)
3d grade	4.3	4.4	4.1	3.8	3.7
	(42)	(41)	(37)	(36)	(32)
4th–7th grade	4.4	4.5	4.1	3.9	3.7
	(69)	(61)	(67)	(63)	(50)
Never-retained pupils					
All never-retained	4.3	4.3	4.1	3.8	3.7
	(422)	(357)	(295)	(231)	(209)
Poor-performing comparison group	4.2	4.3	4.2	3.8	3.7
	(103)	(79)	(68)	(53)	(50)

Table 7.A5. *Locus-of-control averages for retained groups, never-retained pupils, and the poor-performing comparison group*

	Spring Year 1	Spring Year 2	Spring Year 4	Fall Year 8
Year of retention				
1st grade	8.9	9.3	10.1	10.7
	(111)	(89)	(101)	(80)
2d grade	8.9	9.5	10.1	11.0
	(63)	(53)	(58)	(52)
3d grade	9.2	9.8	10.2	11.0
	(42)	(41)	(37)	(33)
4th–7th grade	9.2	9.9	10.6	11.1
	(69)	(60)	(67)	(61)
Never-retained pupils				
All never-retained	9.3	9.8	10.4	10.7
	(420)	(356)	(293)	(215)
Poor-performing comparison group	9.4	9.6	10.4	10.5
	(102)	(79)	(68)	(51)

8

Retention in the broader context of elementary and middle school tracking

Thus far we have seen that retention has mainly positive effects. It seems that having children repeat a grade bolsters their academic skills, and for that reason their self-confidence. Concerns remain. One is that repeaters do not fully catch up. Another involves children's other program placements, both in elementary school and later. This arises because retention is a form of "educational tracking" that causes children to be off time in their grade level, usually permanently.

Curiously, the literature on retention has been almost silent on how retention ties in with other "sorting and selecting" arrangements used by schools for placing children, for example, special education and placement in low-level instructional groups. Moreover, there is little information on whether retention closes off opportunities in middle school and beyond, when formal tracking begins (an exception is the study by Stevenson et al. 1992, which finds evidence of such constraints using the NELS-88 data). We say "curiously" because retention is quintessentially an organizational phenomenon, yet research and commentary on the practice rarely take an organizational perspective (e.g., Sorensen 1970, 1987). If they did, the parallels between retention and other forms of tracking would be hard to miss.

Retention, like other placements, is a creation of school policy. It is an educational treatment that places children in an instructional setting where, among other things, they might have a better chance of keeping up. This placement puts repeaters off time relative to others their age, but offers them a class environment and a span of time more suited to their educational needs. Matching educational delivery to students' presumed needs is at the heart of all educational tracking. We see this in the creation of small, relatively homogeneous groups for instruction, a nearly ubiquitous practice in the primary grades (e.g., McPartland, Coldiron, and Braddock 1987) and in the provision of special education services, whether in pull-out programs or in separate classes. The same rationale supports dividing the curriculum into separate "tracks" in the upper grades. In middle schools and junior high schools, track distinctions usually involve the level or depth at which topics are addressed (e.g., differences among advanced academic, basic, and remedial courses); whereas in high school, tracks often imply completely different subjects, sometimes even distinct programs of study (e.g., auto mechanics, business, college prep., etc.).

All these forms of tracking have legitimate educational objectives, but nevertheless arouse concerns that parallel those for retention: selections or placements may not be fair; the education provided in "low" tracks may be inferior to that provided in "higher" tracks; and children consigned to low tracks may be looked down upon, treated unfairly, and denied opportunities (i.e., they may encounter the stigma issue).

There are extensive literatures on each of these sorting and selecting mechanisms; the themes of selection, stigma, and reduced learning opportunities are prominent in all of them.[1] These parallels come about because the issues are intrinsic to all kinds of educational sorting, and hence overlap its specific forms. Practices merit careful scrutiny when they set some children apart from others, treat them differently, and confer upon them organizational identities that may have pejorative connotations.

In this chapter we look to see how these sorting practices articulate over the course of children's early schooling. To our knowledge no such description exists at present, and even the most basic information is lacking. For example, not a single evaluation of retention using the strategy of matched controls has used prior track placement to match retainees and comparison youngsters.

This piecemeal approach to studying educational sorting is a drawback, and potentially a serious mistake. By examining each kind of sorting separately, the consequences of retention could be over- or underestimated, misconstrued, or missed altogether, depending on how these other practices intersect retention and affect students.

Tracking practices are not isolated in students' lives. In the case of retention, children held back are not just "repeaters," even if researchers choose to look at them from that vantage point alone. In elementary school they also are likely to be in low-reading groups or special education classes, or to be receiving special education services in pull-out programs. In middle school they might be taking remedial courses while many of their schoolmates are in regular or advanced ones. All along the way there are multiple facets of tracking in operation. We know, for example, that all first grade repeaters in the BSS failed reading that year. It is reasonable to expect that most of them, if not all of them, were reading below grade level and were in low-reading instructional groups before they were retained.

Experiences such as these around the time of children's retention could reinforce, or even magnify, retention's consequences. However, they could also offset the effects of retention if many children's placements were "cross-cutting," with repeaters being spared low placements in other areas and promoted youngsters having low placements. Low-ability-group membership for instruction in reading, for example, is not limited to repeaters. Teachers use reading groups mainly to help with classroom management, and three or four groups is the typical arrangement regardless of children's ability levels (Dreeben 1984; Hallinan and Sorensen 1983). This being the case, at some point many promoted youngsters with perfectly satisfactory academic records may find themselves in low-reading groups. For that matter, some repeaters may not be tracked low across the board in other areas. For two groups on opposite sides of the retained/never-retained divide, such as retainees versus the poor-performing group, differences grounded specifically in retention could be over- or underestimated depending on how other tracking experiences are aligned.

One consequence of considering retention in isolation from other types of tracking is that it could be faulted for problems that originate elsewhere. As already seen, many of retainees' problems predate retention, as could a history of low-track assignments. As early as first grade, most future retainees may find themselves in low-instruction groups. In Chapter 3 we saw that many repeaters are moved into special education classes after being held back, and that many are held back a second time. With low-ability groups, special education, and multiple retentions all in the picture, it is hard to single out a particular intervention as the source of children's problems. If only retention is considered, however, it will of course be held accountable.

Finally, in ignoring the broader *system* of tracking, we miss altogether the consequences of retention for children's schooling that play themselves out within that system. For example, early retention could close off opportunities in the middle grades, when formal tracking into different kinds of courses begins. Perhaps because of lingering questions about their abilities, retainees are channeled into remedial or low-level courses, even though they might be able to handle a more challenging curriculum. Retention in this way could limit children's educational prospects even as it helped their performance.

Studies of curriculum tracking in high school typically find little movement across tracks once initial assignments have been made, and when children do switch it is more often downward (i.e., out of the college prep program) than upward (i.e., into it; for an overview of this see Rosenbaum 1980).[2] It is likely that children's placements prior to high school are constraining as well, but this has yet to be explored in depth (exceptions include Dreeben 1984; Eder 1986; Gamoran 1989, 1992; Hallinan 1992).

In this chapter we examine the set of organizational pathways within which retention is embedded by profiling children's educational tracking histories over the elementary and middle school years. These pathways are created by administrative interventions that sort and select children for different treatments as they move up the educational ladder. The chapter has three major sections. The first focuses on first grade, when all children are acclimating to the school routine and when those who will repeat first grade suffer their "setback." Children's reading-group placements, their reading instructional level, special education placements, and retention are considered.

The second section examines reading placements in the elementary and middle school period. Reading is central to the curriculum in the primary grades, and is the subject used most often to group children at the elementary level. More than 90% of schools use within-class ability grouping for reading in first grade, while only about 25% of schools group in first grade in math (McPartland et al. 1987).

The third section examines how repeaters' middle school English/reading, math, and foreign language placements in sixth and seventh grade differ from those of on-time youngsters. Seventh grade is as far as our coverage extends for repeaters, because by middle school they are at least a year behind.

In most school systems the curriculum begins to differentiate in middle school. This is when tracking as commonly understood begins. In math, advanced students may take pre-algebra, while others still are working on number skills; in the language curriculum, high-level students often take a foreign language and may move on to literary criticism and creative or expository writing, while children in lower level classes are limited to remedial reading, rules of grammar, vocabulary building, and the like.

Until middle school, children's options de jure remain open even if they have fallen behind; it is still possible to catch up, which presumably is what retention encourages. But often in middle school and beyond, catching up is no longer even theoretically possible. Children placed in general math will not take calculus in 12th grade, nor will children taking functional reading later on be able to enroll in advanced-placement English literature. Doors are irrevocably closed, because the curriculum is sequenced and differentiated. Many college preparatory courses in high school have prerequisites, and so in a very literal sense access to them often is determined years earlier (e.g., Oakes 1988 and 1989/90). Likewise, while formal tracking does not begin until the middle grades, earlier forms of "hidden tracking," such as retention, may also put students onto different pathways.

Tracking in first grade

We again begin with the experience of first grade repeaters. The situation in first grade is especially interesting because it reflects children's first encounters with educational sorting and sets the tone for everything that follows. Children begin to acquire "pupil identities" and an organizational history that will stay with them as long as they remain in school. Unfortunately for many children, especially those later held back, there is a decidedly negative cast to these first encounters. For perspective, experiences of promoted youngsters (both groups) and of children held back after first grade (i.e., in grades 2 through 7) also are reviewed.

Reading-group placements are available for 615 children in the fall and 622 in the spring.[3] Reading instructional level was taken from report cards, while information on retention and special education services was taken from the school system's central records (see Chapter 2 for problems with the school records).

For each placement we identify children's standing as either "low" or "not low." For reading-group placements, low means being in the lowest group maintained by a teacher. We are interested in monitoring placements that might put students at a disadvantage and possibly be stigmatizing. Grouping is part of the immediate classroom context, and the lowest placements should send the clearest signals. Hence, a child in the third of three groups would be classified as low, while one in the third of four would not. Consistent with practices nationally (e.g., Dreeben 1984; Hallinan and Sorensen 1983), most youngsters (501 of the 615 in the fall) are in classes with three or four groups. Forty-seven, though, are in classes with just two groups, and 34 are in classes with five groups (the other 33 are in ungrouped classes).

For reading-instructional level we classify as "low" children who are reading below grade level in a given quarter.[4] Reading level is not itself part of the tracking system, but it plays a role in screening for placements.[5] According to system-wide guidelines in the BCPS, children reading one grade below expectation should not receive marks above "satisfactory"; children reading two or more levels below should get a failing mark; while the highest permissible mark for children reading at expectation is "good." Only children reading one or more levels above expectation are supposed to get marks of "excellent," and to do so requires at least 90% mastery.[6] There is no way of knowing how faithfully these guidelines are honored, but official policy is clear: reading marks ought to reflect reading level.

Special education placements are recorded in the spring of the year. In most instances these represent assignments for the next school year. Our tallies combine pull-out services from regular classrooms (these provide supplemental instruction in reading or math) with assignment to self-contained special education classes.

More than 70% of first grade repeaters were in low-reading groups in the fall and spring, and slightly more than 90% were reading below grade level at year's end. Additionally, some 20% (26 of 127) were placed in special education at that point. These figures compare with about 20% of all children in low-reading groups fall and spring, 23% reading below grade level, and 7% in special education.

These statistics are sobering. Most first grade repeaters received first quarter reading marks of "unsatisfactory" (Chapter 3), and all of them received failing marks at year's end (Chapter 6). We now see that even before being held back, most repeaters have already been placed in low-ability instructional groups, and that a sizable minority are in special education. These low placements reflect the classroom management side of their academic difficulties. They are both symptom and signal, the latter in the form of organizational identities they carry with them in addition to their standing as repeaters.

But these identities are not the exclusive province of repeaters. Only a few of the never-retained (16) are earmarked for special education services in first grade, but 16% were in low-instructional groups in the fall, as were 10% in the spring; 9% were reading below grade level at year's end. The percentages are higher still if we look at all children promoted at the end of Year 1 (including children held back later, in Years 2 through 7); 20% have low fall reading placements, as do 12% in the spring; 14% read below grade level; and 6% are assigned to special education.

These figures give balance to the substantial disproportionalities seen for first grade repeaters. As a group their tracking experiences in Year 1 are extreme; however, as individuals their experience is not all that exceptional. Many promoted children, even some who make it through middle school without being held back, find themselves in precisely the same circumstances as repeaters in first grade. How these several placements combine in children's experience is displayed in Table 8.1. Each row represents a distinctive combination defined by children's reading-group placements (low or not low, fall and spring) and spring instructional level (below or at grade level). The X's signify low placement. The number of children in each pattern is indicated in the left-hand column, along with the percentage this represents of the entire group covered in the chart (N = 543).[7] To fill out the pattern description, for each configuration we also report the number of children assigned to special education at year's end. To see how retainees' first grade placements compare to those of others, tallies by retention status (Year 1, grades 2 through 7; never retained; and comparison group) are reported to the right of the patterns.

Most children – 340 of the 543, or 63% – have no low placements; they were not in low-reading groups in either the fall or spring, and at year's end were reading at least at grade level. Ten of the 340 were designated for special education, but this is only 3.4% of the total, so such assignment is less common in this pattern than in just about any of the others. It is striking that not one of the 340 is a first grade repeater (see the right-side distributions). In comparison, 79% of the never-retained youngsters fall into the group with no low placements, and even the comparison-

Table 8.1. *First-year tracking patterns*

No. with pattern	Low-reading group (fall)	Low reading level (spring)	Low-reading group (spring)	No. in special education	1st grade retainees	2d–7th grade retainees	Never-retained	Poor-performing comparison group[a]
340 (63)[b]	—	—	—	10	0 (0)	79 (57)	261 (79)	46 (62)
75 (14)	X	X	X	15	57 (75)	11 (8)	7 (2)	3 (4)
46 (8)	—	X	—	3	13 (17)	19 (14)	14 (4)	7 (9)
37 (7)	X	—	X	4	0 (0)	12 (9)	25 (8)	10 (14)
26 (5)	X	X	—	4	1 (1)	10 (7)	15 (5)	6 (8)
12 (2)	X	—	—	0	2 (3)	5 (4)	5 (2)	1 (1)
4 (1)	—	—	X	0	0 (0)	2 (1)	2 (1)	1 (1)
3 (1)	—	X	X	1	3 (4)	0 (0)	0 (0)	0 (0)
Total 543					76	138	329	74

Note: Numbers in parentheses are percentages, going down columns. "X" identifies placements in pattern; dashes indicate not part of pattern.

[a]The poor-performing comparison group youngsters are a subset of the never-retained group. Looking across rows, the "No. with pattern" sample size corresponds to the sum of the 1st grade retainees, 2d–7th grade retainees, and never-retained groups.

[b]Percentages in column sum to 101 due to rounding.

group children, as well as those held back in grades 2 through 7, are well represented in it.[8]

First grade repeaters' placements, in contrast, are highly concentrated at the other extreme. Three-fourths (57 of 76) are in the pattern that involves all low placements, and they constitute 76% of the children with this profile. If placements were random with respect to retention status, only 14% would be expected (the percentage of first grade repeaters in the total group, that is, 76 of 543). Retainees thus are greatly overrepresented in this group (20% of whom also have been designated for special education).

Most of the remaining first grade retainees (18 of 19) are reading below grade level. Hence, even when first grade repeaters are spared other low-track placements, almost all are still reading below grade level at year's end. Indeed, only 1 of the 76 repeaters in Table 8.1 is at grade level.

The exceptional nature of repeaters' first grade tracking experiences is also evident when contrasted with the placements of children held back later (in grades 2 through 7), or with the comparison group youngsters. The 138 second through seventh grade retainees are just about a fourth of the total. This fraction matches almost exactly their percentage in the group that was spared all low placements ($79/340 = 23\%$), so in that respect their first-year experience is unexceptional, and clearly better than that of first grade repeaters.

At the other extreme, only 8% of these children are in the all-low pattern. They constitute about 15% (11 of 75) of the children in this pattern, which puts them well below the 75% figure for first grade repeaters (57 of 75), and below the percentage that would be expected for them (25%) if allocations were random.[9]

While low across-the-board placements in first grade are uncommon among children held back later, they are not spared low placements altogether in first grade. On the contrary, they are above expectation in most other low-pattern groups, composing from 32% to 50% of the membership of each. Their low first grade tracking is not nearly as severe as that of first grade repeaters, but is still decidedly more negative than that of never-retained children.

Children held back later also have more negative experiences than does the comparison group. Seventy-four of these youngsters are covered in Table 8.1, representing about 14% of the total. Exactly 14% (46 of 340) of the no-low-track children are members of the comparison group, which puts them at the expected level, and their placements in most of the low slot patterns span a narrow band of percentages, from 8 to 27. There generally are a few more comparison-group children than expected, but no dramatic concentrations, and they are conspicuously underrepresented in the all-low-placement pattern, making up just 4% of it.

In contrast to most first grade repeaters, these children manage somehow to get by despite their low entering test scores (which are nevertheless not as low as those of first grade repeaters). They experience low-track placements somewhat more often than do the never-retained children (only 62% are in the no–low-placement group compared with 79% of the latter), but their placement pattern is more favorable than that of children retained in grades 2 through 7, and vastly better than that of first grade repeaters. These tracking patterns thus reflect the same orderliness across groups seen in earlier chapters for academic and adjustment difficulties in first grade.

To summarize: first grade retainees' placement profile in their year of failure is exceptional. These children are not just repeaters; most also have been in low-reading groups, almost all are still reading below grade level at year's end, and a sizable minority are headed for special education. In each instance retainees are much more likely than the never-retained to be in a low group or to read below grade level, but beyond these differences, comparison by comparison, repeaters much more often show a *pattern* of consistently low placements. The signals, all of which predate retention, thus are loud and clear, and are aligned with retainees' difficulties with both academics and school adjustment.

First grade repeaters' first-year tracking experiences place them outside the mainstream; nevertheless, close examination of tracking practices reveals that many promoted children also experience some form of low placement during the year. About a fifth (21%) of all never-retained youngsters, and almost 40% of the comparison group, have at least one low placement. These could include reading below grade level in the fourth quarter, being in the lowest reading group, or receiving special education.

These sizable percentages remind us that negative signals from early tracking are not limited to repeaters. Educational sorting in first grade also gives many promoted youngsters reason to question their competence. For that matter, a fifth (16 of 76) of the first grade repeaters were not in low-reading groups at the end of first grade (or targeted for special education), so mixed signals cut both ways. The main message of the comparisons made thus far is that repeaters' placement profiles put them more often and more consistently at the low end of the several first grade tracking hierarchies examined. It is important, though, that many promoted children are placed low, too. Even though tracking experiences in first grade are not usually labeled as such, nor are all kinds of tracking acknowledged, the consequences of this early de facto tracking may be as serious, or more so, than those of tracking for older children. These early decisions determine how much children learn in the basic areas of reading and arithmetic, and thereafter achievement patterns tend to be very stable (this is reflected in the performance trajectories reviewed in Chapters 4 through 6).

Tracking across the elementary grades into middle school: placements in reading/English

In this section we examine children's standing in reading and English through elementary school into the first year of middle school (sixth grade). Children who are held back are especially challenged in reading because first grade repeaters are placed disproportionately in low-reading groups in fall and spring of first grade and hardly any of them are reading at grade level when they finish the year. Here we consider whether their standing changes in the years that follow, by looking at reading instructional level in the spring of Years 1 and 2 (their fail–repeat cycle), reading instructional level through the spring of fifth grade (for most, their last year of elementary school),[10] and sixth grade class assignments (the first year of middle school) in reading/English.

We use reading instructional level because it is available from report cards all through the elementary years.[11] It tracks children's proficiency and structures the instructional process in important ways. To some extent it even substitutes for children's reading-group placements. Correspondence between the two is far from perfect, but in first grade only 10% of the youngsters reading at grade level were in low-reading groups, versus 57% of the children reading below grade level. Among the never-retained, the figures are 9% and 27%. Seventy-eight percent of the 77 first grade repeaters reading below grade level were in low-reading groups, and the sole retainee reading at grade level was not.

In middle school, where distinctions among remedial, regular, and advanced classes are drawn, we can look more directly at curriculum tracking. In the BCPS, reading in middle school is remedial. These courses, most of which are special education classes, carry titles like "Developmental Reading," "Remedial Reading," "Supplementary Reading Resource," and "English with Reading/Writing Emphasis." English is the "regular" track (e.g., "English, Level 1" or "Level 2"; "English, Grade 6"). The school system also offers an advanced English program for children who satisfy various screening criteria (e.g., having passed the school system's proficiency tests, scoring above grade level on standardized tests, or receiving grades of 80 or above in all subjects) and/or have been recommended by their teachers. These include courses with such titles as "English Grade 6 – Enriched" and "English Grade 6 – Advanced Academic."

Children in remedial classes work on basic reading skills, while those in advanced classes study "characterization, literary devices, and authors' purposes," "essays of comparison and contrast, interviews, rudimentary research skills and business letter writing," and "writing in a variety of genres and some lower level skills of debate and defense" (these are excerpted from BCPS course descriptions). Enriched courses are available in all middle schools, while the advanced academic program is available in just 11 of the city's 27 middle schools, 2 of which are magnet schools that enroll students from throughout the city. Admission is by application and/or recommendation.

Children taking reading or English courses identified as special education (e.g., SE Language Arts, Grade 6) are considered in the "low track." Children in regular or advanced courses are classified as "not low" in the coding used in this section. The vast majority of children, whether retained or not – some 85% overall and 99% among first grade repeaters – are enrolled in low-level reading/English classes in sixth grade. Many, though, take two language-arts courses in sixth grade, a common practice in middle school (see Epstein and MacIver 1990). The two courses do not always fall on the same side of the divide between low and not low, which complicates matters somewhat.

Course-taking information is available for 495 children in sixth grade. Of this number, 220 are in low-level courses exclusively, whereas just 75 are in not-low courses exclusively. Sixty-one of the 75 are in advanced courses. Another 200 children are in both reading and regular or ad-

Table 8.2. *Percentage of students reading below grade level in elementary school*

	1st grade retainees	2d–5th grade retainees	Never-retained	Poor-performing comparison group[a]
Spring Year 1	90.4	30.2	9.2	21.4
	(104)	(129)	(411)	(98)
Spring Year 2	35.0	35.3	2.0	2.6
	(80)	(116)	(351)	(77)
Spring 3d grade	52.2	31.0	5.8	10.3
	(90)	(126)	(312)	(78)
Spring 4th grade	54.9	37.8	9.7	23.5
	(82)	(111)	(288)	(68)
Spring 5th grade	62.5	38.7	9.7	15.0
	(56)	(93)	(247)	(60)

Note: Numbers in parentheses are sample sizes.
[a]The poor-performing comparison group youngsters are a subset of the never-retained group.

vanced English. Of these, 153 are in regular English courses and 47 are in advanced ones. It is true that 85% of the children followed into sixth grade took low-level courses that year; but if instead we had classified children in terms of their highest-level course, the percentage classified as in low-level classes would drop to 56%. This large difference notwithstanding, we will primarily be examining remedial placements. Our interest in this volume centers around the experience of repeaters, and the advanced curriculum in middle school has very little relevance for them. Almost all children enrolled in advanced courses are from the never-retained pool: only 3 of the 108 are first grade repeaters: 12 others were held back in Years 2 through 5.

As the figures just reviewed suggest, repeaters' sixth grade standing is not good. Only 1 of 92 first grade retainees, and 2 of 115 second through fifth grade repeaters, are *not* in remedial reading/English. Among the never-retained and the comparison-group children, the percentages are 28.6 and 13.8 respectively.[12] It seems that repeating a grade in elementary school virtually guarantees remedial placement at the beginning of middle school, although such placements are in the 70% range even among promoted children.

We know that most first grade repeaters were reading below grade level when they failed first grade. In Table 8.2 we see that after repeating the year, many were reading at grade level. The first year, more than 90% were reading below grade level, but in the second year, only 35% were. Unfortunately, for many children this improvement is not maintained, so that by fifth grade more than 60% again were reading below grade level.

Many second through fifth grade repeaters also read below grade level in elementary school, but their percentages are far lower than those of first grade retainees. The figures for repeaters in the second through fifth grades hover in the range of 30% to 35% most years, and peak at 38.7% just before the middle school transition. Among never-retained youngsters, in contrast, the percentage reading below grade level never gets above 10, and even the comparison group's highest percentages in any year are in the low 20s. In fifth grade, for example, just 15% of the comparison children read below grade level, compared with 62.5% of first grade retainees and 38.7% of those held back after first grade.

These comparisons reveal large differences in children's competencies at the time of the middle school transition, differences that could close doors for them later. That this is a real risk is seen in Table 8.3, which organizes reading/English configurations from first through sixth grade.[13]

There are many such configurations in children's experience, but most children fall into the six largest patterns. These are presented in descending order by size. For completeness, the less-populated patterns are also displayed, but the largest of these includes just 8 youngsters (3% of the total).

The most common profile, covering 44% of the total, has children reading at grade level all through elementary school, yet being placed in low-level middle school reading/English. (About 62% of the 136 children, we should note, took nonremedial English courses at the same time.) Regardless of their reading proficiency in fifth grade, most children are in remedial reading/English in sixth grade. Nevertheless, reading level still plays a role in sixth grade placements: a fourth of the children reading at grade level in fifth grade are not in low sixth grade classes, compared with just 5.6% of those reading below grade level.

The next-largest pattern involves children with "unblemished" placements over the entire interval. These youngsters read at least at grade level through fifth grade, and in sixth grade are placed in regular or

Table 8.3. *Tracking patterns from first grade through sixth grade*

No. with pattern[a]	Low reading level (spring Yr. 1)	Low reading level (spring Yr. 2)	Low reading level (spring gr. 5)	Low read/Eng. course (gr. 6)	1st grade retainees	2d–5th grade retainees	Never-retained	Poor-performing comparison group[b]
136 (44)	—	—	—	X	1 (3)	25 (37)	94 (53)	18 (47)
54 (17)	—	—	—	—	0 (0)	1 (1)	51 (29)	3 (8)
29 (9)	—	—	X	X	3 (8)	16 (24)	8 (4)	3 (8)
28 (9)	X	—	—	X	9 (23)	4 (6)	13 (7)	9 (24)
20 (6)	X	X	X	X	13 (33)	3 (4)	4 (2)	2 (5)
15 (5)	X	X	X	X	10 (26)	4 (6)	0 (0)	0 (0)
8 (3)	—	X	—	X	0 (0)	7 (10)	1 (1)	1 (3)
6 (2)	—	X	X	X	1 (3)	4 (6)	0 (0)	0 (0)
5 (2)	X	X	—	X	1 (3)	4 (6)	0 (0)	0 (0)
3 (1)	—	—	X	—	0 (0)	0 (0)	3 (2)	0 (0)
2 (1)	X	X	—	—	1 (3)	0 (0)	1 (1)	0 (0)
2 (1)	—	—	—	—	0 (0)	0 (0)	2 (1)	1 (3)
1 (0)	X	—	X	—	0 (0)	0 (0)	1 (1)	1 (3)
Total 309					39	68	178	39

Note: Numbers in parentheses are percentages, going down columns. "X" identifies low placements in pattern; dashes indicate not part of pattern.
[a] All children are covered in these pattern totals, so they characterize the experience of the entire cohort. However, children held back for the first time in middle school (sixth or seventh grade) are not included in the right-side subgroup totals. Hence, the left- and right-side row totals will not always be equal.
[b] The poor-performing comparison group youngsters are a subset of the never-retained group. Looking across rows, the "No. with pattern" sample size corresponds to the sum of the "1st grade retainees," "2d–5th grade retainees," and "Never-retained" groups.

advanced English. At 17% of the total, this group is uncommon, as are the youngsters who compose it: 83% are taking advanced English and 81% are reading above grade level in fifth grade. The other patterns with relatively large totals (four in all, with numbers in the 15 to 30 range) all involve multiple low placements, including the one that has children placed low on every occasion.

There are striking contrasts in how the student groups are distributed across these six largest patterns.[14] Only one of the children spared all low placements was held back. Indeed, more than a fourth of the never-retained children fall into this pattern, while another 53% are in the group placed in low middle school reading/English despite having read at grade level all through elementary school (this is also the modal pattern among second through fifth grade repeaters and in the comparison group).

Eighty-one percent of the never-retained can be accounted for by just the two patterns with a minimum of low placements. Indeed, half of the comparison group falls into these two patterns, and another 24% are in the pattern that picks up these children's first-year difficulties (i.e., below-grade reading in Year 1 and low middle school placement). There is not another "problem pattern" that includes even 10% of either group.

The situation of repeaters is quite different. Most of them, including practically all first grade repeaters, are in patterns with multiple low placements. More than a fourth (26%) of first grade retainees are placed low on every occasion; another 33% are low every year except the second, which reflects the "boost" they got while repeating first grade (taking 2 years to get up to grade level). Their next-most-numerous pattern (at 23%, but representing just nine children), has them reading below grade level only in Year 1, accompanied by low placements in middle school. There are thus some first grade repeaters who maintain their reading skills after first grade, but they are a minority.

Repeaters in the second through fifth grades fare a bit better, but their profiles still reflect many more low placements than do those of the promoted children. More than a third read at grade level at each elementary school benchmark,[15] so for these youngsters their only low placement is not until middle school. Yet almost a fourth (24%) read below grade level for the first time in fifth grade, and the rest are scattered widely over other multiple low-placement patterns, including 6% in the pattern with all low placements. While some of these youngsters appear to be doing satisfactorily until middle school, most show problems that overlap levels of schooling.

Not just repeaters are tracked low in middle school, though; most students, regardless of retention status, are placed in remedial sixth grade reading/English. Low middle school placements are much more common among former repeaters, of course, but this can be understood largely in terms of their continuing problems with reading. Apart from those few first grade repeaters who recovered somewhat while repeating a grade, most read below grade level at every benchmark covered in Table 8.3, and practically all read below grade level at their transition to middle school. These youngsters are overrepresented in low-track classes, but their standing as repeaters is not likely responsible; all but 4 of the 24 never-retained children who read below grade level in fifth grade also were in remedial sixth grade reading/English.

Tracking in middle school: reading/English, math, and foreign language

In middle school the main academic subjects are frequently tracked, and within tracks classes are often grouped by ability level (see Epstein and MacIver 1990). In this section, we examine children's placements in sixth and seventh grade reading/English and math, and whether they have begun studying a foreign language. It seems reasonable to assume that middle school English and math placements will affect those in these same areas later, but research indicates that foreign language study is also sometimes used to screen children into (or out of) high school academic programs (e.g., Alexander and Cook 1982; Rosenbaum 1976). There is not much research on continuities in children's track placements across levels of schooling (e.g., Gamoran 1989; Hallinan 1992; Stevenson et al. 1992), and none of it begins in the early primary grades.

Tracking patterns have been the most extensively studied at the secondary level. High school placements generally do not change, but when children switch programs, it is more often out of the academic track than into it (for a review see Oakes, Gamoran, and Page 1992; also Rosenbaum 1980; Hallinan 1993, however, presents different mobility patterns in her recent research). Failing to take prerequisite courses in middle school almost certainly limits options later.

As mentioned, most children take two reading/English courses in

Table 8.4. *Placements in high-level and low-level sixth and seventh grade courses (in percentages)*

	1st grade retainees	2d–5th grade retainees	Never-retained	Poor-performing comparison group[a]
Sixth grade				
Reading, % low	98.9	98.3	71.4	86.2
	(92)	(115)	(245)	(58)
English, % high	3.3	10.4	37.9	15.8
	(92)	(115)	(235)	(57)
Math, % low	48.9	27.8	6.3	5.3
	(92)	(115)	(237)	(57)
Math, % high	3.3	3.5	23.6	5.3
	(92)	(115)	(237)	(57)
% taking a foreign language	9.7	17.4	55.7	24.6
	(92)	(115)	(237)	(57)
Seventh grade				
Reading, % low	100.0	95.3	70.3	83.9
	(81)	(107)	(236)	(56)
English, % high	3.7	4.7	33.1	19.6
	(81)	(106)	(236)	(56)
Math, % low	55.6	21.5	4.7	5.4
	(81)	(107)	(236)	(56)
Math, % high	0.0	0.9	28.0	14.3
	(81)	(107)	(236)	(56)
% taking a foreign language	12.3	36.4	66.9	55.4
	(81)	(107)	(236)	(56)

Note: Numbers in parentheses are sample sizes.
[a]The poor-performing comparison group youngsters are a subset of the never-retained group.

sixth grade (377 of 495, or 76%). A comparable percentage (77%) does so in seventh grade. Table 8.4 shows how these enrollments are distributed in terms of high- and low-level courses, along with enrollment patterns in math and foreign languages.

The sixth and seventh grade details are generally similar. In all groups a higher percentage takes a foreign language in seventh grade than in sixth, but differences across years are not dramatic, and contrasts across the divide between retained and never-retained students are similar in both years.

Almost all repeaters are in the remedial reading/English program both years, and hardly any are in high-level English. As expected, remedial placements are also more common in the comparison group than overall (86% vs. 71% in sixth grade). Most never-retained youngsters are in the remedial program too, but their percentages are below those of repeaters.

Retained and never-retained placements differ most outside the remedial program. In sixth grade, 38% of those never retained take high-level English, as do 16% of the comparison-group youngsters. The corresponding figures for seventh grade are 33% and 20%. For all practical purposes, these curricular options are beyond the reach of elementary school retainees. Is this unfair? Possibly, but there are large differences among these groups in preparation and qualifications. Hardly any first grade repeaters were reading at grade level at the end of fifth grade, which certainly bears on sixth grade placements. It turns out that three-fourths of the never-retained children and half of the comparison-group children in high-level sixth grade English were reading *above* grade level in fifth grade.

Differences in children's fifth grade CAT-R performance were similarly large. In the spring of fifth grade, the first grade retainees averaged 441 on the CAT-R. The corresponding figures for promoted children ($N = 86$) and those in the comparison group ($N = 8$) in high-level sixth grade English were 571 and 549, respectively. The lowest-scoring advanced English student was 28 points above the retainees' CAT-R average, and only 2 of 127 first grade repeaters had scores above the averages of either never-retained group.

Standard deviations for the three groups' fifth grade CAT-R distributions are 50.9 points, 64.5 points, and 64.6 points (never-retained students, first grade repeaters, and comparison group, respectively). This means that the 130-point gap separating repeaters from those never retained is at least 2 standard deviations, while the 108-point gap separating them from the comparison group is in the vicinity of 1.6 standard deviations. These huge disparities show that first grade repeaters do not match other children's qualifications for high-level middle school coursework. Are first grade retainees denied opportunities when they get to middle school simply because of their status as repeaters? The answer seems to be "No." Their history as repeaters is not at issue here so much as their poor academic skills at the beginning of middle school. The examples given represent the most extreme contrasts, but the general point holds throughout.

The same trends appear in the other areas covered in Table 8.4. Fewer children overall fall outside the regular math curriculum, but among those who do, mainly repeaters take lower-level courses (most of which are special education classes); promoted children, primarily, take upper-level courses. In both sixth and seventh grades, about half of the first grade repeaters are tracked low in math (49% and 56% respectively), as are about a fourth of the second through fifth grade retainees. The corresponding figures among never-retained youngsters are all in the 4% to 6% range; that is, they are about as rare as repeaters in high-level courses.

At the other end of the scale, in the sixth and seventh grades, about a fourth of the never-retained group is in upper-level math. This sizable minority is well beyond the levels realized by any of the other groups. Just as with the English curriculum, then, the high-level math program appears beyond the reach of elementary school retainees.

Disparities involving foreign language study are less pronounced, but the figures still favor those never retained. About 10% to 12% of first grade retainees take a foreign language each year, the only high-level area in which they are above 5%. Figures for the never-retained students, at 56% in sixth grade and 67% in seventh grade, are much higher, with the comparison group and second through fifth grade repeaters falling between these extremes.

These parallels in how youngsters are distributed throughout the middle school curriculum are not simply coincidental; children with strong academic records in one area tend to be strong in others, too. However, administrative considerations also play a role. Some schools use "block scheduling" in making class assignments. Under this arrangement, children move together as a group from class to class throughout the day. This has the effect of placing children in the same track for all their academic courses. In sixth grade, for example, 94% of the children in low-level math also are in low-level reading/English, and 88% of those in high-level math also are in high-level English.

Foreign language enrollments also align with other placements. In sixth grade, for example, 92% of the children enrolled in remedial math are not taking a foreign language, while 83% of those in advanced math are. For high- and low-level English, the corresponding percentages are 91 and 78.

Overlap in middle school placements is thus substantial. To see this more clearly, along with exactly where repeaters fit in, we again have developed placement profiles (see Table 8.5). The patterns shown here, which overlap sixth and seventh grade, identify children's placements each year in reading/English, math, and foreign language as low or not low. The number of children receiving special education services each year, and the number held back in middle school, are also indicated.

Again, most patterns are sparsely populated. Only six apply to as many as 20 children and these encompass 89% of the total in the table (354 of 400). These common patterns warrant particular attention, but the other patterns should not be disregarded altogether, as they reveal much of the complexity of middle school tracking. In fact, there are 33 different curricular configurations in the BSS youngsters' middle school experience.[16] The 14 displayed in Table 8.5 apply to 1% or more of the study group. These configurations overlay additional distinctions involving special education placement and middle school retention, not to mention the children's history of tracking that follows them into the middle grades from elementary school. It is a complicated picture, much more so than is generally appreciated.

The most heavily populated patterns show significant parallels across student groups. The largest pattern involves low reading/English and foreign language placements (which means *not* taking a foreign language) for both years, along with regular or advanced math. In a strictly empirical sense, this turns out to be the "regular" middle school curriculum for our study youngsters: regardless of what else they might be doing in the English program, a fourth of the entire study group takes remedial reading, does not take a foreign language, and is in a nonremedial math sequence.

This configuration is more than a third again the size of the next-largest pattern, and includes many youngsters from each group (including first grade repeaters). Included are a fifth of the never-retained students, about a third of the children held back after first grade, and roughly a third of the comparison-group youngsters. Considering how divergent placement patterns have been thus far, this degree of similarity is unusual; if there is a middle school "melting pot," this is it.

Table 8.5. *Middle school tracking*

No. with pattern[a]	Low rdg/Eng grade 6	Low math grade 6	No foreign language grade 6	Low rdg/Eng grade 7	Low math grade 7	No foreign language grade 7	No. in spec. ed. grade 6	No. in spec. ed. grade 7	6th or 7th grade ret	1st grade retainees	2d–5th grade retainees	Never retained	Poor-perf. comparison group[b]
105 (26)	X	—	X	X	—	X	7	5	15	24 (33)	28 (30)	44 (22)	17 (37)
68 (17)	X	—	X	X	—	—	4	3	14	2 (3)	24 (26)	31 (16)	12 (26)
61 (15)	X	X	X	X	X	X	52	47	4	36 (50)	16 (17)	6 (3)	1 (2)
56 (14)	X	—	—	X	—	—	1	0	10	4 (6)	8 (9)	38 (19)	4 (9)
44 (11)	—	—	—	—	—	—	1	0	1	0 (0)	1 (1)	42 (21)	3 (7)
20 (5)	X	X	X	X	—	X	0	0	3	2 (3)	5 (5)	10 (5)	0 (0)
9 (2)	X	—	X	X	—	X	5	4	0	1 (1)	6 (6)	2 (1)	1 (2)
7 (2)	X	—	X	—	—	—	0	0	0	0 (0)	1 (1)	6 (3)	1 (2)
7 (2)	X	—	X	—	X	—	0	0	0	0 (0)	1 (1)	6 (3)	3 (7)
6 (2)	X	—	X	X	X	X	1	0	0	2 (3)	3 (3)	1 (0)	1 (2)
6 (2)	—	—	—	X	—	—	0	0	0	1 (1)	0 (0)	5 (3)	1 (2)
4 (1)	—	—	X	—	—	X	0	0	0	0 (0)	0 (0)	4 (2)	1 (2)
4 (1)	—	—	—	—	—	—	0	0	0	0 (0)	0 (0)	4 (2)	1 (2)
3 (1)	X	—	X	—	—	X	0	0	2	0 (0)	1 (1)	1 (0)	0 (0)
Total 400							70	60	49	72	94	200	46

Note: Numbers in parentheses are percentages, going down columns. "X" identifies low placements in pattern; dashes indicate not part of pattern.

[a] All children are covered in these pattern totals, so they characterize the experience of the entire cohort. Children held back for the first time in middle school (sixth or seventh grade) are not included in the right-side subgroup totals. Hence, the left- and right-side row totals will not always be equal.

[b] The poor-performing comparison group youngsters are a subset of the never-retained group. Looking across rows, the "No. with pattern" sample size corresponds to the sum of the "1st grade retainees," "2d–5th grade retainees," and "Never-retained" groups.

Another 68 youngsters have the same sixth grade placements, and in seventh grade the same reading/English and math pattern. In seventh grade, though, they begin a foreign language, which is what distinguishes this pattern from the first. For many youngsters, then, selection for foreign language study occurs as they move into seventh grade. This pattern, too, is relatively "open," at least for all but first grade repeaters. Sixteen percent of the never-retained youngsters are included in it, along with 26% each of the second through fifth grade repeaters and of the comparison group.

Relatively large percentages of these same groups also appear in the pattern with only low placements in reading/English both years (the fourth-largest pattern, $N = 56$). Nineteen percent of the never-retained, and 9% each of the comparison group youngsters and of those held back after first grade, are in this group. These youngsters begin foreign language study in sixth grade and are never in low-track math. The percentages in this pattern favor never-retained children somewhat, just as the previous pattern favors the other groups.

The never-retained thus more often take a foreign language and tend to begin it earlier; nevertheless, overall we are impressed that disparities are not larger. Substantial common ground in middle school placements is indicated in these three patterns, which cover roughly one-half to two-thirds of never-retained children and those held back in elementary school after first grade.[17]

In this respect, many elementary school repeaters blend in, more or less, in middle school. Few of them, though, are first grade repeaters, whose single largest pattern involves across-the-board low placements both years (the third pattern). With 15% of the total, this is the third largest pattern overall in Table 8.5. Half the first grade retainees covered there have this combination of placements (36 of 72), and they dominate the pattern, constituting 59% of its membership (another 26% involves children held back in grades 2 through 5). First grade repeaters, as we have seen, have a long history of academic difficulties that parallel an equally long history of low-track placements. These problems obviously continue into middle school, as 52 of the 61 children in this all-low pattern receive special education services in sixth grade, and 47 do in seventh grade.

At the opposite extreme of the all-low pattern is the one that entails no low placements. Forty-four children have this profile, 11% of the total.

Just one of these is an elementary school retainee; 42 were never retained.[18]

Disproportionalities at the extremes are thus pronounced: hardly any of the "low end" children are drawn from the never-retained pool; conversely, only one of the "high end" children is from the retained pool. In these details, retained and promoted children's middle school tracking patterns are radically different. These two patterns account for about a fourth of the total (11% in the no-low pattern; 15% in the all-low pattern), so the numbers involved are far from negligible. Still, for most youngsters other than first grade repeaters, middle school tracking patterns overlap substantially. This would not have been easy to see had the various dimensions of tracking been examined piecemeal, as they usually are.

Tracking and retention: some concluding thoughts

This chapter has examined retention from the perspective of educational tracking. Tracking is an administrative device for placing together students deemed to have like needs and / or competencies. There are many forms of tracking, and their use is widespread. In this chapter we examined, in addition to retention, reading-group placements in first grade, reading instructional level all through the primary grades (a proxy for grouping as well as a measure of children's competencies), special education placements, and middle school children's placements in the core academic subjects.

Each of these interventions has legitimate educational objectives, yet each also has been faulted for failing to meet its objectives, and for unintentionally burdening children in ways often not even recognized. The fairness of tracking has been questioned, as has its effectiveness, especially for low-track youngsters.

Here we have been concerned mainly with how the various placements intersect. At every point of comparison, retainees, as we have seen, tend to be relegated to the lowest educational slots, while never-retained children are most often spared low placements. This tracking emerges in first grade, before anyone has been held back, and also in middle school, after all primary grade retentions have been registered. That the lines are so rigidly drawn is part of the reality of retention, and in middle school a majority of first grade repeaters are on separate tracks from their classmates. However, such extreme patterns are not the rule: middle school tracking patterns are not especially distinctive for promoted children and repeaters held back after first grade.[19]

The variety and complexity of tracking profiles seen in this chapter illustrate why neglecting dimensions of tracking other than retention could frustrate attempts to get a proper reading of retention's consequences. Rigid tracking is most severe in the case of first grade repeaters, who consistently fall far off everyone else's standard. These youngsters' track placements are low before their retention and remain so around the time of it; their skill levels when they get to middle school continue to lag far behind everyone else's.

An important concern is whether being held back in elementary school closes doors for children when they get to middle school. If not shut, these doors are certainly not opened wide; almost all first grade repeaters take remedial reading in sixth and seventh grade, about half are in low-level math, and only about 10% study a foreign language, a much lower percentage than in the other groups. Since so many first grade repeaters have consistently low placements and so few others are similarly situated, it looks as though early retention throws up daunting barriers.

Appearances can be misleading, however. Retention is not the only problem. Most of these children were already "locked out" in first grade, before anyone was held back. Their placements for instruction in reading were consistently low, and most of them were assigned to special education at some point. The initial academic and adjustment difficulties of first grade repeaters were extreme, and these difficulties continued all through elementary school.

Under such circumstances it is hard to tell exactly what underlies first grade repeaters' middle school placements. The effectiveness of any educational program is evaluated nonexperimentally by comparing the later experiences of children who are alike in all relevant respects save exposure to the "treatment" at issue, in this case retention. These first grade repeaters are so different from others that such comparisons may be impossible. Matched control studies typically do not match on factors *prior* to retention or on children's track placements, so the kinds of comparisons made in this chapter ordinarily are not even attempted. But even if the need for such comparisons were understood, in a typical student population there very likely would be too few never-retained children with early placements comparable to those of retainees to accomplish suitable matches. Retention is highly confounded with other low placements and with prior academic difficulties, so the power of statistical adjustments like those used in the present volume is greatly diminished.

Such limitations are disquieting, but it is important to understand the limits of what research can accomplish. The tracking patterns reviewed in this chapter are a sobering reminder that definitive answers may not always be possible. However, not all repeaters' problems and placements are as extreme as those of first grade retainees. Indeed, middle school patterns for later repeaters and promoted youngsters are highly varied, with considerable overlap across the divide between retained students and those who never are.

How repeaters are affected by the broader tracking system is unknown, but they are certainly touched by it. Negative consequences usually attributed to retention could actually be the result of other placements that exercise a stronger pull on children's daily experience, like special education or ability-group assignments. It also is reasonable to suspect that consequences magnify when children's placements are consistently low, both across many tracking dimensions and across years.

Effects of sorting practices early in children's school careers clearly are more complicated than is generally appreciated. To help sort out these complications, research is needed on educational sorting or tracking as a comprehensive system, as distinct from research on parts of the system – on retention alone, special education, ability grouping, or curriculum tracking. We need to know whether the overlap of retention with these other tracking mechanisms aggravates or cushions problems surrounding retention.

This chapter's glimpse of retainees' administrative standing in the context of elementary and middle school tracking reveals that retention is not an isolated experience, easily separated from other aspects of children's schooling. Rather, it is part of a complex of administrative interventions, all designed to treat – and channel – students in different ways. Each treatment interacts with the others. The tracking patterns reviewed in this chapter reveal at least the outlines of how treatments overlap. It is a complicated picture, one we hope encourages further inquiry into the many facets of elementary and middle school tracking.

9

The retention puzzle: problem, solution, or signal?

This volume began by asking whether retention helps children, as intended, or harms them, as critics of the practice believe. The question, it now seems, is too simple, as is the expectation that there will be a simple answer.

Although the analyses in this book indicate that retention has mainly positive consequences, this was not true for all repeaters under all circumstances. Positive effects are found mainly for youngsters held back only once, and for youngsters held back after first grade. Despite the preponderance of positive effects, retention does not cure children's problems. The distinction between "solution" and "some help" is critical, and glossing it over has created much of the confusion surrounding retention. The boost children get from repeating a grade, though real, is limited: most one-time repeaters realize some benefits, but remain far behind their agemates.

These complications notwithstanding, the main thrust of our conclusions is clear; it is also much at odds with the view that retention impedes children's academic development, and especially so with the view that retention assaults their sense of self. Though widely held, this picture of retention does not fit the experience of BSS youngsters. Instead of impeding their progress, repeating a grade helped retainees do better in their repeated year and for some years thereafter, although in diminishing amounts, until they made the transition into middle school. Rather than harming these children emotionally, retention led to improvement in their attitudes about self and school during the repeated year, and gave children a boost that often persisted until middle school.

These conclusions probably accord well with teachers' understandings, because most teachers see a useful role for retention in helping poor-performing students overcome problems before they have fallen too far behind (e.g., Byrnes 1989; Lombardi, Odell, and Novotny 1990; Smith 1989; Smith and Shepard 1988; Tomchin and Impara 1992). However, most researchers and commentators convey a very different sense of how retention works. Remarks by Ernest House (1989: 210), a distinguished scholar in the area of educational policy research, are representative: "The evidence is extensive and unequivocal. It includes test scores, surveys, personality and emotional adjustment measures, case studies – everything from elaborate statistical analyses to asking students how they feel. Almost everything points in the same direction – retention is an extremely harmful practice."

What accounts for such wildly differing views? House (1989: 210) offers several reasons teachers' thinking might be "askew" (his word). Teachers, he argues, see only the temporary improvement that may result from going over the same curriculum for a second time, illustrated vividly in BSS children's "recovery" year in the fail–repeat cycle. Because teachers' contact with children is limited and short-term, they do not observe the problems that emerge later, including dropping out of high school. Nor can teachers compare students' progress with what might have happened had they been passed along. House also believes that most practitioners subscribe to an achievement-oriented ideology that throws up blinders to retention's problems.

All these opinions are reasonable, but there are equally good reasons to suspect that it is the thinking of researchers, not that of teachers, that is "askew." If retention's consequences are actually more positive than negative, how could opinions in the social science research community stray so far off the mark?

The practice of retention: positive effects, bad press

There are any number of reasons individual studies, and assessments of them, might be misleading.[1] In Chapter 1 we mentioned several weaknesses in the available research on retention. With evidence from the BSS now in hand, we should revisit these concerns.

As noted earlier, much of the available research is old, so perhaps the conclusion that retention is harmful is simply dated. Social promotion was in vogue when much of this research was conducted, and it is certainly possible that retention had a different connotation when it was out of favor (for a good overview of historical changes in retention policy, and of the philosophical differences that underlay them, see Larabee 1984). That most of the studies favoring retention are relatively recent is consistent with this possibility.

Much of the research is also suspect on scientific grounds. Earlier in this book we outlined some of the reasons it is so hard to do a proper evaluation. It also is important that prior research is not nearly so consistently lined up against retention as quotes like that from House, and others presented in the first chapter, would suggest. Reynolds (1992: 3), for example, observes that only 25 of the 63 studies covered in Holmes's (1989) meta-analysis use matching or statistical adjustments in evaluating retention's effects. Of these, only 16 match on students' prior achievements, and only 4 match "on attributes that are consistently found to be predictive of the decision to retain including prior achievement, sex and socioeconomic status." We saw in Chapters 5 and 6 that such adjustments can make a big difference in how results are patterned.

Reynolds does not mention that one of the four studies that employs all these controls finds positive effects for retention, but he does go on to say that "this hardly constitutes conclusive evidence for or against retention." Later he notes that the studies reviewed by Holmes find "only marginally negative effects [of retention] on attitudes toward school and positive (though negligible) effects on self-concept." Positive effects on self-concept are also indicated in Reynolds's own analysis, as in ours, and positive effects on performance have recently been reported by Pierson and Connell (1992), and by Peterson et al. (1987), among others. The evidence, it seems, is not nearly as extensive or unequivocal as often assumed (for a balanced overview see Karweit 1992).

We also wonder whether the studies now in the literature overrepresent children who are especially susceptible to retention's damaging effects. Retention no doubt is harder on children in some circumstances than others, and it could work differently in schools where just a handful of retainees stand out in comparison with a large majority of successful students. Little retention research has been conducted on children like those in the BSS, that is, minority and disadvantaged student populations in urban school systems where retention rates are high overall, and where many students fit the so-called at-risk profile. In situations in which repeaters are less conspicuous, it seems plausible that social stigma would not be as much of a problem. Still, we have seen throughout this volume that conventional wisdom can be off the mark, so stigmatization shouldn't just be assumed. In other recent studies, the positive effects of retention are not limited to urban school systems with large poverty-level and minority enrollments. Nor, for that matter, does research on such children always find positive effects (e.g., Reynolds 1992).

School context and student characteristics no doubt play a role in determining the effects of retention, but the confusion in the literature runs deeper. Most central, we believe, are the challenges involved in getting a proper sense of retention's effects. Most studies have not addressed these challenges adequately.

For one thing, repeaters have multiple problems; after retention their test scores are depressed, their marks are poor, and they misbehave, but these difficulties plague repeaters before they are held back. It is understandable that people concerned about retainees and their welfare find the picture troubling on the face of it. It also is understandable that retention would be blamed if just the "after" problems are perceived, as would be the case in everyday, casual observation. Unfortunately, the typical matched-control study looks forward from the point of failure, not backward, and so also lacks perspective on retainees before they are held back.

Few studies are like the present one, in which future repeaters are "captured" in a random sample from a well-defined cohort of students, and then their academic progress and personal development is monitored over a long interval that predates and overlaps the retention experience. An exception is Reynolds's study, already mentioned. In addition to targeting a poverty-level, entirely minority inner-city population, his study also tracks their experiences over time, from kindergarten to the end of fourth grade. His study finds positive effects on attitudes and no achievement differences in same-grade comparisons (which Reynolds does not emphasize), but large shortfalls in same-age comparisons. We, too, found large same-age differences at roughly the same point (spring of Year 4), at least among first grade repeaters, but these differences sometimes were considerably below these children's shortfall from before retention.

This longitudinal approach allows us to view repeaters' standing after retention in light of their circumstances before they were held back, and in terms of academics, self-regard, and liking for school. This sense of retainees' history is absolutely essential, because repeaters in the BSS sample began school with serious academic and adjustment problems that worsened over time. Once in school, linguistic barriers, poor work habits, lack of social support, and perhaps troubled relationships with their teachers no doubt aggravate many of these children's problems. This, though, is part of the *backdrop* to retention. In the fall of first grade, eventual retainees' CAT-R average was 24 points below that of never-retained children, and their CAT-M average was 29 points lower. Both disparities were much larger for first grade repeaters, whose scores were below those of never-retained children by 34 and 41 points respectively. Such large shortfalls signal that repeaters were far behind their class-mates at the start of their formal schooling. We also saw large differences in early school adjustment.

Throughout their elementary and middle school years we have moni-tored BSS children's progress in reading and math, the two subjects that dominate the curriculum in the early grades (see Rosenshine 1980). They are the foundation for almost all schooling that comes later. A child who can't keep up in reading, or who is weak in basic number skills, will not suddenly spurt ahead when the teacher gets to the next lesson or moves on to the next subject. Knowledge of the fundamentals is hierarchical and cumulative: children cannot learn fractions if they cannot add and subtract, and reading skills below grade level will guarantee that every other subject is a challenge.

Knowing retainees' problems were more severe before retention than after tells us that retention itself has not created, or even compounded, their problems. House (1989) reminds us that most teachers do not see repeaters' problems that emerge after the repeated year; nevertheless, for a proper reading of retention's effects the time frame needs to stretch in both directions. Most retention studies gloss over or omit entirely prob-lems that exist before children are held back.

Also ignored in most commentary and research on retention are track-ing systems – such as reading-group placements in first grade, reading level in the upper elementary years, course placements in middle school, and special education placements – that could be even more relevant to children's day-to-day experience at school than their standing as re-tainees. Retention, for example, does not affect children's daily schedule, but the other placements do. Special education is no doubt the most dramatic, but high and low reading groups in elementary school, and high- and low-track classes in middle school, differ markedly in status as seen by students, parents, and classmates. They also differ in student composition and group dynamics, as well as in instructional pace, style, and content (for an excellent overview of these issues see Oakes et al. 1992). More salient than retention, these other administrative decisions also could have more substantial impact, and since retainees tend to occupy low "slots" in other dimensions of tracking, the effects of tracking can be confused with those of retention.

Problems that distinguish single repeaters from children who experience multiple retentions, or from those placed in special education after being held back, also tend to get slighted. These latter youths account for much of retainees' later performance deficit, but the literature is silent on how problems that are peculiar to particular categories of retainees ought to be construed.

The question is whether all the problems overlapping retention are viewed as its consequences, because most studies of retention start with a group of repeaters and then compose a comparison group of promoted children who are "like the repeaters" in ways deemed relevant. Such research lacks the broad purview and long time frame of the Beginning School Study, and studies of retention rarely take a perspective that is sensitive to the broader organizational context. The "pathways" of Chapter 2 and the "bundling" of track placements in Chapter 8 show that retainees are placed in low tracks much more than other students, but most evaluations of retention simply ignore tracking. The confusion created may be one reason so many people perceive retention in a negative light. They see low placements or special education as consequences rather than as concomitants of retention.

Finally, preconceptions no doubt play a role as well. Much of the literature on retention and tracking reflects a negative mind-set. In part, these predispositions are grounded in equity or fairness concerns (Chapter 1). But there is also a critical perspective on schooling and social inequality that emphasizes the role played by schools in preserving patterns of advantage and disadvantage across generations. The well-to-do, it is argued, pass along their good fortune by ensuring that their children do well in school, and schools cooperate by making more resources and opportunities available to them. The tracking system, in this view, is a key instrument for selective sorting on the basis of social privilege, legitimated through reliance on "merit" criteria – test scores, grades, and the like (see, for example, Bowles and Gintis 1976; and more recently Oakes 1992).

Minority and disadvantaged children tend to be overrepresented in lower-track placements. Similarly, they are more likely to be held back than whites or children from higher SES families. The experience of the BSS youngsters shows this too, although much more in terms of socio-economic than race/ethnicity disparities. When children are separated along racial/ethnic and class lines (even if the separation is based on educationally appropriate criteria), assigned to roles that are low in the school's hierarchy of values, and treated differently thereafter, the risk of harm is real.

The other risk, though, is that of accepting evidence too readily just because it accords with one's worldview. We fear this is the case with retention. Weak, inconclusive evidence has been presented as robust. Bad science, when taken seriously, spills over to bad practice. Teachers by and large want desperately to help, but they have been cast as villains in the retention controversy and made to feel guilty for holding "un-enlightened" ideas. Worse yet, some children who might be helped by having an extra year to consolidate their skills probably have been pushed along unprepared when they would have been better served by being held back.

Whether to have a child repeat is the implicit question in most evalua-tions of retention. The picture is mixed, but the preponderance of favor-able indications in our data for single-grade repeaters is clear. Had we started at the point when children were held back, as most research does, we would have missed not just the depth of their earlier problems, but also the course they were running prior to retention. If not seen from this perspective, the turnaround reflected in children's progress while going through a grade the second time would have been obscured. And even when repeaters' standing slipped after retention, in many comparisons they still were relatively better off than they had been before repeating a grade.

Repeaters only rarely kept up, in the sense of having test scores or marks on a par with those of promoted children. Sometimes the com-parisons were not favorable, as in the case of first grade repeaters (and others) when they arrived at the middle school period. But after adjusting repeaters' later performance for their standing before retention, they usually did keep up, and in many of the same-grade comparisons they were well ahead of what would be expected for children "like them." Furthermore, for these children retention apparently left few if any psychological scars.

Our data show little harm from retention, and we can think of no reason for expecting social promotion to repair anything. It seems better to give children a chance to consolidate their skills by repeating a grade, despite the currently negative social climate that militates against this choice. Educators, administrators, and parents have limited options to deal with children who have fallen far behind. Later we will discuss alternatives to retention that go beyond the simple either / or dilemma we have posed, but when the only available options are to promote or retain, as they often are for educators and administrators in school systems like that of Baltimore, our advice would be to judge each case on its merits and to recommend retention if it seems warranted.

Marginal students and educational transitions

The problems that our analyses identify have little to do with retention. The particular burdens that weigh on children when they start formal schooling, and when they move from the elementary grades into middle school, are critical. How these key educational transitions are weathered is likely more important for children's schooling than anything having to do with retention policy. The more important question is how to structure children's school experience so that the formidable hurdles presented at these transition points can be successfully negotiated.

A life-course perspective points to transitions as times of stress in people's lives (for a general overview see Elder 1985, 1991). The life transitions that usually come to mind are encountered in adulthood – marrying, becoming a parent, embarking on a new career, entering retirement. But children's role transitions can be as dramatic, as challenging, and possibly even more overwhelming than those experienced by adults, because children have less control over their lives, and fewer resources with which to meet the challenges. Just as with adults, some will be better positioned than others to weather transition pressures. Those not well positioned need help.

This volume considers two school transitions: that into full-time schooling, representing children's first encounters with the student role and with the attendant educational bureaucracy that defines its parameters; and the transition from elementary to middle school, when the role demands and the bureaucracy undergo significant changes. Our data suggest that both transitions are more difficult for repeaters to manage, precisely because they are already shaky academically.

The beginning school transition and early school failure

The relevance of transition pressures at the time of school entry is obvious. Indeed, failure in the early grades is virtually a synonym for unsuccessful adaptation to the student role. Time and again throughout this volume we have seen striking parallels between the severity of children's difficulties and the scheduling of their retention. First grade retainees, the largest single repeater group by far in the BSS sample, are also the most severely stressed. Children's first year in full-time school is the most problematic for falling behind in every data set we have seen, including national data on modal age in grade. It thus seems that the retention situation in Baltimore is not unusual. Shepard and Smith's (1989) survey of 13 states, for example, reveals that primary grade retention peaks in first grade in all 13.[2] Several states also have high rates in kindergarten.

The beginning school period entails a transition into a new social world (Entwisle and Alexander 1989, 1993). Children add "schoolchild" to their role set and must learn to function in an institutional context governed by conventions different from those at home. The norms and expectations surrounding teacher–pupil relations are very different from those for parents and offspring. Relations with teachers, for example, are instrumental, impersonal, and achievement oriented (for a thoughtful discussion of these issues see Dreeben 1968). These new and different role relationships challenge all youngsters, but for children who have fewer resources outside school, and who have grown up outside the middle class mainstream, home and school may seem like entirely different worlds.

Differences across class lines in family socialization practices give children from higher SES families an academic advantage before they begin school, and a continuing advantage all through their years there. More often, their parents read with them and are seen reading; there are more magazines and other reading materials in the home; they take more trips to libraries; and their parents value literacy more and hold their children to higher standards. Middle and upper class families in general are more supportive of things academic, and they have the resources to make that support tangible (see Hess and Holloway 1984; Slaughter and Epps 1987).

Children who lack these advantages are victims of resource shortfalls in their family and community environments. They often get off to a shaky start academically, and once they have fallen behind, their prospects for recovery are not good. Among the BSS youngsters, for example, children who lose ground in terms of test scores and marks over the first year tend to hold that position all along the way. Children's achievement trajectories are established early (e.g., Bloom 1964; Kraus 1973), as data for the first 8 years of school covered in this volume testify. Retention calls attention to children's problems, but it neither causes them, nor, as best we can determine, compounds them.

Academic failure, not retention, is what needs fixing; unfortunately, failure is what awaits too many children in places like Baltimore. That it sets in so early and for so many is the price children pay for growing up in highly stressed (economically and otherwise) home and community circumstances (e.g., Coleman and Hoffer 1987). The BSS children all began first grade in 1982. Most of their parents were in their 20s at that time, when being young, poorly educated, a single parent, or African-American often also meant living in or at the edge of poverty. The national statistics on poverty and family disorganization among the "forgotten half" of the population who do not go to college are sobering. Indeed, their situation during this period has been likened to a "New Depression" (*Forgotten Half* 1988: 16).

In Baltimore, as in other old-line cities, whites and the well-to-do have been abandoning the city, moving to the suburbs and beyond in large numbers. In 1980, near the time when the BSS started, Baltimore's population was 55% African-American, up from 47% a decade earlier. The white population that remained was much older than the African-American population, with a median age of 37.0 versus 26.2 (U.S. Bureau of the Census 1973, 1983). Forty-one percent of Baltimore households with children under 18 were headed by a female in 1980, and half of these fell below the poverty line. Overall, 19% of families were living in poverty, with about the same percentage receiving public assistance. Nearly a third of 16- to 19-year-olds were identified as not enrolled in school and not high school graduates, while more than half the adults 25 years and older had not completed high school (U.S. Bureau of the Census 1983). Baltimore placed 14 among the nation's 15 largest cities in 1983 in the percentage of 20- to 24-year-olds completing high school (Szanton 1986).

These conditions in the early eighties were the social backdrop to the time our study youngsters were starting first grade. They are not limited to the early eighties, however, as hard times prevailed during the rest of the decade. In 1990, for example, the percentage of female-headed families with children under 18 had risen to 49, and poverty levels remained high at 18% overall (U.S. Bureau of the Census 1991). A recent analysis (Children's Defense Fund 1992) shows a 32.5% percent 1990 poverty rate in Baltimore for persons under age 18; 39.1% for African-Americans, and 16.9% for whites. Of the 200 cities with populations of at least 100,000 in 1990, 112 had African-American poverty rates higher than Baltimore's; 55 had higher white poverty rates. The situation in Baltimore thus is bad, but hardly exceptional.

Moreover, the population served by the public schools is even more disadvantaged than in the city overall, and this imbalance, too, is very likely typical. As mentioned in the Preface, in 1988, 60% of Baltimore's public school students were receiving free lunches[3] (Citizens Planning and Housing Association 1990). In almost half the elementary schools, the figure was above 70%, and in 26 of the 106 schools it was more than 80%!

The families in the BSS sample similarly reflect high levels of socioeconomic disadvantage, even though our sampling intentionally over-represented white and better-off families. Forty-seven percent of the BSS children were living in single-parent households when they started school, 67% of the families received free or reduced-price meals at school, and 38% of the mothers of study children had not completed high school. More sobering still are first grade benchmarks for children who remained in city schools over the entire 8-year period covered in this volume: 52% of the children were in single-parent households, 76% of the families qualified for free or reduced-price meals, and 42% of the mothers were high school dropouts. All of these are well documented as academic risk factors (Natriello, McDill, and Pallas 1990).

For youngsters who are not regularly promoted over the first three grades, failure is not a sharply demarcated experience that occurs when they are held back. Rather, they have been "failing" or "near failing" all along. The administrative decision to have them repeat a grade is mainly a public signal vouching for the severity of their problems. Critics of retention sometimes seem to assume that simply doing away with the decision will solve the basic problem. This is obviously untrue. What needs to be changed is not the retention decision, but the sorry experience of youngsters who fail to negotiate the beginning school transition successfully.

Programs to help children manage this difficult time in their lives are not well described. Head Start, the only federally funded preschool program for poor children, currently serves fewer than one in five 3- to 5-year-olds who live in poor families, a ratio that has not changed significantly since the mid-eighties. Programs to ease school adjustment during kindergarten generally are piecemeal, and rarely do they have the standing of formal policy. Although most school personnel do not view kindergarten adjustment as especially problematic, according to Love and Logue's National Transition Study (1992) the data indicate otherwise. A third of schools in which 50% or more of students qualify for free meals, for example, report that children have great difficulty adjusting to academic demands. These schools also report more transition classes (e.g., an extra year between kindergarten and first grade) and kindergarten retention, two practices that have escalated nationwide in recent years (e.g., Epstein 1987; for commentary and research overviews see Shepard 1989, as well as Shepard and Smith 1988). Whatever the merits of such practices, the trends themselves clearly signal the same problem indicated in the high rate of early failure seen for BSS children; too many children start school unprepared or not well-enough prepared for what awaits them.

The middle school transition and the fading of retention's benefits

Getting off to a bad start in school is the backdrop for early retention. Recovering from early failure is hard, but children do recover to some extent after being held back a year. The recovery is not complete, though, because most retainees remain behind both their previous classmates and their new ones. The recovery also is only temporary, which is the concern addressed in this section.

The gains children realize by repeating a grade are hard won, and costly, so to see them fade over time is a disappointment. In fact, though, most interventions designed to shore up the academic skills of at-risk children have transient effects. Benefits of preschool programs for the disadvantaged like Head Start raise test scores only temporarily (e.g., Lazar and Darlington 1982; Schweinhart, Berrueta-Clement, Barnett, Epstein, and Weikart 1985; Schweinhart and Weikart 1985).

Children usually show a significant IQ spurt in the year following their participation in such programs, but after a couple of years their scores typically are no better than those of children who did not go to pre-school.[4] This pattern left early commentators skeptical about the useful-ness of large-scale compensatory education programs as a remedy for the academic difficulties of children from impoverished backgrounds (e.g., Jensen 1969; McDill, McDill, and Sprehe 1969; but see also Bron-fenbrenner 1974, who emphasizes the gains themselves as signifying effectiveness).

The "spurt–fade out" pattern is not limited to preschool programs, though. It also is seen in comparisons of half-day versus full-day kinder-garten programs (Entwisle, Alexander, Cadigan, and Pallas 1987; Kar-weit 1989a), and in assessments of Chapter 1, the major federal program for assisting schools that service large numbers of poverty-level children (e.g., Carter 1984; Gabriel et al. 1985; Myers 1986; for good overviews of these issues see Haskins 1989; Slavin 1989).

None of these efforts to help children represents a well-defined inter-vention model. Head Start and Chapter 1 are mainly funding mecha-nisms, and exactly how the funding is deployed varies greatly at the local level. Similarly, extending kindergarten to a full day simply buys more time for children in school, and the use to which that time is put is not standardized. Indeed, attempts in all of these areas to isolate specific program features that could be used to inform future planning have not been especially successful (e.g., Karweit 1989a; Schweinhart, Weikart, and Larner 1986; White 1985–86; White, Taylor, and Moss 1992).[5] Castro and Mastropieri (1986), for example, caution that four nostrums about preschool programs – that earlier is better, as are more parental involvement, high levels of structure, and greater intensity – are not consistently supported by the literature. Some may not hold up at all, and others may do so only for certain kinds of children under particular circumstances (e.g., highly structured instruction seems to work best for disadvantaged populations).

Retention, too, lacks programmatic coherence, and exactly what part of the experience helps children has yet to be isolated. In this volume, for example, we have been able to compare only children who have been held back with those who have not been, and this is typical of retention evaluations. Many localities provide supplemental services for retainees, but rarely are alternative service models systematically compared. The pattern for retention thus parallels that seen for other interventions; such programs seem to help, but absent an effective program to consolidate and sustain children's improved performance, the advantages they bring about do not last.

Our results tell us a little more, however. Retainees' academic standing in some instances still shows improvement several years after retention. This is an uncommonly long interval; or, equivalently, an uncommonly slow fade. Moreover, it is critical, we think, that in several comparisons both academic performance and attitudes dropped off most noticeably around the time of the middle school transition. Recall that most schools in the Baltimore system have a K–5, 6–8 grade structure. By the upper elementary grades most repeaters are already a year or two behind their on-time peers, so they are considerably older than their classmates when they enter middle school. In most instances retainees are closer to 13 or 14 than to 12, children's typical age at the start of sixth grade.

"Settling in" issues arise whenever children switch schools. Having to learn one's way around a new physical environment, getting to know new teachers and administrators, possibly being separated from one's long-time friends, and going from "top dog" to the bottom of the school's social hierarchy are very real concerns for children. All of these problems are magnified when the move is from a smaller school to a bigger one, as is typical in the middle-grades transition. These transition changes alone would complicate children's lives, but for retainees the changes encountered in the middle grades are much more challenging, and the accommodations required of them are correspondingly greater.

Compared with elementary schools, middle and junior high schools are larger and more departmentalized, teaching is more specialized, standards of performance are higher, and academic achievement is emphasized more, all of which encourage a more competitive atmosphere. There are also differences in the character of pupil–teacher relations: teachers tend to be more distant and controlling; they rely more on whole-class instruction; evaluation is more public; and tracking tends to be more formalized and rigid.

This middle school or junior high environment is very different from that of the primary grades, and under the old junior high grade structure (K–6, 7–9), it was imposed on children just when most of them also were wrestling with the changes that define adolescence – changes in their bodies, in their personal identities, in their relations with peers, and so forth. The situation is even more complicated, however, because the very features of schooling in the middle grades that are new in children's experience tend to run counter to their needs as adolescents. Eccles and Midgley (1989: 141) describe the situation as follows:

> These changes are *particularly* harmful at early adolescence in that they emphasize competition, social comparison and ability self-assessment at a time of heightened self-focus; they decrease decision-making and choice when the desire for control is growing; and they disrupt social networks at a time when adolescents are especially concerned with peer relationships and may be in special need of close adult friendships.

That the middle-grades transition is hard on children now seems well established, and this problem is increasingly understood as one shared by middle schools and junior highs alike. Children's attitudes toward self and school, along with their performance, tend to deteriorate as they move from the primary grades to later ones (for an overview see Eccles and Midgley 1989; Stipek 1984; Weisz and Cameron 1985), but there is an especially precipitous decline right around the middle-grades transition. Some studies (e.g., Simmons and Blyth 1987) find a large falloff at the transition between the sixth and seventh grades (that is, into junior high school); nevertheless, moving the transition back to between the fifth and sixth grades (into middle school) does not help consistently (see Eccles and Midgley 1989), perhaps because organizational arrangements in middle schools and in junior high schools are not all that dissimilar (e.g., Cuban 1992; Eccles et al. 1991).[6]

The experience of the BSS youngsters suggests that the middle school transition especially challenges elementary school repeaters. Retainees are off-time (and older) when making the middle school transition, so for them the adolescent and school transitions may still overlap.[7] Although these youngsters were doing better in the postretention period than before, they still were barely hanging on. They remained highly vulnerable, so it is reasonable to suppose that any of several middle school features mentioned – elevated standards, a more rigid tracking system, or the larger, more impersonal bureaucracy – could set them back. These are problems for everyone, but repeaters probably are not as well positioned as others to manage them.

The middle school dip experienced by repeaters in the Beginning School Study points to this transition as a time of particular vulnerability. Research on compensatory education, as well as the present assessment of retention, indicates that we know more about how to help at-risk children succeed academically than is generally appreciated, but finding a formula for lasting benefits has proven elusive. The rather substantial benefits registered in the short term wash out; after a few years the children who have been helped are no better off than they had been before. The challenge is to preserve these hard-won victories. Extra support at the middle-grades transition conceivably could make a great difference, as might extra support at the beginning-school transition, where the issue is how to sustain the momentum induced by compensatory preschool programs and/or full-day kindergarten.

Retention and remediation: avoiding failure, preserving gains

Although the BSS data indicate that 1-year retentions have positive effects on scholastic competence, this does not mean that we have any particular enthusiasm for holding children back. Quite the contrary. Retention is an admission of failure, both for the children who will spend at least 2 years in a grade and for the schools that are supposed to help them make satisfactory progress. Yet under a social promotion regime most repeaters would lag even farther behind in the upper grades than they do after having been held back, and this relative advantage is important. Retention helps children recover in the short term, and for a number of years afterward it keeps many above where they would have been had their earlier performance trajectories simply been extrapolated. We judge retention a qualified success – the "success of failure" alluded to in this volume's title.

The qualifications, though, are critical. Regardless of exactly how the comparisons are made (whether through statistical adjustments or comparison groups), evaluations of retention basically all look to see whether retainees, or promoted children with a similar academic prognosis, make greater strides.[8] We accept this as a reasonable standard for judging retention's effectiveness, just as does virtually everyone else (if only implicitly) who has worked in this area. But going beyond the narrow question of whether retention helps or hurts, one has to question a system of education that leaves so many children, retained and promoted alike, so far behind. Similar concerns have been raised by Travers (1982: 273) in commenting on the debate over special education versus regular placement, and by Hebbeler (1985) regarding the effectiveness of preschool programs. Program evaluations give us a sense of what would have been expected absent the intervention at issue, but the prognosis for poor-performing children all together is not good, and we should not be content to see repeaters just keep pace if the pace itself is unacceptable. Retention does not turn failures into academic superstars, or even into average students. At best it helps them hang on, and by the time they get to the middle grades they are mainly relegated to remedial, slow-track courses. It is a useful clarification to know that lower-level middle school placements should not be attributed to retention, but it is small comfort if we wish to launch as many children as possible onto successful middle school trajectories. The real need is to figure out how to avoid failure in the first place; and when children do have to be held back, we need to know how to make retention even more effective than it is, and how to keep children's performance elevated once they get back into the regular promotion sequence.

There is as yet no clear way to help all children succeed academically, but that does not mean good ideas are completely lacking. Within the context of retention, there are many alternatives to simply "recycling" children for a year, and it is reasonable to think some of them should be more effective. Medway (1985), for example, mentions as possibilities transition classes (for problems detected in kindergarten), promotion with supplemental services, retention with supplemental services, partial promotion (in which only part of the curriculum is repeated), and summer school. Some recent restructuring proposals may even prove useful, such as the resurgence of interest in ungraded schools (e.g., Willis 1991). These group children for instruction on the basis of readiness or competence in the instructional area, rather than on age, and often supplement whole-class instruction with individualized instruction and team teaching. Assessments are made frequently, and children move through a sequence of learning levels that can encompass the entire span of grades in the school's grade structure. This approach creates large, reasonably homogeneous instructional groups without separating "low" from "high" within an age cohort. It also allows for flexibility in placing students and relieves some of the calendar-driven pressures that leave many children behind when the teacher has to move on (see Gutierrez and Slavin 1992; Slavin 1987).

Although the evidence thus far on transition classes (e.g., Leinhardt 1980; Shepard and Smith 1986) and summer programs (e.g., Carter

1984; Heyns 1987) is not very encouraging, none of these options has been thoroughly evaluated, and there should be ways to make them work. In the early primary grades, for example, at-risk children overall make impressive academic strides during the school year, keeping pace with children from more advantaged backgrounds in terms of test score gains, and in some cases doing even better. However, these children regress or stay even over the summer months, when school is not in session, while others advance. This pattern prevails for the BSS youngsters (Entwisle and Alexander 1992, 1994), and has been documented for children in Atlanta (Heyns 1978) and in New Haven (Murnane 1975), as well as in at least one large national survey (Heyns 1987). Schooling, this pattern suggests, very likely is more effective than generally appreciated for disadvantaged youngsters.

If some school is good, shouldn't more be better? Reflecting this logic, proposals to lengthen the school year, extend the school day, and begin school at earlier ages have been advanced.[9] We favor more early schooling for those at risk, and extra supports all through the primary grades to help preserve gains associated with compensatory interventions, including preschool, full-day kindergarten, and retention. Time, though, is little more than an empty box, and simply stretching the school day or the school year will not by itself fix anything. What counts is the use to which time is put, and probably also how programs are followed up at home. Much time in school is devoted to procedural matters and the like, and even when children are supposed to be working on academic tasks, their attention is frequently elsewhere (for time logs in the primary grades see Rosenshine 1979, 1980; for research reviews see Karweit 1985, 1989b). Wasted time is one concern; ineffective use of engaged time is another. In surveying the relevant literature, Karweit (1989b: 91) concludes that the effects of time on learning are weak and inconsistent, and that "there is little evidence to suggest that increasing time for learning in and of itself will be an effective educational strategy."[10] To make progress academically children must be taught well, with appropriate techniques, in a supportive educational environment. This holds for all youngsters, but especially for children at risk of being held back (Leinhardt and Bickel 1989).

A thorough treatment of the literature on instructional practices that seem to work especially well with at-risk children is outside the purview of this volume, but Slavin, Karweit, and Madden (1989) identify several themes that seem to have considerable support. These are cogent and worth repeating (355–56):

1. The setting in which remedial or special education services are provided makes little difference. What does matter is the quality of the programs implemented in that setting.
2. Prevention and early intervention are much more promising than waiting for learning deficits to accumulate.
3. Effective classroom and pull-out programs tend to accommodate instruction to individual needs while maximizing direct instruction. They frequently assess student progress through a structured hierarchy of skills, and adapt instructional strategies to the results of these assessments. When pull-out programs are used they should be intensive (e.g., one-to-one tutoring or computer-assisted instruction), brief, and designed to quickly catch students up with the rest of the class, not to support them indefinitely.
4. Effective preschool programs tend to emphasize exploration, language development, and play, not academics. Effective kindergarten programs build language and prereading skills using structured, well-organized, comprehensive approaches.
5. Remedial and special education services are too often poorly integrated with the regular education program. Collaboration and consistency between regular, remedial, and special education are essential.
6. Teacher behaviors associated with outstanding achievement gains for students in Chapter 1 pull-out programs, and for mainstreamed academically handicapped students in regular classrooms, tend to be similar to behaviors found effective for all students. Effective practices for students at risk tend not to be qualitatively different from the best practices of general education.

These principles are sensible, and most are well supported through extensive research. If they could be applied sensitively in regular and supplementary programs throughout children's schooling, and combined with effective home–school "partnership" programs (e.g., Epstein 1992; for evaluations of Success for All, which embodies many of these principles, see Madden, Slavin, Karweit, Dolan, and Wasik 1993; and Slavin, Madden, Karweit, Livermon, and Dolan 1990), we suspect there would be less need for retention altogether, and that when it was needed, students would backslide far less often later.

Concluding remarks

The retention question can be framed narrowly or broadly. By the standards of a narrow assessment, in which we ask whether poor-performing children are better or worse off having been held back, we find in favor of retention. This is important, because although the weight of sentiment in the research literature would have us believe otherwise, having children repeat a year can and does help academically; moreover, at least for children like those in Baltimore, it does not compromise self-regard. It would be unfortunate if this useful tool in the school's arsenal were discarded because of unwarranted conclusions drawn from a weak and inconsistent research literature. However, if the goal is to have children who are not well prepared *succeed* in school, retention is not a solution. Policies need to be especially conscious of difficulties surrounding educational transitions, when problems tend to mount. Performing at acceptable levels before moving on is key in our view. Retention supplies the additional time needed by some students, but a lasting solution requires more than simply going over the same material twice.

Notes

1. Retention: many questions, few answers

1. The report states (p. 3) that the 6-year-olds below first grade are "late starters," although it is not clear how this was determined.
2. Ethnicity is self-reported in Census surveys, and Hispanics may be of any race. There is thus some double counting in these tallies. Changes over time in patterns of ethnic self-identification could confound trends in the case of Hispanics.
3. But see Slavin et al. (1989) for a thoughtful overview of practices that might reduce the need for retention.
4. For the time being we set aside alternatives other than routine promotion (e.g., promotion with special remediation efforts; see, for example, Leinhardt 1980). These other possibilities will be considered in the concluding chapter.
5. We suppose it also would have to be stipulated that there are no advantages accruing to other classes of students large enough or important enough to justify the harm to some. Research evaluations rarely consider such possible tradeoffs, but they are commonplace in the real world, and to somehow resolve them is one of the heavy burdens of education administration.
6. Wilson (1990) also criticizes Holmes for favoring same-age over same-grade comparisons in evaluating retention's effectiveness.
7. Although these very same factors could, and probably would, contribute to individual differences in performance *within* groups.
8. Fortunately, the youngsters with complete records closely approximate the characteristics of those lost from the analysis owing to gaps in the testing series.
9. Peterson et al.'s use of the normal curve metric is a minor problem here, as this results in a different "fulcrum" being used for the various comparison groups (e.g., the performance of retained first graders is scaled relative to the distribution of first graders, while that of second graders is referenced to other second graders). It would obviously be useful to know whether re-

tainees are doing better or worse than promoted youngsters at some specified time after retention, and normal score equivalents don't tell that particular story. Since the various CAT levels are vertically calibrated, it would have been a simple matter to report raw score means as well. These use a common metric across levels, and would have informed such questions.

10. Mantzicopoulos and Morrison (1992) also report significant same-grade differences favoring repeaters in the repeated year, but again this is largely a consequence of the way the comparisons were structured.

11. We reluctantly decided not to inquire about income or welfare status, fearing that such inquiries would discourage many parents from participating in the study.

2. Children's pathways through the elementary and middle school years: retention+

1. Many of the other records were also problematic in that they were either incomplete or seemingly inconsistent in some way. These, though, we were able to resolve, mostly by assuming an orderly promotion history in the absence of indications otherwise (e.g., if the spring code for a given year was missing, but the previous fall code was one grade level behind the subsequent fall code).

2. Many midyear reassignments involve special education students, which complicates matters. Special education classes typically include pupils from all grade levels, and the BCPS central records are inconsistent in how children are classified. Sometimes a grade level is indicated, sometimes not. In Figure 2.1 we do not report grade levels for children while they are in special education classes. This circumvents the problem of uneven coverage, but obscures to some degree the overlap between retention and special education, because the retention experience of students who are placed in special education before being retained is not displayed. This omission turns out to be of minor consequence, however, since only a handful of retained students enter special education before being retained. Most special education assignments occur after at least one retention. All retentions will be covered in the text, whether they occur before or after special education assignment.

3. Candidates for special education whose problems are judged insufficiently severe to require placement in separate classes receive special education pull-out instruction in reading and / or math. In Figure 2.1 these youngsters are included in the tally for their grade level. During the 8-year period, 144 children received such services at some point, 60 in Year 1, 59 in Year 2.

4. Identifying the sample of retained students in Figure 2.1 is complicated by

the timing of special education assignment. In general, a horizontal line between boxes across 2 years indicates that children were retained in that year. Thus, 126 students were retained in first grade in the first year, 61 in second grade in the second year, 45 in third grade in the third year, and so on. The total number of retainees in these years is slightly higher, however. If students were assigned to special education in the spring of the year, before being retained, then they are added to the special education category at the bottom of Figure 2.1. Their grade placement following that assignment is not displayed. The numbers in the upper section of the figure thus somewhat undercount retentions. The complete tally of retainees, year by year, is as follows: first grade, 127; second grade, 68; third grade, 47; fourth grade, 21; fifth grade, 10; sixth grade, 22; and seventh grade, 22.

5. Children who left the BCPS are not included in Figure 2.1 after their departure even if they later returned. There may be as many as 12 youngsters who came back at some point, but their school records may not be reliable in all cases. Six of the 12, for example, seemingly returned for just one semester and then left again.

6. In fact, this figure is very likely on the low side in terms of what is happening in the city school system generally. A simple tally of the grade-specific retention rates for grades 1 through 5 in the city school system for the 1988–89 school year yields a "cumulative risk of retention" of 52%. The highest elementary school rate is in first grade, with 16.3% of the city system's first graders being held back (Kelly 1989). Our sampling design overselected whites and children from higher SES households, and so it is not surprising that the BSS figures should fall a bit short of those citywide. These kinds of young people have a lower probability of being held back (see Chapter 3).

7. The most common grade-span arrangement in the BCPS is the typical middle school structure, although many others are also represented. At the end of fifth grade, 84% of BSS students with school code data were in schools with a prekindergarten, kindergarten, or first through fifth grade structure (479 of 569). Another 7% attended elementary schools that had only third through fifth grades. The remaining 49 students were in schools with other grade spans: Pre-K–6, K–6, K–8, 4–6, Pre-K–8, and 1–6. At the end of eighth grade all but 12% of students (54/469) were in middle schools that spanned sixth through eighth grades. The remaining students attended schools with five other patterns: 6–9, 7–8, 7–9, K–8, and Pre-K–8.

8. As noted earlier, because of prior special education assignment the figures displayed in Figure 2.1 are on the low side. The actual fifth, sixth, and seventh grade tallies are 10, 22, and 22 respectively.

9. Retainees seem much more attached to the city system than never-retained youngsters. Only 29% of first grade retainees leave the system by Year 8, as

against 52% of never-retained children. More is said about this pattern of selective outflow later in this chapter.

10. Only 767 children are covered in Table 2.1, down a bit from the 775 included in Figure 2.1. These additional exclusions are due to problems with the central record information on school moves.

11. But even for children "retrieved" in Year 4, pupil and parent interviews from the early years are often unavailable. In addition, no parent or child interviews were conducted in the third year, and no child interviews were conducted in the fifth year, so annual coverage of various data sources is uneven for reasons other than "missing cases." These complications will be discussed more fully when the data at issue are used.

12. Disagreement as to the year of retention is greater, but even at this level of detail the two sources are reasonably well aligned. There are 241 youngsters for whom school records and self-reports both indicate retention. The two sources agree on the year of retention for 66% of the 241 ($N = 160$) and are a year off for another 15% ($N = 37$). The other 44 almost all report more recent retention than is indicated in school records. This could be a memory problem, but some may have responded in terms of a second, and therefore later, retention (we asked separately about second retentions, but the questioning format could have confused some youngsters).

13. The data sources used in Table 2.2 are described fully later in the volume. California Achievement Test (CAT) scores and report card marks are from school records.

14. Case base shrinkage for other measures reflects both sample attrition and incomplete coverage on that particular data source.

3. Characteristics and competencies of repeaters: who is held back?

1. Our study extends through 8 years, but consequences of retention can be evaluated only after children are held back. For this reason, only retentions through seventh grade are considered in this and the remaining chapters.

2. On the first parent interview, we asked only the educational level of the parent respondent, 86% of whom were the study child's mother or step-mother. Only 65 (or just over 8%) were fathers. In the second, fourth, and sixth years we asked specifically about mothers and fathers, and so some gaps from the first year were filled in. Many parents resided in households with no father present (see Table 3.1 for figures from the first year), which accounts for some of the missing data that remain.

3. The denominators for these last calculations are the standard deviations reported in the first column, those for all children.

238   *Notes to pp. 53–60*

4. We saw in the last chapter, however, that more white than African-American students leave the BCPS over time. These figures could be misleading if many white retentions are missed, because retention data come from BCPS records. However, only 14 of the 123 Exiters for whom we have self-reported grade-level data were first retained after leaving the BCPS. Even though most of these were white (10 of 14), so few are involved that the figures presented are probably reasonably accurate.
5. Only spring scores are available for the 1988–89 and the 1989–90 school years (Years 7 and 8), the last years covered in this volume.
6. These two subtests were also less subject to "ceiling constraints" in the early years than were some others. For example, about 12% of the sample received the highest possible scores on the Vocabulary and Math Computation subtests in the spring of 1983; only 3% to 4% scored at the top on the CAT-R and CAT-M subtests.
7. Technical documentation on the CAT battery indicates that it has good psychometric properties. Kuder–Richardson 20 (homogeneity) reliabilities for the entire battery are reported to range between .83 (beginning of first grade) to .92 for tests designed for the first three years. The test manual reports fall to spring correlations of .69 and .81 for the first and second years. The corresponding correlations for the BSS data are .64 and .77. Test norms (California Achievement Test 1979: 53) show BSS students were 5 points below the norming sample (less than 0.2 standard deviations) when they began first grade.
8. However, even when looking at children with comparable testing levels and early marks, social factors still predicted the risk of retention: boys were still somewhat more likely to be held back than girls, and children from low-income families more so than those better off economically.
9. Here we are using teachers' ratings only from first grade, but similar ratings were also secured in Years 2 and 4. Alpha reliability for the three scales ranges from .74 for the Attention Span–Restlessness scale to .83 for the Cooperation–Compliance scale, and stability correlations across years generally are in the range of .3 to .5.
10. These evaluations were secured in the spring of the year from first grade homeroom teachers, who in most instances were also subject area instructors. For first grade repeaters, these opinions are no doubt partly behind the retention decisions. In the next section, though, we will see that children held back in second grade and later also score below never-retained youngsters on all these first grade teacher evaluations. The link between poor school adjustment and retention thus does not simply reflect unfavorable attitudes on the part of retaining teachers. Rather, these youngsters actually appear to be behaving differently, because ratings from first grade anticipate who will be held back later.

11. Validation studies of the MSTOI have found correlations ranging from .30 to .85 with second grade reading achievement (Cooper 1979; Suhorsky and Wall 1978), and a correlation of .33 with third grade reading achievement (Kaufmann 1982).

12. Differences revolving around the five subscale scores are similar to those indicated by the at-risk distinction in all three comparisons made in this chapter, and are generally of similar magnitude. They have been excluded here to conserve space.

13. We again must be cautious in using ratings from first grade teachers because these are the ones who recommend that first grade repeaters be held back. In these instances, the MSTOI ratings, as well as others like the classroom behavior ratings, may not be independent of the promotion decision. However, when we look only at ratings provided by kindergarten teachers, the pattern is very much the same.

14. Incidentally, the overrepresentation of minority youths among retainees can be accounted for almost entirely by their lower family SES levels. When socioeconomic factors are adjusted for, African-American youngsters are no more likely than whites to be held back. See Dauber et al. (1993) for additional detail.

15. Never-retained youngsters are not included in these tables.

16. Meisels and Liaw (1991) also compare demographic characteristics of early and late retainees over the elementary and middle school grades, using retrospective reports from the NELS-88 project. In some of their comparisons, background differences are smaller among early repeaters than among later, whereas we find them to be larger. However, their comparisons of early versus late contrast children held back in kindergarten through third grade with those retained in the fourth through eighth grades, and so are not strictly comparable to those reported in Table 3.2. By "early" we mean first grade repeaters, specifically. Their results do accord with ours, however, in finding much larger differences across the divide between retained students and those never retained than in comparing earlier with later repeaters.

17. Indeed, when using just kindergarten teachers' ratings, 65% of first grade repeaters are picked up by the at-risk designation. The figure for retainees in the second through seventh grades is 29%.

18. To the contrary, in fact, academically they fall even farther behind over the course of the year, as seen in later chapters.

19. None is large enough for us to be confident in generalizing them to the larger population from which the BSS sample was drawn. This is similar to the comparisons of early vs. late retention reviewed in the previous section.

20. The differences on the three classroom behavior scales range from slightly less than 2 points (0.35 standard deviations) to a bit more than 3 points (0.61 standard deviations).

4. Monitoring academic performance: test scores before and after retention

1. By way of comparison, just under half (147 of 317) of the retainees are encompassed by these cutoffs.
2. The gains reported here, and throughout this chapter, are computed for individuals with scores available at the beginning and end of the interval at issue. These will not always correspond to the differences in average scores at the beginning and end points because of differences in case coverage. So, for example, the first entry in Table 4.1 shows a 31.5-point first grade CAT-R gain for first grade repeaters, based on data for 104 youngsters. In Table 4.A1, though, first grade repeaters are reported to have fall and spring averages of 257.0 ($N = 106$) and 287.1 ($N = 118$) respectively. The difference between these is 30.1 points. There will be such minor differences throughout. The first approach, which we think is more appropriate, is the average individual gain; the second is the difference in Time 1 and Time 2 averages.
3. The second-year component overlaps the summer months between the first and second time through the grade, and so credits any summer gains to the repeated year. While poor-performing children generally do not advance much on these sorts of cognitive tests when school is not in session (e.g., Entwisle and Alexander 1992; Heyns 1978), in this instance combining summer and winter gains for repeaters does alter the picture somewhat because second and third grade repeaters make unusually large strides in the summer following their failed year. Such improvement in their fall testing levels is very likely an artifact of test-wiseness. Retained children take the same version of the CAT battery in the repeated year as in the failed year. The various versions of the CAT battery are grade-specific, so this is not a problem among promoted youngsters. Same-grade comparisons that simply compare spring averages across years (e.g., Mantzicopoulos and Morrison 1992; Peterson et al. (1987) are susceptible to the same distortion. How patterns of summer and school year gains differ is an important topic, but one that cannot be treated thoroughly here. Later in this chapter, when we review preretention and postretention gains over the same interval, we note how this seasonal pattern affects the gains comparisons reported in Figures 4.1 and 4.2 (along with Table 4.1). Here we are interested how youngsters' performance changes from when they begin a particular grade to when they finish it, and in the case of repeaters this takes 2 full school years.
4. The exception involves CAT-M gains (Figure 4.2), where first grade retainees advance less in second grade than do second grade retainees.
5. The large gains registered by fourth through seventh grade retainees in the early grades are an exception, but these youngsters here serve mainly as

another comparison group, and so the "exception" in this instance helps prove the rule.

6. The same holds for 9 points of the third grade repeaters' second-year gains, but for them even a 36-point advance represents substantial progress. First grade repeaters, in contrast, lost ground over the first summer.

7. Again, though, if summer gains are subtracted out, the improvement is less than indicated in Table 4.1; 2 points for first grade repeaters, 1 point for third grade repeaters.

8. This does not mean retainees have been brought up to the level of those never retained. Retainees started so far back that even better-than-average gains still leave them far behind. Nevertheless, some lost ground has been made up, which might not have happened had these children been promoted.

9. About all that is known is whether they received special education pull-out instruction in reading or math. Otherwise, the formal curriculum should be the same, although individual teachers no doubt sometimes make their own adjustments.

10. This is what we think is indicated by second and third grade repeaters' unexpected improvement in the fall of their repeated grade.

11. Since the comparisons here involve retainees after retention and yet-to-be retained youngsters before retention, the over-time decline seen for everyone is confounded with age differences across groups. In these grade-specific comparisons, retainees' gains are being evaluated against gains for the yet-to-be-retained from the previous year. Their average increase should be lower for this reason alone, and so might have nothing to do with postretention fade. Same-age comparisons beginning in the year after retainees have moved beyond the retained grade also point in the same direction, however, with gains prior to retention generally exceeding those after it. This is especially the case for CAT-R comparisons. Same-age comparisons are aligned chronologically, so they more clearly isolate differences that revolve around retention. To look at retainees after retention, these same-age comparisons can be implemented only for Years 3 through 6, as fall scores are not available in Years 7 and 8, and they mainly are possible only for comparing grade 4–7 retainees with earlier ones. These same-age comparisons thus are more limited than we would like, but they seem to support the conclusion based on same-grade comparisons in Figures 4.1 and 4.2: there indeed is a postretention fade in excess of the general developmental drop in test score gains seen for everyone.

12. The interval for retainees spans 8 years, versus 7 years for promoted children.

13. The figures are not identical because somewhat different intervals are used

in calculating gains for repeaters the second time through the repeated grade. In Table 4.1, the failed-year component is the first year's fall-to-spring gain (31.5 points on the CAT-R). So that the entire interval is covered, the repeated-year component (54.5 CAT-R points) goes from spring to spring. In Table 4.3, gains are computed for fall to spring throughout, so the pre- and postretention figures are directly comparable.

14. We say elementary years here because the longest interval extends only through Year 6. All retainees at this point would still be in elementary school, and even on-time youngsters would just be finishing their first year of middle school.

5. How retention affects performance on standardized tests

1. The father's education was considered for inclusion as well, but preliminary analyses indicated that this measure made no difference when the others were included. Since coverage on the father's education measure is the lowest of all background characteristics ($N = 489$), we decided not to use it.

2. We originally had thought to contrast "any" with "none" of these problems, but the checks in Chapter 4 suggested that special education status might be more problematic than double retention. Of the 317 retainees covered in these analyses, 184 were neither held back a second time nor assigned to special education; 48 were assigned to special education but not held back a second time; 43 were held back a second time but not put into special education; and 42 were both held back a second time *and* put into special education.

3. These are metric regression coefficients, computed on the basis of pairwise present variance–covariance matrices. The "pairwise present" stipulation means that all cases having data on both variables involved were used in computing covariances, even if those cases were missing some data needed to calculate other covariances. The alternative approach, "listwise present," screens out cases lacking information on any variable, and loses too many cases to be employed. The two approaches yield very similar estimates here.

4. As indicated in the table note, this figure comes from an equation in which differences between the other retainee groups and those never retained are also estimated. These figures are −21.5 for second grade repeaters, −18.0 for third grade repeaters, and −13.0 for fourth through seventh grade repeaters. To keep the presentation manageable, these other comparisons are not reported in our tables, but they were included in all analyses. Because of this, the unadjusted differences reported in the first row of results in these regression analyses will differ some from the corresponding unadjusted differences reported in the previous chapter. This happens because somewhat different

sets of youngsters are covered in the two approaches. The computations here use the test scores of first grade repeaters and never-retained children having fall testing data, which will be the same as the data reported previously. However, these statistical adjustments also use data from second through seventh grade retainees, and this can alter the picture slightly. For example, the corresponding differences computed from Table 4.A1 are quite close but not identical to those just reported: −33.8 for first grade repeaters (i.e., 290.8 to 257.0), −21.2 for second grade repeaters, −18.1 for third grade repeaters, and −12.9 for fourth through seventh grade repeaters.

5. The single asterisk in the tables uses a somewhat less stringent criterion of significance: 1 in 20 times (5%).

6. The inability to construct a comparison group that is an exact match, even on one variable, points up a weakness in the matched-group approach.

7. Analyses not shown indicate that their early testing levels are the major factor here. Socioeconomic differences play only a minor role.

8. This happens because the poor-performing comparison group makes above-average gains in the second year, exceeding even those registered by the full sample of promoted youngsters. It may be that some of these children's poor first-year scores were unusually low, and hence gave a false reading of their levels of competence. This phenomenon, known as "regression toward the mean," is not at all uncommon when very low or very high scores are selected out. If this is behind retainees' unfavorable comparison with the "poor performers," then not too much should be made of their poor showing. The regression phenomenon occurs for statistical and other reasons that have no bearing on the efficacy of retention. Larabee (1984) explores this regression phenomenon in some detail in his study of promotion practices.

9. In the eighth year this amounts to 0.6 standard deviations, whereas in the earlier period this same absolute difference was equivalent to 1.0 standard deviations, so retainees in this instance are relatively better off, though still behind.

10. In these tables, unlike those already reviewed for first grade repeaters, entries in the corresponding same-grade and same-age comparisons differ even in the first couple of columns because for second and third grade retainees, a same-grade "offset" is required in all comparisons. By the fall of second grade, first grade repeaters have already been held back, so their fall scores for the first analysis are from the third year (when they are going into second grade). In Table 5.1, the baseline score was from the fall of first grade, before anyone had repeated. Hence there was no difference between averages from the "fall of first grade" and averages from the "fall of Year 1." The differences in the first couple of columns comparing results in Tables

5.3 and 5.4, and in Tables 5.5 and 5.6, are all slight, but that they are different at all reflects the same-grade offset for children held back before the grade at issue.

11. There are, however, differences of detail. For example, shrinkage between the unadjusted and the adjusted estimates generally is a good bit larger in these tables than was seen previously for first grade repeaters, and the differences that remain after adjustment are correspondingly smaller.

12. When second grade repeaters are compared with the poor performers, we see pretty much the same pattern against the earlier benchmarks after adjustment as before. Even this, though, has a positive cast to it, as the differences after retention are not much larger than those from before, so there is little indication of postretention trailing off.

13. Exceptions are the figures seen at the very start and at the very end.

14. The unadjusted estimates for the repeated year are negative and one is large (–35.5). These both represent significant improvement over retainees' standing at the end of their failed year, but without the adjustments we cannot tell how much of the remaining shortfall should be attributed to prior difficulties and other risk factors.

6. Teachers' classroom evaluations of repeaters: report card marks in reading and math

1. Research nevertheless indicates that children's school performance generally goes down over time; see, for example, Simmons and Blyth 1987.

2. In middle school, some of these might be one-semester courses, and so marks would be from midyear, rather than from year's end. The scheduling of middle school courses will be described later in this chapter.

3. Retainees' entries in columns beyond their repeated grade reflect a same-grade offset. Their seventh grade averages, for example, come from Year 8, while never-retained youngsters' seventh grade averages come from Year 7.

4. We have compared the end-of-year and end-of-semester marks with those from the final quarter, and they all yield averages that are virtually interchangeable.

5. The only major lack of coverage involves elementary school records from Year 7. Only double repeaters should still be in elementary schools in Year 7, and because of administrative problems that year, our coverage of these youngsters' records is off. Year 7 marks are available for just 49 double retainees, compared with 69 in Year 6 and 71 in Year 8. We will mention possible implications of this later when marking trends are reviewed.

6. Since fifth grade is the end of elementary school, this "blip" may be the school's way of wishing them well.

7. There are two exceptions to this pattern. The first involves fifth grade marks, which we have seen are high for everyone. Retainees' middle school marks in most instances are below their fifth grade marks, but this is true for promoted youngsters too. Also, second grade repeaters' math marks consistently fall below their averages from the second through fourth grades.

8. We were concerned that this relatively favorable showing for retainees in middle school might be misleading because of missing elementary school records from Year 7. Most double repeaters would still be in elementary school in Year 7, and because of how these same-grade comparisons are structured (i.e., the 1-year offset) this would mainly affect our figures for sixth grade. Indeed, our coverage of double retainees is sparser for sixth grade marks than for either fifth or seventh grade marks, and the sixth grade averages that are available for them are generally lower than those of other retainees. One implication of this is that if we were to look only at single repeaters the picture would be even more favorable than it is in Table 6.1; all but one of their sixth and seventh grade math averages is 2.0 or higher, for example. But in terms of the comparisons presented, it turns out that sparse coverage of double retainees in sixth grade does not change the picture at all. We checked this by recalculating the sixth grade averages using the larger of the fifth or seventh grade subsamples as the sixth grade base for double repeaters (e.g., for first grade repeaters in math, the number of double re-tainees used in computing the new average was 42, as opposed to the 26 for whom marks actually were in hand; we assume that these 42 would have the same average as is observed for the 26). None of these new averages differs by as much as 0.1 marking units from those reported in Table 6.1. Since the averages in Table 6.1 are rounded to one decimal place, the recomputed entries are identical to those reported.

9. Marks get more variable over time just as test scores did, but not as dra-matically so. Partly this is because we collapsed to middle school metric from percentages into four categories akin to the marking distinctions used in the primary grades. The reading standard deviation from the fall of first grade is 0.82; that from the spring of seventh grade is 0.90; and all but one from the intervening years fall between these values. The corresponding figures for math marks are 0.81 and 0.92, and in math all the others are in between.

7. The stigma of retention: effects on children's sense of self, attitudes toward school, and achievement orientations

1. In Year 7 only children making the transition to middle school that year were interviewed.

2. Additional detail is available in Pallas, Entwisle, Alexander, and Weinstein (1990).

3. Spring scores were used when available because these reflect children's reactions to experiences throughout the year. In the upper grades, only fall responses are available.

4. In Table 7.A1 we see additionally that third grade repeaters and fourth through seventh grade repeaters start out with self-esteem averages close to those of the poor-performing comparison group.

5. The next-largest increase – that is, 0.3 points – is registered by second grade repeaters, which seems anomalous since this is the year they will be held back.

6. As mentioned, we also interviewed children in Year 7 who were just entering middle school, including some 63 first grade repeaters. Their Year 7 average on the academic self-esteem scale was 18.6, just a bit above their Year 8 average, and well below the figure from Year 6. The dropoff for them seen in Figure 7.1 thus does seem to be a middle-grades phenomenon, documented in Simmons and Blyth (1987) and in reports of Eccles and her colleagues (1984; 1989; 1990; 1991).

7. Interviews were also conducted in the fall of the year, before first report cards were issued. We focus here on the children's spring responses, as these reflect their reactions to experiences during the year.

8. In Years 1, 2, and 4 we asked expectations in reading. In Year 6, when some children were still in elementary school and some were in middle school, we asked expectations in "reading/English." Some of the on-time children at this point were taking English instead of reading, as English is introduced in middle school as part of the regular curriculum. In Year 8 we asked separately about expectations in reading and English. When a response was not available in reading, the English expectation was used, collapsed to the elementary school metric. This parallels the procedure used for marks in middle school.

9. Year 6 data are not available on this measure.

10. In the fall of first grade, first grade repeaters' average was 9.1, a bit higher than the spring figure reported in Table 7.5. They are the only group whose average dropped from fall to spring, so it appears that their academic difficulties during the year inclined them toward more of an external orientation.

11. Their decline from the spring of Year 1 to fall of Year 2 is 0.3 points, from 8.9 to 8.6. This is the largest decline in the interval. Two other groups went down 0.1 point, while the other averages increased modestly.

12. As has been the case throughout this volume, we need to be careful here that trend comparisons reflect real changes in children's thinking and not those

in sample composition over time. To check on this, all the averages reported in this section were recomputed using only children for whom data were available in Year 8. Most of these are youngsters who remained in Baltimore City Public Schools for the entire period of this study, and for them data are reasonably complete throughout. This restriction reduces group sizes in the early years by 50% to 65% in most instances, as attrition across years is appreciable. Despite such large reductions, most of the averages change very little, and the minor changes that are registered only sharpen interesting comparisons. For instance, in several of the tables, the Year 1 averages for first and second grade repeaters are a bit lower, while most of the others are unchanged. This puts them even farther back at the beginning, making first grade repeaters' later progress even more impressive. In these attrition checks their second-year improvement and Year 8 relative decline both remain vivid.

13. That we see any correlation between Year 1 and Year 8 expressions of academic self-esteem is noteworthy, given the length of the interval and the modest reliability of the measures. Over-time stability in children's ideas about self increases as they get older. The Year 8 measure correlates .12 with the Year 1 measure, .22 with that in Year 2, .29 with the Year 4 measure, and .45 with that in Year 6. This pattern holds for most of the measures considered in this chapter. There are two important implications: first, that children's sense of self becomes more stable as they mature (in Year 8, most are age 14); second, and conversely, that their ideas about self are more malleable, and hence more susceptible to influence, during the early formative years. This is one reason for being especially interested in young children's reactions to retention.

14. The tables also report levels of explained variance – the R statistics at the bottom of each column – for the most inclusive equations. Most are in the vicinity of .10 or less, indicating that variance in these attitudes is not well explained by the set of predictors being used. A relatively low proportion of explained variance is typical in studies of attitude and personality development involving young children.

15. Differences between fourth through seventh grade repeaters and never-retained children are not reported but were included in the analysis.

16. These adjustments are not of great consequence in any of the regression analyses, which is rather different from consequences observed in the academic area.

17. This chapter contains only same-age comparisons. This seems most appropriate when considering children's attitudes about self and school, as these typically grow more negative as children get older.

18. The results for math mark expectations in Table 7.3 are an exception. Here

retainees' expectations lag behind in Year 2 as well as in Year 1, and in the comparison with all never-retained children in Year 4 as well. However, none remains significant after adjustments are made for background differences and early test scores.

19. Third through sixth grade repeaters did score lower on perceived competence in comparisons with a random sample of promoted children, however.

8. Retention in the broader context of elementary and middle school tracking

1. In Chapter 1 we discussed some of the literature on retention. For an overview on grouping / tracking see Good and Marshall 1984; Oakes, Gamoran, and Page 1992; Rosenbaum 1980. On special education, see Heller 1982; Leinhardt and Pallay 1982; and Madden and Slavin 1983.

2. Hallinan (1993), however, shows high mobility rates altogether and considerable movement in both directions. Tracking may be less rigid nowadays than previously, as many schools have moved away from across-the-board program placements in favor of more flexible programs (e.g., Harvard Education Letter 1992a,c).

3. These data come from teacher questionnaires administered in first grade. Fifty-one of 57 homeroom teachers, most of whom also were subject-area instructors, responded.

4. This classification does not necessarily mean that they are reading below expectation. Children at the beginning of the year generally are not expected to be reading at grade level. In the BCPS, for example, the average expectation for children's reading level in the first quarter of first grade is beyond beginning preprimer; children reading at the primer level are above average.

5. It also affects instruction. Barr and Dreeben (1983), for example, found large differences in the first grade basal readers used in three Chicago area school districts. The readers differed in both the number and difficulty of words introduced, and this influenced the number of words learned during the year. In addition, teachers paced their coverage of materials differently as a function of both ability-group level and reading level.

6. At the end of first grade, children in the BCPS are expected to be reading either in the second half of a level-1 book or in the first half of a level-2 book.

7. The figure covers only children with information on all the tracking measures. The largest loss (137 youngsters) revolves around reading-group placements. This includes the 33 children in classes where small groups were not used.

8. Overall, 63% of the cohort is in the no-low pattern. Figures for the comparison group and later repeaters, at 60% and 57%, fall just a bit short of this level.

9. Even so, they are relatively more numerous in this group than never-retained children (at 9%, that is, 7 of 75) and than comparison-group children (at 4%; 3 of 75).

10. Here, as in the previous section, the distinction is between those reading below grade level and those reading at or above grade level. For first grade repeaters, reading at grade level in the second year means they are in a level-1 reader; for all others the standard is level 2. The criterion thus is grade specific, which seems appropriate. Still, the standard is different, and this needs to be kept in mind. By fifth grade, the comparisons are offset for all elementary school repeaters, much like under the same-grade approach used in previous chapters. All children are rated at the end of fifth grade, regardless of how long it took for them to get to that point.

11. It would be preferable to monitor children's reading-group placements, but these data are available only in the first 2 years, and hardly any first grade repeaters are covered in the second year.

12. For perspective, using enrollment in a nonremedial course (whether regular or advanced) as the criterion, the corresponding percentages are: 28.3 for first grade repeaters; 46.9 for second through fifth grade repeaters; 73.2 for all never-retained children; and 50.9 for comparison-group youngsters.

13. In Table 8.3, placements and reading instructional levels are grade appropriate throughout, even for double retainees. For these youngsters, sixth grade reading/English courses reflect their Year 8 enrollments.

14. Children not held back until middle school are included in the left-side pattern tallies in Table 8.3 ($N = 309$), but not in the right-side group comparisons. This is why the subgroup pattern totals sometimes are less than the "No. with pattern" total in the first column.

15. By fifth grade all these youngsters have been held back at least once, so the pattern for all of them is grade-adjusted. The spring of fifth grade for most is the end of their sixth year, so at some point all have had the benefit of an extra year to get to grade level.

16. Indeed, many more than 33 patterns would be indicated if we also distinguished high-level placements in English and Math from regular-level courses.

17. Incidentally, there are not many children receiving special education services in these three groups, but 39 of the 49 youngsters in Table 8.5 held back in sixth or seventh grade are in them. These "routings" off a common middle school experience suggest very different trajectories: for many, it is into a foreign language, but for others it is retention. These may be the middle school "success stories" and the "failures," respectively.

18. The group subtotals in Table 8.5 do not sum to the full-row total in this instance because children held back for the first time in sixth or seventh

grade are not displayed separately. There are 54 such youngsters altogether, dispersed across many patterns, including some not displayed in the chart.

19. Partly, though, this is because most never-retained children have at least one low placement, usually in the reading curriculum.

9. The retention puzzle: problem, solution, or signal?

1. A technical one (see Schmidt 1992) is that the type II error – failure to detect an effect when one exists – is generally ignored in considering studies one at a time. Only when effect sizes are pooled over many studies are differences of reasonable magnitude likely to be detected.

2. The exact level at which they "peak" varies greatly across localities, however, ranging from a high of 20% in Arizona to a low of 1.6% in Hawaii.

3. The cutoff for free meals is 1.3 times the current poverty level, figured according to income and family size.

4. Even though gains in IQ and achievement are only short-term phenomena, they should not be dismissed as inconsequential. They could, for example, be the reason that poor preschooled children are less often held back or assigned to special education. Retention rates are highest in first grade, so an edge at this point might well be enough to tip the scales. Woodhead (1988: 447–48) discusses how such temporary improvement can "trigger a more positive cycle of achievement and expectation [and] carry the child through the later grades long after the original cognitive benefits had washed out." Then, too, IQ gains and performance on standardized tests are not the only considerations. The same research shows significant lasting benefits of pre-school participation on other important criteria; preschool participants are less likely to be held back or assigned to special education, for example. Follow-up studies that track children beyond high school also find that participants more often graduate from high school, are less likely to experi-ence unemployment afterward or to be on public assistance, are more likely to be living with a spouse or companion, and are less likely to be in jail.

5. This holds, too, for evaluations of the Project Follow Through planned variation experiment (Stebbins, St. Pierre, Proper, Anderson, and Cerva 1977). Follow Through was a federal program intended to build upon the successes of Head Start by providing extra services and resources to chil-dren during the early elementary years. Even though funding for Follow Through waned during the seventies, controversy raged for years over whether different Follow Through sites did in fact differ in effectiveness and whether particularly effective program features could be identified (e.g., Bereiter and Kurland 1981–82; Gersten 1984; House, Glass, McLean, and Walker 1978).

6. This conclusion may be too sweeping, however. Epstein and MacIver (1990), in their comprehensive overview of middle-grades practices, conclude that most middle schools "have not yet developed educational programs based on recommended practices for the middle grades" (p. 73); nevertheless, they still see some differences of detail that reflect more responsive practices in middle schools. These include more opportunities for remedial instruction, activities designed to ease transition pressures, and a greater commitment to interdisciplinary teaming.
7. The timing issue is complicated for girls by the lowered age of menarche in recent years.
8. We have already commented at length on the difficulties that arise in trying to make such comparisons. We will not repeat that discussion here, but such problems should be understood as the backdrop to all this literature.
9. See Kagan and Zigler (1987), for example, on the pros and cons of proposals to begin school at age 4.
10. Good studies showing positive time effects would include Brown and Saks (1986), as well as Taylor, Frye, and Maruyama (1990).

Bibliography

Abidin, R. R., W. M. Golladay, and A. L. Howerton. "Elementary School
Retention: An Unjustifiable, Discriminatory and Noxious Policy." *Journal
of School Psychology* 9 (1971): 410–17.

Alexander, K. L., and M. A. Cook. "Curricula and Coursework: A Surprise End-
ing to a Familiar Story." *American Sociological Review* 47 (1982): 626–40.

Alexander, K. L., D. R. Entwisle, and S. Bedinger. "When Expectations Work:
Race and Socioeconomic Differences in the Efficacy of Children's and
Parents' School Performance Expectations." *Social Psychology Quarterly*,
in press.

Alexander, K. L., D. R. Entwisle, and S. L. Dauber. "First Grade Classroom
Behavior: Its Short- and Long-term Consequences for School Performance." *Child Development* 64 (1993): 801–14.

"Children in Motion: School Transfers and Elementary School Performance." Unpublished manuscript, Johns Hopkins University, 1994.

Bachman, J. G., S. Green, and I. D. Wirtanen. *Dropping Out: Problem or Symptom?* Vol. 3 of Youth in Transition series. Ann Arbor, MI: Institute for
Social Research, 1971.

Barr, R., and R. Dreeben. *How Schools Work*. University of Chicago Press, 1983.

Bereiter, C., and M. Kurland. "A Constructive Look at Follow Through Results." *Interchange* 12 (1981–82): 1–22.

Bianchi, S. "Children's Progress Through School: A Research Note." *Sociology
of Education* 57 (1984): 184–92.

Blake, J. *Family Size and Achievement*. Berkeley and Los Angeles: University of
California Press, 1989.

Bloom, B. B. *Stability and Change in Human Characteristics*. New York: Wiley,
1964.

Blumenfeld, P., P. Pintrich, J. Meece, and K. Wessels. "The Formation and Role
of Self Perceptions of Ability in Elementary Classrooms." *Elementary
School Journal* 82 (1982): 401–20.

Bowler, M. *The Lessons of Change: Baltimore Schools in the Modern Era.* Baltimore, MD: Fund for Educational Excellence, 1991.

Bowles, S., and H. Gintis. *Schooling in Capitalist America: Educational Reform and the Contradictions of Economic Life.* New York: Basic, 1976.

Bronfenbrenner, U. "Is Early Intervention Effective?" *Teachers College Record* 76 (1974): 279–303.

Brown, B. W., and D. H. Saks. "Measuring the Effects of Instructional Time on Student Learning: Evidence from the Beginning Teacher Evaluation Study." *American Journal of Education* 94 (1986): 480–500.

Byrnes, D. A. "Attitudes of Students, Parents and Educators Toward Repeating a Grade." In *Flunking Grades: Research and Policies on Retention,* edited by L. A. Shepard and M. L. Smith, pp. 108–31. London: Falmer, 1989.

Cairns, R. B., B. D. Cairns, and H. J. Neckerman. "Early School Dropout: Configurations and Determinants." *Child Development* 60 (1989): 1437–52.

California Achievement Tests. *California Achievement Tests: Norms Tables, Level 18, Forms C and D.* Monterey, CA: CTB/McGraw Hill, 1979.

Carter, L. F. "The Sustaining Effects Study of Compensatory and Elementary Education." *Educational Researcher* 13 (1984): 4–13.

Castro, G., and M. A. Mastropieri. "The Efficacy of Early Intervention Programs: A Meta-analysis." *Exceptional Children* 52 (1986): 417–24.

Catterall, J. S. "On the Social Costs of Dropping out of School." *The High School Journal* 71 (1987): 19–30.

Children's Defense Fund. *City Poverty Data from the 1990 Census.* Washington, DC: Children's Defense Fund, 1992.

Citizens Planning and Housing Association. *Report Card on the Baltimore City Public Elementary Schools.* Baltimore, MD: Board of School Commissioners, 1990.

Coleman, J. S., E. Q. Campbell, C. J. Hobson, J. McPartland, A. Mood, F. D. Weinfeld, and R. L. York. *Equality of Educational Opportunity.* Washington, DC: U.S. Government Printing Office, 1966.

Coleman, J. S., and T. Hoffer. *Public and Private Schools: The Impact of Communities.* New York: Basic, 1987.

Consortium of Longitudinal Studies. *As the Twig Is Bent: Lasting Effect of Preschool Programs.* Hillsdale, NJ: Erlbaum, 1983.

Cooper, C. "The Relationship Between Early Identification of Potential Learning Problems Using the Maryland Systematic Teaching Observation Instrument and Later Reading Achievement in Elementary School." Ph.D. diss., University of Maryland, 1979.

Crandall, V. C., W. Katkovsky, and V. J. Crandall. "Children's Beliefs in Their Own Control of Reinforcement in Intellectual-achievement Situations." *Child Development* 36 (1965): 91–109.

254   *Bibliography*

Cuban, L. "What Happens to Reforms That Last? The Case of the Junior High School." *American Educational Research Journal* 29 (1992): 227–51.

Dauber, S. L., K. L. Alexander, and D. R. Entwisle. "Characteristics of Retainees and Early Precursors of Retention in Grade: Who is Held Back?" *Merrill-Palmer Quarterly* 39 (1993): 326–43.

Dreeben, R. *On What is Learned in School.* Reading, MA: Addison-Wesley, 1968.

"First-grade Reading Groups: Their Formation and Change." In *The Social Context of Instruction: Group Organization and Group Process,* edited by P. L. Peterson, L. C. Wilkinson, and M. Hallinan, pp. 69–84. San Diego, CA: Academic, 1984.

Eccles, J. S., S. Lord, and C. Midgley. "What Are We Doing to Adolescents? The Impact of Educational Contexts on Early Adolescents." *American Journal of Education* 99 (1991): 521–42.

Eccles, J. S., and C. Midgley. "Stage/environment Fit: Developmentally Appropriate Classrooms for Early Adolescents." In *Research on Motivation in Education,* vol. 3, edited by R. E. Ames and C. Ames, pp. 139–86. San Diego, CA: Academic, 1989.

"Changes in Academic Motivation and Self-perception During Early Adolescence." In *From Childhood to Adolescence: A Transitional Period?* edited by R. Montemayor, G. R. Adams, and T. P. Gulotta, pp. 134–55. Newbury Park, CA: Sage, 1990.

Eccles, J. S., C. Midgley, and T. Adler. "Grade-related Changes in the School Environment: Effects on Achievement Motivation." In *The Development of Achievement Motivation,* edited by J. G. Nicholls, pp. 283–331. Greenwich, CT: JAI, 1984.

Eder, D. "Organizational Constraints on Reading Group Mobility." In *The Social Construction of Literacy,* edited by J. Cook-Gumperz, pp. 138–55. Cambridge University Press, 1986.

Elder, G. H. Jr. "Perspectives on the Life Course." In *Life Course Dynamics: Trajectories and Transitions, 1968–1980,* edited by G. H. Elder Jr., pp. 23–49. Ithaca, NY: Cornell University Press, 1985.

"The Life Course." In *The Encyclopedia of Sociology,* vol. 2, edited by E. F. Borgatta and M. L. Borgatta, pp. 1120–30. New York: Macmillan, 1991.

Entwisle, D. R., and K. L. Alexander. "Early Schooling as a 'Critical Period' Phenomenon." In *Sociology of Education and Socialization,* vol. 8, edited by K. Namboodiri and R. G. Corwin, pp. 27–55. Greenwich, CT: JAI, 1989.

"Summer Setback: Race, Poverty, School Composition, and Mathematics Achievement in the First Two Years of School." *American Sociological Review* 57 (1992): 72–84.

"Entry Into Schools: The Beginning School Transition and Educational Stratification in the United States." In *Annual Review of Sociology,* vol. 19, edited by J. Blake and J. Hagen, pp. 401–23. Palo Alto, CA: Annual Reviews, 1993.

"Winter Setback: School Racial Composition and Learning to Read." *American Sociological Review* 59 (1994): 446–60.

Entwisle, D. R., K. L. Alexander, D. Cadigan, and A. M. Pallas. "Kindergarten Experience: Cognitive Effects or Socialization?" *American Educational Research Journal* 24 (1987): 337–64.

Entwisle, D. R., and L. A. Hayduk. *Too Great Expectations: The Academic Outlook of Young Children.* Baltimore, MD: Johns Hopkins University Press, 1978.

"Academic Expectations and the School Attainment of Young Children." *Sociology of Education* 54 (1981): 34–50.

Early Schooling: Cognitive and Affective Outcomes. Baltimore, MD: Johns Hopkins University Press, 1982.

Epstein, J. L. *School and Family Partnerships.* Report No. 6. Baltimore, MD: Center on Families, Communities, Schools and Children's Learning. Johns Hopkins University, 1992.

Epstein, J. L., and D. J. MacIver. *Education in the Middle Grades: National Trends and Practices.* Columbus, OH: National Middle School Association, 1990.

Epstein, J. L., and J. M. McPartland. "The Concept and Measurement of the Quality of School Life." *American Educational Research Journal* 13 (1976): 15–30.

Epstein, K. K. "Latest Trend: Flunking Kids in First Grade." *Baltimore Sun,* April 5, 1987, p. C5.

Felner, R. D., and A. M. Adan. "The School Transitional Environment Project: An Ecological Intervention and Evaluation." In *Fourteen Ounces of Prevention: A Casebook for Practitioners,* edited by R. H. Price, E. L. Cowen, R. P. Lorion, and J. Ramos-McKay, pp. 111–22. Washington, DC: American Psychological Association, 1988.

Felner, R. D., M. Ginter, and J. Primavera. "Primary Prevention During School Transitions: Social Support and Environmental Structure." *American Journal of Community Psychology* 10 (1982): 277–90.

Fine, M. *Framing Dropouts: Notes on the Politics of an Urban Public High School.* Albany, NY: SUNY Press, 1991.

Finlayson, H. J. "Non-promotion and Self-concept Development." *Phi Delta Kappan* 59 (1977): 205–06.

The Forgotten Half: Pathways to Success for America's Youth and Young Families. Washington, DC: Youth and America's Future: William T. Grant Commission on Work, Family and Citizenship, 1988.

Gabriel, R. M., B. L. Anderson, G. Benson, S. Gordon, R. Hill, J. Pfannenstiel, and R. M. Stonehill. *Studying the Sustained Achievement of Chapter 1 Students.* Washington, DC: U.S. Government Printing Office, 1985.

Gallup, A. M. "The 18th Annual Gallup Poll of the Public's Attitudes Toward the Public Schools." *Phi Delta Kappan* 68 (1986): 43–59.

Gamoran, A. "Rank Performance and Mobility in Elementary School Grouping." *Sociological Quarterly* 30 (1989): 109–23.

——— "Access to Excellence: Assignment to Honors English Classes in the Transition to High School." *Educational Evaluation and Policy Analysis* 3 (1992): 185–204.

Gersten, R. "Follow Through Revisited: Reflections on the Site Variability Issue." *Educational Evaluation and Policy Analysis* 6 (1984): 411–23.

Goethals, G. R. "Social Comparison Theory: Psychology from the Lost and Found." *Personality and Social Psychology Bulletin* 12 (1987): 261–78.

Good, T., and S. Marshall. "Do Students Learn More in Heterogenous Groups?" In *The Social Context of Instruction: Group Organization and Group Process*, edited by P. L. Peterson, L. C. Wilkinson, and M. Hallinan, pp. 15–39. San Diego, CA: Academic, 1984.

Grissom, J. B., and L. A. Shepard. "Repeating and Dropping Out of School." In *Flunking Grades: Research and Policies on Retention*, edited by L. A. Shepard and M. L. Smith, pp. 34–63. London: Falmer, 1989.

Gutierrez, R., and R. E. Slavin. "Achievement Effects of Nongraded Elementary Schools: A Best-evidence Synthesis." *Review of Educational Research* 62 (1992): 333–76.

Haddad, W. D. "Educational and Economic Effects of Promotion and Repetition Practices." Staff Working Paper No. 319. Washington, DC: World Bank, 1979.

Hall, W. F., and D. R. Demarest. "Effect on Achievement Scores of a Change in Promotion Policy." *Elementary School Journal* 58 (1958): 204–07.

Hallinan, M. T. "The Organization of Students for Instruction in the Middle School." *Sociology of Education* 65 (April 1992): 114–27.

——— "Track Mobility in Secondary School." Paper presented at the annual meeting of the American Sociological Association. Miami, FL, 1993.

Hallinan, M. T., and A. B. Sorensen. "The Formation and Stability of Instructional Groups." *American Sociological Review* 48 (1983): 838–51.

Hammack, F. M. "Large School Systems' Dropout Reports: An Analysis of Definitions, Procedures, and Findings." *Teachers College Record* 87 (1986): 324–41.

Harvard Education Letter. "Repeating a Grade: Does It Help?" *Harvard Education Letter* 2 (1986): 1–4.

——— "After Tracking – What? Middle Schools Find New Answers." *Harvard Education Letter* 8 (Sept.–Oct. 1992a): 1–5.

——— "The Seventh-grade Slump and How to Avoid It." *Harvard Education Letter* 8 (Jan.–Feb. 1992b): 1–4.

——— "The Tracking Wars: Is Anyone Winning?" *Harvard Education Letter* 8 (May–June 1992c): 1–4.

Haskins, R. "Beyond Metaphor: The Efficacy of Early Childhood Education." *American Psychologist* 44 (1989): 274–82.

Hebbeler, K. "An Old and a New Question on the Effects of Early Education for Children from Low Income Families." *Educational Evaluation and Policy Analysis* 7 (1985): 207–16.

Heller, K. A. "Effects of Special Education Placement on Educable Mentally Retarded Children." In *Children in Special Education: A Strategy for Equity*, edited by K. A. Heller, W. H. Holtzman, and S. Messick, pp. 262–99. Washington, DC: National Academy Press, 1982.

Hess, R. D., and S. D. Holloway. "Family and School as Educational Institutions." In *The Family*. Vol. 7 of *Review of Child Development Research*, edited by R. D. Parke, pp. 179–222. University of Chicago Press, 1984.

Hetherington, E. M., K. A. Camara, and D. L. Featherman. "Achievement and Intellectual Functioning in One-parent Families." In *Achievement and Achievement Motives*, edited by J. Spence, pp. 205–84. San Francisco: Freeman, 1983.

Heyns, B. *Summer Learning and the Effects of Schooling.* San Diego, CA: Academic, 1978.

"Schooling and Cognitive Development: Is There a Season for Learning?" *Child Development* 58 (1987): 1151-60.

Holmes, C. T. "A Synthesis of Recent Research on Nonpromotion: A Five Year Follow-up." Paper presented at the annual meeting of the American Educational Research Association. San Francisco, 1986.

"Grade Level Retention Effects: A Meta-analysis of Research Studies." In *Flunking Grades: Research and Policies on Retention*, edited by L. A. Shepard and M. L. Smith, pp. 16–33. London: Falmer, 1989.

Holmes, C. T., and K. M. Matthews. "The Effects of Nonpromotion on Elementary and Junior High School Pupils: A Meta-analysis." *Review of Educational Research* 54 (1984): 225–36.

House, E. R. "Policy Implications of Retention Research." In *Flunking Grades: Research and Policies on Retention*, edited by L. A. Shepard and M. L. Smith, pp. 202–13. London: Falmer, 1989.

House, E. R., G. V. Glass, L. D. McLean, and D. E. Walker. "No Simple Answer: Critique of the 'Follow Through' Evaluation." *Harvard Educational Review* 48 (1978): 128–60.

Jackson, G. B. "The Research Evidence on the Effects of Grade Retention." *Review of Educational Research* 45 (1975): 613–35.

Jencks, C. "How Much Do High School Students Learn?" *Sociology of Education* 58 (1985): 128–53.

Jensen, A. R. "How Much Can We Boost IQ and Scholastic Achievement?" *Harvard Educational Review* 39 (1969): 1–123.

Kagan, S. L., and E. F. Zigler. *Early Schooling: The National Debate.* New Haven, CT: Yale University Press, 1987.

Karweit, N. "Should We Lengthen the School Term?" *Educational Researcher* 14 (1985): 9–15.

———. "Effective Kindergarten Practices for Students at Risk." In *Effective Programs for Students at Risk,* edited by R. E. Slavin, N. L. Karweit, and N. A. Madden, pp. 103–42. Boston: Allyn & Bacon, 1989a.

———. "Time and Learning: A Review." In *School and Classroom Organization,* edited by R. E. Slavin, pp. 69–95. Hillsdale, NJ: Erlbaum, 1989b.

———. "Retention Policy." In *Encyclopedia of Educational Research,* edited by M. Alkin, pp. 1114–18. New York: Macmillan, 1992.

Kaufmann, R. M. *An Investigation of the Relationship Between Early Identification Procedures During Kindergarten and Subsequent Third Grade Reading.* Dissertation Abstracts International, 42, 1909A (University Microfilms No. 8226474), 1982.

Kellam, S. G., J. D. Branch, K. C. Agrawal, and M. E. Ensminger. *Mental Health and Going to School: The Woodlawn Program of Assessment, Early Intervention, and Evaluation.* University of Chicago Press, 1975.

Kelly, S. P. "15,000 City Students Failed Despite Debate Over Promotions." *Evening Sun,* July 25, 1989, p. C1.

Kraus, P. E. *Yesterday's Children.* New York: Wiley, 1973.

Larabee, D. F. "Setting the Standard: Alternative Policies for Student Promotion." *Harvard Educational Review* 54 (1984): 67–87.

Lazar, I., and R. Darlington. "Lasting Effects of Early Education: A Report from the Consortium for Longitudinal Studies." *Monographs of the Society for Research in Child Development* 47, nos. 2–3 (1982).

Leinhardt, G. "Transition Rooms: Promoting Maturation or Reducing Education?" *Journal of Educational Psychology* 72 (1980): 55–61.

Leinhardt, G., and W. Bickel. "Instruction's the Thing Wherein to Catch the Mind That Falls Behind." In *School and Classroom Organization,* edited by R. E. Slavin, pp. 197–226. Hillsdale, NJ: Erlbaum, 1989.

Leinhardt, G., and A. Pallay. "Restrictive Educational Settings: Exile or Haven?" *Review of Educational Research* 54 (1982): 557–78.

Lloyd, D. N. "Prediction of School Failure from Third-grade Data." *Educational and Psychological Measurement* 38 (1978): 1911–1200.

Lombardi, T. P., K. A. Odell, and D. E. Novotny. "Special Education and Students at Risk: Findings from a National Study." *Remedial and Special Education* 12 (1990): 56–62.

Love, J. M., and M. E. Logue. *Transitions to Kindergarten in American Schools: Executive Summary.* Final report to the Office of Policy and Planning, U.S. Department of Education, Contract No. LC88089001, 1992.

Madden, N. A., and R. A. Slavin. "Mainstreaming Students with Mild Handicaps: Academic and Social Outcomes." *Review of Educational Research* 53 (1983): 519–69.

Madden, N. A., R. E. Slavin, N. L. Karweit, J. Dolan, and B. A. Wasik. "Success for All: Longitudinal Effects of a Restructuring Program for Inner-city Elementary Schools." *American Educational Research Journal* 30 (1993): 123–48.

Mantzicopoulos, P., and D. Morrison. "Kindergarten Retention: Academic and Behavioral Outcomes Through the End of Second Grade." *American Educational Research Journal* 29 (1992): 182–98.

McDill, E. L., M. S. McDill, and J. T. Sprehe. *Strategies for Success in Compensatory Education: An Appraisal of Evaluation Research.* Baltimore, MD: Johns Hopkins University Press, 1969.

McDill, E. L., G. Natriello, and A. M. Pallas. "A Population at Risk: Potential Consequences of Tougher School Standards for Student Dropouts." *American Journal of Education* 94 (1986): 135–81.

McPartland, J. M., J. R. Coldiron, and J. H. Braddock. *School Structures and Classroom Practices in Elementary, Middle and Secondary Schools.* Report No. 14. Baltimore, MD: Johns Hopkins University Center for Research on Elementary and Middle Schools, 1987.

Medway, F. J. "To Promote or Not to Promote?" *Principal* 64 (1985): 22–25.

Meisels, S. J., and F. Liaw. "Failure in Grade: Do Retained Students Catch Up?" Paper presented at the annual meeting of the American Educational Research Association. Chicago, April 1991.

Mischel, W., R. Zeiss, and A. Zeiss. "Internal–External Control and Persistence: Validation and Implications of the Stanford Preschool Internal–External Scale." *Journal of Personality and Social Psychology* 29 (1974): 265–78.

Morris, D. R. "Patterns of Aggregate Grade-retention Rates." *American Educational Research Journal* 30 (1993): 497–514.

Mueller, E. J. "The Long-term Effects on Reading Achievement of Failing First Grade." Paper presented at the annual meeting of the American Educational Research Association. San Francisco, March 1989.

Murnane, R. J. *The Impact of School Resources on the Learning of Inner City Children.* Cambridge, MA: Ballinger, 1975.

Myers, D. E. *An Analysis of the Impact of Title 1 on Reading and Math Achievement of Elementary School Aged Children.* Washington, DC: Office of Educational Research and Improvement, U.S. Department of Education, 1986.

National Center for Education Statistics. *A Profile of the American Eighth Grader: NELS-88 Student Descriptive Summary.* U.S. Department of Education, Office of Educational Research and Improvement, Report No. 90-458. Washington, DC: U.S. Government Printing Office, 1990.

National Commission on Excellence in Education. *A Nation at Risk: The Imperative for Educational Reform.* Washington, DC: U.S. Government Printing Office, 1983.

Natriello, G., E. L. McDill, and A. M. Pallas. *Schooling Disadvantaged Children: Racing Against Catastrophe.* New York: Teachers College Press, 1990.

Oakes, J. "Tracking in Mathematics and Science Education: A Structural Contribution to Unequal Schooling." In *Class, Race and Gender in American Education,* edited by L. Weis, pp. 106–25. Albany, NY: SUNY Press, 1988.

"Opportunities, Achievement and Choice: Women and Minority Students in Science and Mathematics." *Review of Research in Education* 16 (1989–90): 153–222.

"Can Tracking Research Inform Practice? Technical, Normative and Political Considerations." *Educational Researcher* 21 (1992): 12–21.

Oakes, J., A. Gamoran, and R. N. Page. "Curriculum Differentiation: Opportunities, Outcomes and Meanings." In *Handbook of Research on Curriculum,* edited by P. W. Jackson, pp. 570–608. New York: Macmillan, 1992.

Otto, H. J., and E. O. Melby. "An Attempt to Evaluate the Threat of Failure as a Factor in Achievement." *Elementary School Journal* 35 (1935): 588–96.

Pallas, A. M. "The Determinants of High School Dropouts." Ph.D. diss., Johns Hopkins University, 1984.

School Dropouts in the United States. Issue paper CS87-426, Center for Education Statistics, Office of Educational Research and Improvement. U.S. Department of Education, 1987.

Pallas, A. M., D. R. Entwisle, K. L. Alexander, and P. Weinstein. "Social Structure and the Development of Self-esteem in Young Children." *Social Psychology Quarterly* 53 (1990): 302–15.

Pallas, A. M., G. Natriello, and E. L. McDill. "The High Costs of High Standards: School Reform and Dropouts." *Urban Education* 22 (1987): 103–14.

"The Changing Nature of the Disadvantaged Population: Current Dimensions and Future Trends." *Educational Researcher* 18 (1989): 16–22.

Peterson, S. E., J. S. DeGracie, and C. R. Ayabe. "A Longitudinal Study of the Effects of Retention/Promotion on Academic Achievement." *American Educational Research Journal* 27 (1987): 107–18.

Pierson, L. H., and J. P. Connell. "Effect of Grade Retention on Self-system Processes, School Engagement and Academic Performance." *Journal of Educational Psychology* 84 (1992): 300–07.

Reynolds, A. J. "Grade Retention and School Adjustment: An Explanatory Analysis." *Educational Evaluation and Policy Analysis* 14 (1992): 101–21.

Richer, S. "Reference-group Theory and Ability Grouping: A Convergence of Sociological Theory and Educational Research." *Sociology of Education* 49 (1976): 65–71.

Rose, J. S., F. J. Medway, V. L. Cantrell, and H. S. Marus. "A Fresh Look at the Retention/Promotion Controversy." *Journal of School Psychology* 21 (1983): 201–11.

Rosenbaum, J. E. *Making Inequality.* New York: Wiley, 1976.

"Some Implications of Educational Grouping." *Review of Research in Education* 8 (1980): 361–401.

Rosenshine, B. V. "Content, Time and Instruction." In *Research on Teaching: Concepts, Findings and Implications,* edited by P. L. Peterson and H. J. Walberg, pp. 28–56. Berkeley, CA: McCutchan, 1979.

"How Time is Spent in Elementary Classrooms." In *Time to Learn,* edited by C. Denham and A. Lieberman, pp. 107–26. Washington, DC: National Institute of Education, 1980.

Rotter, J. B. "Generalized Expectancies for Internal Versus External Control of Reinforcement." *Psychological Monographs* 1, no. 609 (1966).

Royce, J. M., R. B. Darlington, and H. W. Murray. "Pooled Analyses: Findings Across Studies." In *As the Twig Is Bent: Lasting Effects of Preschool Programs,* edited by the Consortium for Longitudinal Studies, pp. 411–459. Hillsdale, NJ: Erlbaum, 1983.

Rumberger, R. W. "High School Dropouts: A Review of Issues and Evidence." *Review of Educational Research* 57 (1987): 101–21.

Schmidt, F. L. "What Do Data Really Mean? Research Findings, Meta-analysis and Cumulative Knowledge in Psychology." *American Psychologist* 47 (1992): 1173–81.

Schweinhart, L. J., J. R. Berrueta-Clement, W. S. Barnett, A. S. Epstein, and D. P. Weikart. "The Promise of Early Education." *Phi Delta Kappan* 66 (1985): 548–51.

Schweinhart, L. J., and D. P. Weikart. "Evidence That Good Early Childhood Programs Work." *Phi Delta Kappan* 66 (April 1985): 545–48.

Schweinhart, L. J., D. P. Weikart, and M. B. Larner. "Consequences of Three Preschool Curriculum Models Through Age 15." *Early Childhood Research Quarterly* 1 (1986): 15–45.

Shepard, L. A. "A Review of Research on Kindergarten Retention." In *Flunking Grades: Research and Policies on Retention,* edited by L. A. Shepard and M. L. Smith, pp. 64–78. London: Falmer, 1989.

Shepard, L. A., and M. L. Smith. "Synthesis of Research on School Readiness and Kindergarten Retention." *Educational Leadership* 44 (1986): 78–86.

"Escalating Academic Demand in Kindergarten: Counterproductive Policies." *Elementary School Journal* 89 (1988): 135–45.

"Introduction and Overview." In *Flunking Grades: Research and Policies on Retention,* edited by L. A. Shepard and M. L. Smith, pp. 1–15. London: Falmer, 1989.

Simmons, R. G., and D. A. Blyth. *Moving Into Adolescence: The Impact of Pubertal Change and School Context.* Hawthorn, NY: Aldine, 1987.

Slaughter, D. T., and E. G. Epps. "The Home Environment and Academic Achievement of Black American Children and Youth: An Overview." *Journal of Negro Education* 56 (1987): 3–20.

Slavin, R. E. "Ability Grouping and Student Achievement in Elementary Schools: A Best-evidence Synthesis." *Review of Educational Research* 57 (1987): 293–336.

——. "Students at Risk of School Failure: The Problem and Its Dimensions." In *Effective Programs for Students at Risk,* edited by R. E. Slavin, N. L. Karweit, and N. A. Madden, pp. 3–19. Boston: Allyn & Bacon, 1989.

Slavin, R. E., N. L. Karweit, and N. A. Madden. *Effective Programs for Students at Risk.* Boston: Allyn & Bacon, 1989.

Slavin, R. E., N. A. Madden, N. L. Karweit, B. J. Livermon, and L. Dolan. "Success for All: First-year Outcomes of a Comprehensive Plan for Reforming Urban Education." *American Educational Research Journal* 27 (1990): 255–78.

Smith, M. L. "Teachers' Beliefs About Retention." In *Flunking Grades: Research and Policies on Retention,* edited by L. A. Shepard and M. L. Smith, pp. 132–50. London: Falmer, 1989.

Smith, M. L., and L. A. Shepard. "What Doesn't Work: Explaining Policies of Retention in the Early Grades." *Phi Delta Kappan* 66 (1987): 129–34.

——. "Kindergarten Readiness and Retention: A Qualitative Study of Teachers' Beliefs and Practices." *American Educational Research Journal* 25 (1988): 307–33.

Sorensen, A. B. "Organizational Differentiation of Students and Educational Opportunity." *Sociology of Education* 43 (1970): 355–76.

——. "The Organizational Differentiation of Students in Schools as an Opportunity Structure." In *The Social Organization of Schools: New Conceptualizations of the Learning Process,* edited by M. T. Hallinan, pp. 103–29. New York: Plenum, 1987.

Stebbins, L. B., R. G. St. Pierre, E. C. Proper, R. B. Anderson, and T. R. Cerva. *Effects of Follow Through Models.* Vol. 4-A of *A Planned Variation Model.* Washington, DC: U.S. Office of Education, 1977.

Stevenson, D., K. Schiller, and B. Schneider. "Sequences of Opportunities for Learning Mathematics and Science." Paper presented at the annual meeting of the American Sociological Association. Pittsburgh, PA, 1992.

Stipek, D. J. "The Development of Achievement Motivation." In *Research on Motivation in Education,* edited by R. Ames and C. Ames, pp. 145–74. San Diego, CA: Academic, 1984.

Stipek, D. J., and J. R. Weisz. "Perceived Personal Control and Academic Achievement." *Review of Educational Research* 51 (1981): 101–37.

Stroup, A. L., and L. N. Robins. "Elementary School Predictors of High School Dropout Among Black Males." *Sociology of Education* 45 (1972): 212–22.

Suhorsky, J., and R. Wall. *A Validation Study of Early Identification and Intervention Program Screening Instruments: A Longitudinal Study*. Baltimore, MD: Maryland State Department of Education (ERIC Document Reproduction Service No. ED 171 777), 1978.

Szanton, P. L. *Baltimore 2000: A Choice of Futures*. Baltimore, MD: Morris Goldseker Foundation, 1986.

Taylor, B. M., B. J. Frye, and G. M. Maruyama. "Time Spent Reading and Reading Growth." *American Educational Research Journal* 27 (1990): 351–62.

Tomchin, E. M., and J. C. Impara. "Unraveling Teachers' Beliefs About Grade Retention." *American Educational Research Journal* 29 (1992): 199–223.

Travers, J. R. "Testing in Educational Placement: Issues and Evidence." In *Children in Special Education: A Strategy for Equity*, edited by K. A. Heller, W. H. Holtzman, and S. Messick, pp. 230–61. Washington, DC: National Academy Press, 1982.

Tuck, K. D. "A Study of Students Who Left: D.C. Public School Dropouts." Paper presented at the annual meeting of the American Educational Research Association. San Francisco, March 1989.

U.S. Bureau of the Census. *Characteristics of the Population. Part 22, Maryland*. Vol. 1 of *Census of the Population: 1970*. Washington, DC: U.S. Government Printing Office, 1973.

Characteristics of the Population. Part 22, Maryland. Vol. 1 of *Census of the Population: 1980*. Washington, DC: U.S. Government Printing Office, 1983.

1990 Census of the Population and Housing, Summary Tape File 3A, Maryland Computer File. Washington, DC: Department of Commerce, Bureau of the Census, Data Users Service, 1991.

Wagenaar, T. C. "What Do We Know About Dropping Out of High School?" In *Research in Sociology of Education and Socialization*, edited by A. C. Kerckhoff, pp. 161–90. Greenwich, CT: JAI, 1987.

Weiss, J. A., and J. E. Gruber. "The Managed Irrelevance of Federal Education Statistics." In *The Politics of Numbers*, edited by W. Alonso and P. Starr, pp. 363–91. New York: Russell Sage, 1987.

Weisz, J. R., and A. M. Cameron. "Individual Differences in the Student's Sense of Control." In *Research on Motivation in Education. Vol. 2: The Classroom Milieu*, edited by C. Ames and R. Ames, pp. 93–139. San Diego, CA: Academic, 1985.

White, K. R. "Efficacy of Early Intervention." *Journal of Special Education* 19 (1985-86): 401–16.

White, K. R., M. J. Taylor, and V. D. Moss. "Does Research Support Claims

About the Benefits of Involving Parents in Early Intervention Programs?" *Review of Educational Research* 62 (1992): 91–125.

Willis, S. "Breaking Down Grade Barriers: Interest in Nongraded Classrooms on the Rise." *ASCD Update* 33 (1991): 1–4.

Wilson, M. "Book Review of 'Flunking Grades: Research and Policies on Retention.'" *Educational Evaluation and Policy Analysis* 12 (1990): 228–30.

Wood, D., N. Halfon, D. Scarlata, P. Newacheck, and S. Nissim. "The Impact of Family Relocation on Children's Growth and Development, School Function and Behavior." *Journal of the American Medical Association* 270 (1993): 1334–38.

Woodhead, M. "When Psychology Informs Public Policy: The Case of Early Childhood Intervention." *American Psychologist* 43 (1988): 443–54.

Index

Wasik, B. A., 232
Weikart, D. P., 225, 226
Weinfeld, F. D., 166
Weinstein, P., 246
Weiss, J. A., 3
Weisz, J. R., 156, 160, 166, 228
Wessels, K., 166
White, K. R., 226
whites: age and gender trends of, 4–5; in
    Baltimore, 223–24; in Beginning School
    Study, 45; demographics for, 6; retention
    rates among, 5

Willis, S., 230
Wilson, M., 234
Wirtanen, I. D., 7–8
Wood, D., 35
Woodhead, M., 250

York, R. L., 166

Zigler, E. F., 251
Zeiss, A., 166
Zeiss, R., 166

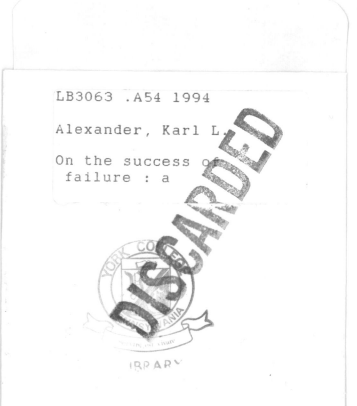